AMC'S BEST DAY HIKES NEAR
PHILADELPHIA

Four-Season Guide to 50 of the Best Trails
in Eastern Pennsylvania, New Jersey, and Delaware

SUSAN CHARKES

Appalachian Mountain Club Books
Boston, Massachusetts

The AMC is a nonprofit organization and sales of AMC books fund our mission of protecting the Northeast outdoors. If you appreciate our efforts and would like to make a donation to the AMC, contact us at Appalachian Mountain Club, 5 Joy Street, Boston, MA 02108.

www.outdoors.org/publications/books/

Distributed by The Globe Pequot Press, Guilford, Connecticut.

Front cover photographs (top) © T.L. Gettings, (bottom) © SuperStock
Back cover photographs (l-r) © iStock; © iStock; © Purestock / Kwame Zikomo / SuperStock
All interior photographs © Susan Charkes
Maps by Ken Dumas, © Appalachian Mountain Club
Book design by Eric Edstam

Library of Congress Cataloging-in-Publication Data
Charkes, Susan.
  AMC's best day hikes near Philadelphia : four-season guide to 50 of the best trails in eastern Pennsylvania, New Jersey, and Delaware / Susan Charkes.
    p. cm.
  Includes bibliographical references and index.
  ISBN 978-1-934028-33-9 (alk. paper)
  1. Hiking—Pennsylvania—Philadelphia Region—Guidebooks. 2. Trails—Pennsylvania—Philadelphia Region—Guidebooks. 3. Philadelphia Region (Pa.)—Guidebooks. I. Appalachian Mountain Club. II. Title. III. Title: Appalachian Mountain Club's best day hikes near Philadelphia. IV. Title: Best day hikes near Philadelphia.
  GV199.42.P4P553 2010
  796.510974—dc22
                    2009045893

The paper used in this publication meets the minimum requirements of the American National Standard for Information Sciences-Permanence of Paper for Printed Library Materials, ANSI Z39.48-1984. ∞

Outdoor recreation activities by their very nature are potentially hazardous. This book is not a substitute for good personal judgment and training in outdoor skills. Due to changes in conditions, use of the information in this book is at the sole risk of the user. The author and the Appalachian Mountain Club assume no liability for accidents happening to, or injuries sustained by, readers who engage in the activities described in this book.

Interior pages contain 30% post-consumer recycled fiber. Cover contains 10% post-consumer recycled fiber. Printed in the United States of America, using vegetable-based inks.

© **Mixed Sources**
Product group from well-managed forests, controlled sources and recycled wood or fiber
www.fsc.org   Cert no. SCS-COC-002464
© 1996 Forest Stewardship Council

FSC

10 9 8 7 6 5 4 3 2 1   10 11 12 13 14 15 16

This book is dedicated to my parents,
who first took me to the woods
and then let me go to walk on my own

and to my son,
who is on the verge

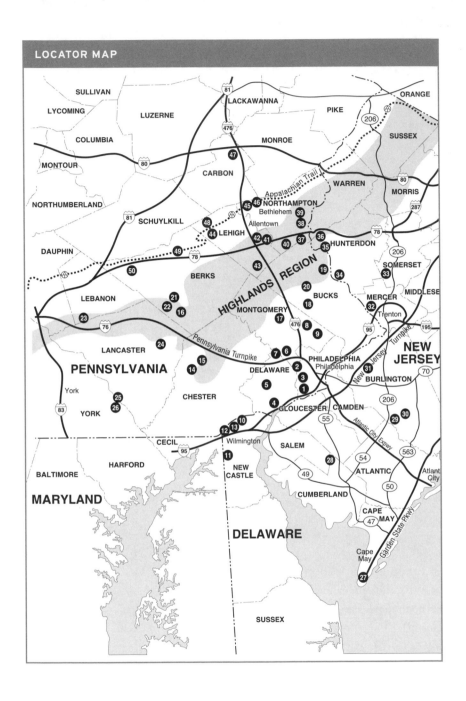

CONTENTS

SECTION 2: CENTRAL AND SOUTHERN NEW JERSEY

SECTION 3: LEHIGH VALLEY

NATURE ESSAYS

APPENDICES

AT-A-GLANCE TRIP PLANNER

#	Trip	Page	Location	Difficulty	Distance and Elevation Gain
SOUTHEASTERN PENNSYLVANIA AND DELAWARE					
1	Fairmount Park Loop (Art Museum)	3	Philadelphia, PA	Easy	9.0 mi, minimal
2	Wissahickon Valley Park	8	Philadelphia, PA	Moderate-Difficult	7.0 mi, 250 ft
3	Pennypack Park	13	Philadelphia, PA	Moderate	8.0 mi, 50 ft
4	John Heinz National Wildlife Refuge at Tinicum	18	Philadelphia and Folcroft, PA (Delaware County)	Easy	5.0 mi, minimal
5	Ridley Creek State Park	23	Newtown Square, PA (Delaware County)	Moderate	5.5 mi, 225 ft
6	Valley Forge National Historical Park–Mount Misery and Mount Joy	29	King of Prussia, PA (Chester and Montgomery Counties)	Moderate	5.0 mi, 450 ft
7	Valley Forge National Historical Park–River Trail	34	King of Prussia, PA (Chester and Montgomery Counties)	Easy	6.0 mi, 25 ft
8	Green Ribbon Trail	39	Lower Gwynedd, PA (Montgomery County)	Easy-Moderate	7.5 mi, minimal

Estimated Time	Fee	Good for Kids	Dogs Allowed	Public Transit	X-C Skiing	Snow-Shoeing	Trip Highlights
3.5 hrs			🐕	🚌	🎿	⛷⛷	River at the heart of the city
3.5 hrs			🐕	🚌	🎿	⛷⛷	Rugged wild gorge, old-growth forest
3.0 hrs			🐕	🚌	🎿	⛷⛷	Picturesque wooded valley on the city's edge
2.0 hrs		🚶	🐕	🚌		⛷⛷	Freshwater tidal marsh and pond, great birding
2.75 hrs		🚶	🐕		🎿	⛷⛷	Steep forested hills along a winding creek
3.0 hrs		🚶	🐕	🚌	🎿	⛷⛷	Woods and hills near Washington's Headquarters
2.75 hrs		🚶	🐕	🚌	🎿	⛷	Historic, placid Schuylkill River greenway
3.0 hrs			🐕	🚌	🎿	⛷⛷	Rail-accessible wooded creekside walk

Estimated Time	Fee	Good for Kids	Dogs Allowed	Public Transit	X-C Skiing	Snow-Shoeing	Trip Highlights
3.5 hrs		✔	✔				Extensive meadows
2.0 hrs		✔	✔	✔		✔	Urban oasis
3.0 hrs	$		✔		✔	✔	Scenic, forested pond
4.5 hrs			✔		✔	✔	Two states, one creek, many hills
3.5 hrs	$		✔		✔	✔	Steep, forested blue-rock valley
1.25 hrs		✔	✔		✔	✔	Rocky, gently rolling hills
2.25 hrs		✔	✔		✔	✔	Open fields and large lake
3.0 hrs		✔	✔		✔	✔	Forested hills in Daniel Boone country
4.0 hrs			✔			✔	Deep woods surrround a quiet lake
3.0 hrs		✔	✔		✔	✔	Diverse rural landscape
4.0 hrs			✔		✔	✔	Spectacular High Rocks gorge
3.0 hrs		✔	✔			✔	Rocky forest with lake views
2.5 hrs		✔	✔			✔	Rugged hike with scenic summit views
3.0 hrs			✔		✔	✔	Extensive conifer and hardwood forests
1.25 hrs		✔	✔			✔	Large contiguous forest

Estimated Time	Fee	Good for Kids	Dogs Allowed	Public Transit	X-C Skiing	Snow-Shoeing	Trip Highlights
1.5 hrs		✓	✓		✓	✓	Rugged rock formations, extensive forests
3.5 hrs			✓				Wild, rugged gorge in old-growth forest
3.5 hrs			✓			✓	Eagles soar above rocky riverside ravines
3.25 hrs	$		✓				Ocean beach and dune forests
2.5 hrs		✓	✓		✓	✓	Diverse forests on the edge of the Pinelands
4.0 hrs			✓		✓	✓	Soft pine-needle trails, cedar-brown river
4.0 hrs			✓		✓		Marvelous view; highest point in Pine Barrens
2.0 hrs		✓				✓	Westernmost Pine Barrens park
3.25 hrs (shuttle hike) or 3.75 hrs (loop)			✓			✓	Mountain in miniature
2.25 hrs		✓	✓		✓	✓	Ridge-top boulder amusement park
4.0 hrs			✓		✓	✓	Along the wild and scenic Delaware River
2.0 hrs			✓				Clifftop views of the Delaware River
3.0 hrs		✓	✓			✓	Moist, rich rocky woods

Estimated Time	Fee	Good for Kids	Dogs Allowed	Public Transit	X-C Skiing	Snow-Shoeing	Trip Highlights
2.0 hrs		✓	✓			✓	Steep, rocky forested hills
1.25 hrs		✓	✓		✓	✓	Open, grassy area
1.75 hrs		✓	✓			✓	Meadows, old trees, ravine and history
3.0 hrs		✓	✓				Historic Bethlehem
2.0 hrs		✓	✓		✓	✓	Rocky hardwood forest
2.75 hrs		✓	✓		✓	✓	Flat, creekside hike; historic and cultural sites
1.5 hrs		✓	✓		✓	✓	Looping hillside trails, boulders
5.5 hrs			✓				Exposed rock ridge-top with great views
4.0 hrs		✓	✓			✓	Scenic Lehigh Valley
2.0 hrs			✓				Challenging scramble in barren landscape
5.0 hrs			✓			✓	Numerous rich forests, diverse terrain
4.5 hrs			✓			✓	Magnificent waterfalls, riverside walk
4.5 hrs			✓			✓	Most celebrated Appalachian Trail view in Pennsylvania
2.75 hrs		✓	✓			✓	Hemlock ravines, walled sand spring

PREFACE

THERE'S NO SUCH THING AS A BAD HIKE. HOW COULD THERE BE? You're outdoors; you're walking: all's right with the world.

I was raised in the western Philadelphia suburbs, where I picked up the hiking habit from my parents. On weekends we'd go day-hiking in the area, so I grew up thinking it was only natural that hiking was what you did for fun outdoors: all that beauty, all that fresh air, all those interesting things to look at for free. Unlike much of the rest of my early type-A life, hiking was noncompetitive. It didn't matter how fast you got to the end; what mattered was how you got there.

From my father, the scientist, I inherited a voracious appetite for observation, identification, classification, and contextualization. I could hardly take a step without noticing something interesting—some rock or tree or creature—and trying to figure out more about it. What's that rock saying about how the land got to be the way it is? Why is that tree growing here and not there? How did this tree get to be shaped like this? Why are birds singing in these woods and not those?

From my mother, the humanist, I inherited a craving to make stories out of what I observed. With British novelist E. M. Forster, she could say, "Only connect." There is an emotional, spiritual significance to everything in nature that goes beyond what we can see. Discovering the stories is half the joy; sharing them is the other half.

A hike is a time to enjoy the good feeling we get from propelling ourselves forward, straining against gravity going uphill, and braking against it going downhill. But a hike can be more. When we learn about a place—really learn it by walking through it and observing it—we open ourselves up to the possibility of falling in love with it. The place becomes part of our life story.

I continued hiking after I left home, got married, and formed a family. My family and I hiked on weekends and on vacations, wherever we went. After I went back to being on my own and moved to new locales, hiking led me to new friends and helped me feel like I was almost home even in a strange place. It was a familiar activity that I could apply to new ground.

Affection for the Philadelphia area drew me home after living away; hiking helped cement my determination to remain. Besides helping me nurture emotional bonds with the area's forests and parks, hiking has also helped me nurture comparable ties with my hiking companions. The strongest of these is the bond I've developed with my son (now 19) as we have hiked together in the region where both of us grew up. Handing down what I am passionate about, the way my parents handed down their passions to me, has been my greatest hiking joy.

I'm still learning about new places to go—new trails, and trails new to me. The region is so full of places to hike that I could take a different hike every day of the year. But every hike is different, even if you hike the same path every day. There's always something new because every day is different.

To paraphrase Ernie Banks, "It's a beautiful day for a hike—let's take two!"

ACKNOWLEDGMENTS

THIS BOOK IS THE PRODUCT OF AN ENORMOUS AMOUNT OF HARD WORK, determination, and vision. Heather Stephenson, publisher of AMC Books, has been the guiding force behind the project from the beginning and never wavered in her commitment to it. Books editor Dan Eisner made sure that what needed to get done did, and always maintained a calm, centered presence in the midst of a whirlwind. Kristen Sykes, Mid-Atlantic project manager for the Appalachian Mountain Club and vice chair for the Highlands Coalition—a can-do person if there ever was one—has tirelessly spearheaded Highlands protection initiatives. On a personal level, she is an endless font of ideas and support; without her encouragement I would never have considered this project. Jennifer Heisey, AMC's Mid-Atlantic recreation planner, has devoted countless hours to promoting (and doing) hiking in the Highlands.

When gathering background information, I was delighted to meet and speak with numerous public servants who are engaged in park and trail management, as well as volunteers who spend their spare time working to preserve, protect, and share the places they love. Among these were Claire Mickletz (Brandywine Creek State Park); Steve Heitzer (Delaware Canal State Park); David Bartoo (Delaware State Parks); David Long (Durham Township, Bucks County); Laurie Goodrich and Mary Linkevich (Hawk Mountain Sanctuary); Kevin Blair (Hickory Run State Park); Karen Ament and Lissette Santana

(Holtwood Preserve); Bill Clother (Hunterdon County Parks); Gary Stolz and Bill Buchanan (John Heinz National Wildlife Refuge); Dan Kunkle (Lehigh Gap Nature Center); Lisa Frittinger (Mercer County Parks); Tim Ciotti (Montgomery County Parks); Brent Burke (The Nature Conservancy, Cape May); Gretchen Ferrante (New Jersey Audubon Society, Cape May); Martin Rapp (New Jersey Natural Lands Trust); Alan Hershey (New Jersey Trails); Daniel Hewko (Nolde Forest State Park); Craig Olsen and Gail Hill (Peace Valley Nature Center); David J. Robertson, Ph.D. (Pennypack Ecological Restoration Trust); Drew Brown (Philadelphia Water Department, Fairmount Waterworks Interpretive Center); Claire Adair (New Jersey Audubon Society, Rancocas); Roger McChesney (Ridley Creek State Park); Phil Richard and Dave Dendler (Somerset County Park Rangers); Mike Wilson (Trout Unlimited); Deirdre Gibson (Valley Forge National Historical Park); Jeannie Ford (Wharton State Forest, Batsto); Barbara Woodford (Wilmington State Parks); and Carol DeLancey (Wissahickon Valley Watershed Association).

To a great degree the book reflects input from AMC's Delaware Valley Chapter (AMCDV) hike leaders and volunteers. The AMCDV Chapter—of which I am a member, hike leader, and former conservation chair—hikes regularly throughout the Philadelphia area and beyond. To select and map the best hikes from the hundreds possible around the area, I depended heavily on the expertise of many people who cheerfully offered their advice, including Al Schwartz (also of Allentown Hiking Club), Pete Jarrett, Charlie Phy, Kathy Kelly-Borowski, Rich Wells, Seth and Sue Bergmann, Lennie and Bill Steinmetz, Dan and Noelle Schwartz, Phil Mulligan, Tom Sherwood, Bill Lotz, Jerry Goldstein, Jeff Lippincott, Pat McGill, Alan and Bette Male, Mike and Tina Lawless, Cliff Hence, Dwayne Henne, Terry Stimpfel, and Kevin Burkman. There are other fine hiking clubs in the Philadelphia area, and I also appreciated the input of Mike Hughes and Milt Cannan of the Batona Hiking Club, and Jim Hooper of the York Hiking Club and Mason-Dixon Trail System.

Special thanks go to those hikers who not only helped with selection and routing but also accompanied me on hikes, including AMCDV's Jim Sayne (also of Chester County Trail Club), Dave "Wissahickon Man" Stein (also of Batona Hiking Club), Joan Aichele, Ron Phelps, Dale Brandreth, and Rich Benningfeld, as well as Batona's Allen Britton, Lisa Sandler, and Paul Piechowski. Many happy hiking hours were spent in the company of my son Nick Stevick and my cousin Ann Summer. My father, David Charkes, a longtime AMC member, hikes with me now vicariously. Finally, my intrepid companion Ref deserves the most prominent mention for never ending a hike without a smile.

INTRODUCTION

WHY HIKE? WHY NOT JUST STAY HOME?

We hike, in the first place, to leave home, in the sense of "home" as the place we're used to. People are hard-wired to seek novelty. We want to use our senses, to learn, to develop our skills, and to adapt to change. Hiking is an activity; we take action, engaging our minds as well as our bodies, not passively receiving experience but actively creating it.

And we hike, also, to go home, in the sense of "home" as the outdoors. People evolved outdoors, tramping through forests, scrambling along riverbanks, surveying grassy valleys, climbing mountains, kicking sand along the shore, listening to birds, spotting fish, avoiding snakes. When we hike, we reconnect with what we give up for the comforts of indoor life: the body in nature.

The Philadelphia area—southeastern Pennsylvania, central and southern New Jersey, and northern Delaware, or what residents call the Delaware Valley—is home to millions of people. Hiking in the area offers an astonishingly diverse array of experiences. No matter where you live in the region, you're within an hour or two's drive of someplace completely different. That's because the area is where two very different pieces of the earth's crust meet. The meeting is not entirely peaceful—not at all like Edmund Hicks's iconic painting of the treaty between William Penn and the Lenape Indians. No, here the flat Atlantic coastal plain encounters hard rock and breaks it up into pieces. The meeting place is called the Fall Line because innumerable waterfalls cascade down the dislocated rocks along it. It roughly parallels Route 1 in New Jersey, cuts across the Delaware River at Trenton, and runs southwest across the Susquehanna River south of the Conowingo Dam.

Philadelphia itself lies on the Fall Line where the line crosses the Schuylkill River. To the southeast of the city, the sandy flat coastal plain stretches like a table. Northwest of the city, the ridges and valleys of the Appalachian Mountains ripple like folds in a tablecloth. The area in between—a mosaic of rolling hills, open fields, small woods, and meandering streams—is the Piedmont (literally, the foothills of the Appalachians).

This variety of terrain creates a multiplicity of hiking opportunities. You could hike in the morning on a flat, pine-needle-strewn trail along a boggy pond, and in the afternoon climb by a boulder-strewn creek cascading down a rugged ravine. In between you could hike through butterfly-bedecked meadows or sit on a low stone and watch the leaves drift down into a shallow stream.

Diversity, too, can be found in the region's trails. National, state, county, and local parks; state game lands; and nonprofit nature centers abound, all crisscrossed with trails that can be hiked in a day.

Also within easy driving reach in the Philadelphia area are great long-distance trails. The most famous long-distance trail, the Appalachian Trail (AT), runs more than 2,000 miles from Maine to Georgia. In southeastern Pennsylvania it traverses the crest of the Kittatinny Ridge (Blue Mountain), the southernmost mountain of the Appalachian Plateau; hikes in this area provide some glorious valley views and access to deep, rich woods full of wildlife. To hike any portion of the AT is to join a unique community: hikers and trail maintainers fiercely committed to preserving its legacy as the premier long-distance trail in the eastern United States. Other long-distance trails, less well-known, are also avidly hiked and maintained by dedicated volunteers, including the Batona Trail in the New Jersey Pine Barrens (50 miles long) and the Horse-Shoe (140), Mason-Dixon (193), and Conestoga (63) trails in Pennsylvania's Chester and Lancaster counties and in Delaware. The AMC is working to extend the current Highlands Trail in New York and New Jersey by more than 100 miles through Eastern Pennsylvania, an effort the club calls the Pennsylvania Highlands Trail Network (PHTN).

Other long-distance trails are those along canals and old rail beds, which are just as numerous in the region as wilderness trails. These trails, remnants of nineteenth-century industries, remind us that one way to leave home is to travel back in time, to discover that what we know now as home was not always this way. The Philadelphia area is as rich in history as it is in habitat. The nation was born here, and you can hike in some of the now-venerated sites of the American Revolution. The area was also an economic engine for the new nation, due in part to the countless rushing waterways.

There are numerous opportunities to hike in or near sites that were once communities centered on the mills and forges that were the industrial parks of their day, or farms that once fed families and villages. Today these sites, preserved as parkland, have largely reverted to nature. Old stone walls, crumbling foundations, charcoal hearths, dam stub ends, millrace trenches, fencerows marking former fields, and trees lining disused roads are traces—fading but not yet disappeared—of what once was modern life. They, like the hikers who pause to contemplate the passage of time and the stubborn persistence of wild nature, are going home.

HOW TO USE THIS BOOK

WITH 50 HIKES TO CHOOSE FROM, you may wonder how to decide where to go. The locator map at the front of this book will help you narrow down the trips by location, and the At-a-Glance Trip Planner that follows the table of contents will provide more information to guide you toward a decision.

Once you settle on a destination and turn to a trip in this guide, you will find a series of icons that indicate whether the hike is good for kids, if dogs are permitted, if you can go snowshoeing or cross country skiing there, and whether there are fees. This information is also covered in the At-a-Glance Trip Planner.

Information on the basics follows: location, difficulty rating, distance, elevation gain, estimated time, and available maps. The difficulty ratings are based on the author's perception and are estimates of what the average hiker will experience; however, you may find the hikes to be easier or more difficult than stated. The estimated time is also based on the author's perception. Consider your own pace when planning a trip. The elevation gain is calculated by subtracting the elevation of the trip's lowest point from the elevation of the trip's highest point. It does not account for every dip and rise along the route. Information is included about the relevant U.S. Geological Survey (USGS) maps, as well as where you can find trail maps. The trip overview (in boldface type) summarizes what you will see on the trip.

The directions explain how to reach the trailhead by car and, for some trips, public transportation. Global Positioning System (GPS) coordinates for the parking lots are also included for owners of car GPS devices. If you don't own a GPS device, it is wise to consult an atlas before leaving home.

Most of the trips are either loop or out-and-back hikes, beginning and ending at the same trailhead. A few are linear or shuttle hikes, requiring two cars, one at the beginning and one at the end.

In the Trail Description sections, you will find instructions on which trails to hike and where to turn. You will also learn about the history of the area and the flora, fauna, landmarks, and other points of interest you may encounter.

The trail maps that accompany each trip will help guide you along your hike, but it would be wise to also take an official trail map with you. Maps are often—but not always—available online, at the trailhead, or at the office or visitor center. The Appalachian Trail in Pennsylvania is divided into numbered sections, and printed maps and guidebooks for each section are published by the Keystone Trails Association. They can be purchased from its website (www.kta.org) or at bookstores and outfitters throughout the region.

Each trip ends with a More Information section that provides details about the location of restrooms, trail access times, fees (if any), the property's rules and regulations, and contact information for the agency that manages the land where you will be hiking.

TRIP PLANNING AND SAFETY

HIKING IN THE PHILADELPHIA AREA ISN'T LIKE A MOUNTAINEERING TREK that requires intense preparation. The climate is relatively moderate, and information is readily available about weather on a daily, even hourly, basis; the terrain does not require special equipment to traverse; the risk of attack from wild animals is low; and emergency assistance is usually a cell phone call away. Nonetheless, your enjoyment of any hike—even a short hike close by—will be enhanced if you are prepared for the unexpected.

Planning will increase your chances of having an enjoyable, safe hike. In particular, be prepared to get tired, wet, lost, hungry, or injured. The odds are that you won't encounter problems, but if you take simple steps in advance you'll be better able to cope should any arise. Before heading out for your hike, consider the following:

- Select a hike that everyone in your group is comfortable taking. Match the hike to the abilities of the least capable person in the group. If anyone in your group is uncomfortable with the weather or is tired, turn around and complete the hike another day.
- Plan to be back at the trailhead before dark. Before beginning your hike, determine a turnaround time and don't diverge from it, even if you have not reached your destination. Just in case, carry a lightweight flashlight or headlamp, along with spare batteries.

- Check the weather at your hike destination. Temperatures at higher elevations—including the ridges of the Lehigh Valley—are often significantly cooler than they are in the city and suburbs. Temperatures fall very fast after sunset. All over the area, storms are a potential hazard. If rain is in the forecast, bring waterproof gear. Spring and fall bring unstable air masses to the area; summer features late-afternoon thunderstorms. If you are planning a ridge or summit hike, especially in summer, get an early start so that you will be off the exposed area before the late-afternoon hours when thunderstorms most often strike.
- Bring a pack with the following items:
  - ✓ Water (Two quarts per person is usually adequate, depending on the weather and length of the trip.)
  - ✓ Food (Even if you are planning only a 1-hour hike, bring some high-energy snacks such as nuts, dried fruit, or snack bars. Pack a lunch for longer trips. Save some food for when you get back to the trailhead.)
  - ✓ Map and compass (Be sure you know how to use them. A handheld GPS device may also be helpful.)
  - ✓ Headlamp or flashlight, with spare batteries
  - ✓ Extra clothing (Pack rain gear and extra socks; in cool weather bring a wool or fleece pullover, a hat, and mittens, as well as hand- and foot-warmers.)
  - ✓ First-aid kit (Your kit should include adhesive bandages, gauze, non-prescription painkiller, moleskin, and topical antihistamine for insect bites.)
  - ✓ Pocketknife or multitool
  - ✓ Waterproof matches or a lighter
  - ✓ Trash bag to carry out waste
  - ✓ Toilet paper, hand sanitizer
  - ✓ Whistle
  - ✓ Sunscreen
  - ✓ Sunglasses
  - ✓ Cell phone
  - ✓ Insect repellent (optional)
  - ✓ Binoculars (optional)
  - ✓ Camera (optional)
- Wear appropriate footwear and clothing. Wool or synthetic hiking socks will keep your feet dry and help prevent blisters from forming. Waterproof boots help protect your feet from light rain or muddy spots. For hikes on mountain ridges, over-the-ankle hiking boots provide support and good

traction; for foothills or coastal plains hikes, low-top shoes are sufficient and less fatiguing. Avoid wearing cotton clothing, which absorbs sweat and rain; not only are wet clothes unpleasant, but when the temperature drops they can contribute to hypothermia, which can be dangerous. Polypropylene, fleece, silk, and wool all do a good job of wicking moisture away from your body and keeping you warm in wet or cold conditions. Dress in layers, especially for long hikes, so that you can add or remove items as ambient temperatures change; also, your body warms up quickly as you hike and cools when you stop.

- A trekking pole or two is a matter of personal preference. A pole can be useful to help ford streams and to assist going uphill or downhill. Some people use poles for added upper-body exercise. On the other hand, a pole can get in the way when rockhopping, and you may need two hands to grip rocks when scrambling. A collapsible pole can remain in the pack when not in use.

- Tell someone you trust where you will be hiking and when you expect to return. If you see a logbook at a trailhead, be sure to sign in when you arrive and sign out when you finish your hike.

- When you are in front of the rest of your hiking group, wait at all trail junctions until the others catch up. This avoids confusion and helps keep people in your group from getting lost or separated.

- If you see branches or logs that appear to be purposely blocking a trail junction, it probably means the trail is closed.

- If a trail is muddy, walk through the mud or on rocks, never off the trail to the side. Staying in the center will keep the trail from eroding into a wide hiking highway. Waterproof boots will keep your feet comfortable.

- Take extra care when hiking in the rain or next to streams so as not to slip on wet tree roots or rocks.

- Ticks, which can carry diseases, are common in many wooded and grassy areas in suburbs and exurbs (but uncommon on mountain ridges), and are active year-round in this area. To reduce the chance of a tick bite, you may want to wear pants and a long-sleeve shirt. After you finish your hike, check for ticks on your clothes and body. The deer tick, which can carry Lyme disease, can be as small as a pinhead. Run a lint roller over your clothes. Take a shower when you get home and check again.

- Mosquitoes can be common in the woods in summer and fall. Although some can carry diseases, their bite is mostly annoying. As with ticks, you can reduce the chance of bites by wearing long sleeves and pants.

- Poison ivy is often a hazard when hiking. All parts of it—leaves, stems, vines, berries—carry an irritating oil that is absorbed into the skin. To identify the plant, look for clusters of three leaves that shine in the sun but are dull in the shade. The vines are dark brown and woolly-hairy, often wrapped around trees. If you do come into contact with poison ivy, flush the affected area with copious amounts of water as soon as possible; use soap if available (as the oil is not very soluble in water).

- Snakes are common in many hiking areas. Snakes are cold-blooded; their body temperature rises and falls with the ambient temperature. They hibernate during cold months. In summer, snakes may bask on exposed rocks or on open trails. Snakes may also be found near stone walls, brush piles, or fallen logs. Snakes usually avoid confrontation and are not aggressive toward humans; when surprised or provoked, however, snakes may bite. Most snakes in the Philadelphia region are harmless, but northern copperheads and timber rattlesnakes have venomous bites that can be painful or, in very rare cases, fatal. To reduce the chance of an unpleasant encounter for both parties, use proper "snake etiquette," especially when hiking around rocky areas in the warm seasons: look before taking a step or reaching in between rocks; if you see a snake, leave it alone. If you are bitten by a snake, seek medical attention as quickly as possible.
- Bears are resident in wooded mountainous areas and may occasionally be encountered on the trail. Black bears, the only species in the Philadelphia area, are not generally aggressive; most will run from a human. But a female with cubs may, on rare occasions, attack if she feels her young are in danger. If you see a bear, do not provoke it. Retreat from any encounter.
- When hiking anywhere, be alert and aware of your surroundings. Don't hike with earphones on. It is a good general rule not to hike alone, especially on lightly traveled routes.
- Wear blaze-orange items in hunting season. Hats and/or vests are best. Hunting seasons vary. Check with state game commissions for dates:
  Pennsylvania: www.pgc.state.pa.us
  New Jersey: www.state.nj.us/dep/fgw/hunting.htm
  Delaware: www.fw.delaware.gov/Hunting/Pages/HuntingSeasons.aspx

Being prepared, planning ahead, and taking precautions to reduce risks may seem like overkill. Hiking, after all, is supposed to be a stress-free, simple experience. But experienced hikers know that the quality of every hike is increased significantly by putting advance effort into it, to avoid the negative impact of the unexpected. Make every surprise a happy one.

LEAVE NO TRACE

THE APPALACHIAN MOUNTAIN CLUB is a national educational partner of Leave No Trace, a nonprofit organization dedicated to promoting and inspiring responsible outdoor recreation through education, research, and partnerships. The Leave No Trace program seeks to develop wildland ethics—ways in which people think and act in the outdoors to minimize their impact on the areas they visit and to protect our natural resources for future enjoyment. Leave No Trace unites four federal land management agencies—the U.S. Forest Service, the National Park Service, the Bureau of Land Management, and the U.S. Fish and Wildlife Service—with manufacturers, outdoor retailers, user groups, educators, organizations such as the AMC, and individuals.

The Leave No Trace ethic is guided by the following seven principles:

1. **Plan Ahead and Prepare.** Know the terrain and any regulations applicable to the area you're planning to visit, and be prepared for extreme weather or other emergencies. This will enhance your enjoyment and ensure that you've chosen an appropriate destination. Small groups have less impact on resources and the experience of other backcountry visitors.

2. **Travel and Camp on Durable Surfaces.** Travel and camp on established trails and campsites, rock, gravel, dry grasses, or snow. Good campsites are found, not made. Camp at least 200 feet from lakes and streams, and focus activities on areas where vegetation is absent. In pristine areas, disperse use to prevent the creation of campsites and trails.

3. **Dispose of Waste Properly.** Pack it in, pack it out. Inspect your camp for trash or food scraps. Deposit solid human waste in catholes dug 6 to 8 inches, at least 200 feet from water, camp, and trails. Pack out toilet paper and hygiene products. To wash yourself or your dishes, carry water 200 feet away from streams or lakes and use small amounts of biodegradable soap. Scatter strained dishwater.

4. **Leave What You Find.** Cultural or historic artifacts, as well as natural objects such as plants or rocks, should be left as found.

5. **Minimize Campfire Impacts.** Cook on a stove. Use established fire rings, fire pans, or mound fires. If a campfire is built, keep it small and use dead sticks found on the ground.

6. **Respect Wildlife.** Observe wildlife from a distance. Feeding wild animals alters their natural behavior. Protect wildlife from your food by storing rations and trash securely.

7. **Be Considerate of Other Visitors.** Be courteous, respect the quality of other visitors' backcountry experience, and let nature's sounds prevail.

The AMC is a national provider of the Leave No Trace Master Educator course. The AMC offers this five-day course, designed especially for outdoor professionals and land managers, as well as the shorter two-day Leave No Trace Trainer course, at locations throughout the Northeast.

For Leave No Trace information and materials, contact the Leave No Trace Center for Outdoor Ethics, P.O. Box 997, Boulder, CO 80306. Phone: 800-332-4100 or 302-442-8222; fax: 303-442-8217; web: www.lnt.org. For information on the AMC Leave No Trace Master Educator training course schedule, see www.outdoors.org/education/lnt.

1

SOUTHEASTERN PENNSYLVANIA AND DELAWARE

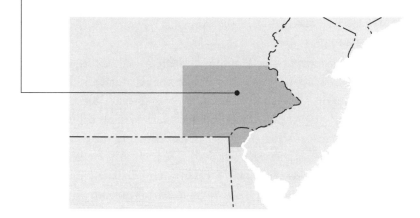

SOUTHEASTERN PENNSYLVANIA AND DELAWARE have the most diverse geography of the regions described in this book. The Atlantic coastal plain meets the rocky foothills of the Piedmont at the Fall Line, which crosses the Delaware River close to Trenton, New Jersey, and continues southwest, crossing the Susquehanna River below the Conowingo Dam. The flat, sandy coastal plain therefore includes some of Philadelphia and all of Delaware south of the Christina River. Hikes in the coastal plain include Fairmount Park Loop (Trip 1), John Heinz National Wildlife Refuge at Tinicum (Trip 4), Lums Pond State Park (Trip 11), and Bull's Island and D&R Canal (Trip 34).

The Fall Line, the change in elevation between the Piedmont and the coastal plain, is marked by dislocations in the bedrock, creating a cliff, or scarp. Not so much a line as a zone of varying width, it is called the Fall Line because waterfalls and rapids form where streams cross the boundary between the soft, sandy soils and the harder rocks of the Piedmont. All that falling water proved an irresistible source of power for mills and other waterwheel-based early industries. On the Wissahickon Creek alone there were more than 70 mills. Philadelphia, located on a bluff along the Delaware formed by piled-up sediments of the coastal plain, was a port city to which the mill products could be shipped for export.

The Fall Line also marks the point at which major rivers—including the Delaware, Schuylkill and Susquehanna—cease to be navigable. The falls of these rivers (at Trenton, East Falls, and Conowingo) are rapids formed by huge rocks displaced from the scarp. It is virtually impossible to hike anywhere along a stream or river near the Fall Line and not encounter reminders of the power of water as it drops down the scarp. Old mill dams, millraces, and mills themselves abound, and even if the structures are gone, the names cling to the places and roads they once occupied. The only hike in the book that directly crosses the Fall Line is the Fairmount Park Loop (Trip 1), most of which is in the coastal plain, but others, including the Pennypack Ecological Restoration Trust (Trip 9), go very near it.

Above the Fall Line north to Blue Mountain, which marks the southern edge of the ridge and valley section, the Piedmont's varying character is illustrated by the diverse topography of its landforms, and these in turn are determined by the dominant bedrock—typically sedimentary rock such as shale or sandstone, or metamorphic rock such as schist or gneiss. In turn, the landforms are shaped by the effects of wind, water, and weather on the rock. There are swampy lowlands, floodplains, dry woods, hills, bluffs, ravines, and diabase ridges. Piedmont hikes typically include a variety of terrain, which not only makes the hikes more fun but also helps support a diverse population of wildlife and thus makes it more likely the hike will continue to be enjoyable for years to come.

Within the Piedmont, the Pennsylvania Highlands are a distinct conservation region, running across the state from South Mountain (Cumberland County) to Easton (Northampton County). Piedmont hikes in the Pennsylvania Highlands include Hibernia County Park (Trip 14), Marsh Creek State Park (Trip 15), French Creek State Park (Trip 16), Green Lane Park/Perkiomen Trail (Trip 17), Ralph Stover State Park/Tohickon Valley Park (Trip 19), Nockamixon State Park (Trip 20), Neversink Mountain Preserve (Trip 21), Clarence Schock Park (Trip 23), and Money Rocks Park (Trip 24).

Other Piedmont hikes include Wissahickon Valley Park (Trip 2), Pennypack Park (Trip 3), Ridley Creek State Park (Trip 5), Valley Forge National Historical Park/Mount Misery and Mount Joy (Trip 6), Green Ribbon Trail (Trip 8), Pennypack Ecological Restoration Trust (Trip 9), Alapocas Run State Park (Trip 10), White Clay Creek Preserve/White Clay Creek State Park (Trip 12), Brandywine Creek State Park (Trip 13), Peace Valley Nature Center (Trip 18), Nolde Forest Environmental Education Center (Trip 22), Kelly's Run (Trip 25), and the Mason-Dixon Trail—Holtwood Preserve (Trip 26).

TRIP 1
FAIRMOUNT PARK LOOP
(ART MUSEUM)

Location: Philadelphia, PA
Rating: Easy
Distance: 9.0 miles
Elevation Gain: Minimal
Estimated Time: 3.5 hours
Maps: USGS Philadelphia; trail maps available online

Art and architecture, boats and bridges, history and nature all converge along the river that has been at the heart of Philadelphia since the city's founding.

DIRECTIONS

Take Kelly Drive or West River Drive (recently renamed Martin Luther King, Jr. Drive) east to the Philadelphia Museum of Art; or take I-676 west to the Benjamin Franklin Parkway exit and turn right onto 22nd Street, then left onto left outer lanes of the Ben Franklin Parkway and continue to the museum; or take I-676 east to the Spring Garden Street exit. Park on the street or in the museum's public garage. (Alternatively, since this is a loop, you can park on the West River Drive (Martin Luther King, Jr. Drive) side for free, except on weekends April–October, by crossing the river at Spring Garden Street.) For more detailed directions, visit www.philamuseum.org/visit/12-453-3.html. *GPS coordinates:* 39° 58.090′ N, 75° 11.031′ W.

To reach the museum area by public transportation, use SEPTA bus routes 7, 32, 38, 43, or 48, or Regional Rail lines to 30th Street Station or Suburban Station. From May 1 through October 31, the Phlash Downtown Visitor Shuttle provides direct service between Penn's Landing, Center City, and the museum between 10 A.M. and 6 P.M.

TRAIL DESCRIPTION

This hike features one of the glories of Philadelphia: the Schuylkill River waterfront. While this is the most urban hike in the book, it is surprisingly close to nature. The path is virtually all paved and level; the only elevation gain is the climb up Fair Mount to the Water Works scenic overview at the end.

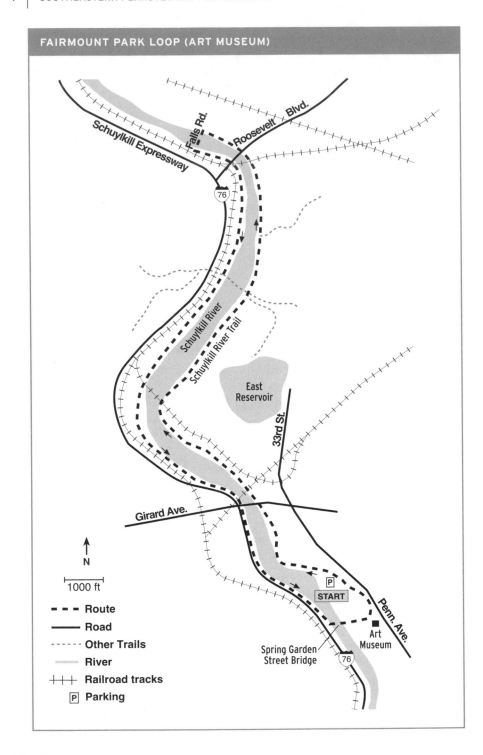

FAIRMOUNT PARK LOOP (ART MUSEUM)

Schuylkill Expressway

Falls Rd.

Roosevelt Blvd.

76

Schuylkill River

Schuylkill River Trail

East
Reservoir

33rd St.

Girard Ave.

N

1000 ft

P

START

Penn. Ave.

Art
Museum

Spring Garden
Street Bridge

76

- - - Route
——— Road
----- Other Trails
River
+++ Railroad tracks
P Parking

Scullers ply the Schuylkill River along Boathouse Row in Philadelphia.

The route follows a portion of the Schuylkill River Trail, a planned riverside trail that will extend 128 miles from the river's source, at Pottsville, Pennsylvania, to its mouth at the Delaware River. In addition to the segment near the Philadelphia Museum of Art, other completed parts of the trail include a 20-mile leg from Philadelphia's Center City district up to Valley Forge (see Trip 7).

The river loop hike is all within Fairmount Park, whose 9,200 acres comprise one of the largest urban parks in world. Beginning on the east bank, at the Fairmount Water Works, the route proceeds upstream to the East Falls of the Schuylkill, crosses the river, and returns on the west side. Some of Philadelphia's most distinguishing features—its ethnic and cultural diversity, passion for athletics, and embrace of arts and history—are on display. The trail is popular not only with walkers but also with runners, cyclists, dog owners, and families. On weekends it is crowded, especially during special events such as regattas.

Begin at the parking area near the Fairmount Water Works, below the Philadelphia Museum of Art. A stroll through the Fairmount Park Azalea Garden, adjacent to the parking lot, makes for a grand prelude in spring. Start the hike itself at a trail marker on the opposite side of the drive. Follow the paved path past Boathouse Row, a cluster of diverse Victorian-era rowing clubhouses; at night their lit outlines shimmer, reflected in the river.

Proceed along the riverbanks to the left. To the right is Kelly Drive—formerly East River Drive, and still known as such to many local residents—named for Jack Kelly, Olympic rower, city councilman, and father of actress Grace Kelly. Look for his sculpture farther down the trail. This section contains many examples of Fairmount Park's renowned collection of public art, honoring people both famous and obscure.

Shortly, the trail bends right along the roadway, but a sidewalk continues along the riverbank. Take the sidewalk. The riverside walk is quieter and provides a superior view of the large sculpture garden devoted to American history. Past the sculpture garden the sidewalk rejoins the trail, passing under the Girard Avenue Bridge, then around Promontory Rock, which hosts innumerable tiny plants that have gained a roothold in its crevices. Notice the rock's wavy layers of gneiss and Wissahickon schist with shiny mica flakes.

After Promontory Rock, the trail meanders by a mile-long grove of cherry trees (many of which are gifts from Japan), which in very early spring burst with pink and white flowers. Pass under several bridges, each with a historical marker. The stone-arched 1866–67 Pennsylvania Railroad Connecting Bridge was featured by Thomas Eakins in his 1871 painting *Max Schmitt in a Single Scull.*

The boathouses spill out rowers in profusion. Rowing is a long-lasting Delaware Valley tradition; it's a rare hike on this trail that doesn't include a glimpse of the powerful, graceful rhythm of a crew.

Past the cherry trees, the riverfront landscape becomes more natural, crowded with floodplain trees: silver maple, box elder, sumac, slippery elm. Across Kelly Drive are looming bluffs covered with plants typical of steep river slopes: oaks, dogwoods, and rhododendrons. If you squint, and cover your ears, it is possible to imagine the wild landscape that flourished before the roadway was built and the Schuylkill dammed—when the river had the Lenape names of Manayunk ("where we drink") and Ganshowahanna ("falling waters").

From here to East Falls, the trail alternately rises above the riverbank and returns to it. On the bluffs are the ornate mausoleums of Laurel Hill Cemetery. East Falls itself is an old commercial district, marking the end of the naturalistic walk. It's a short trek along sidewalks to the Falls Bridge, a steel truss built in 1895. Cross the bridge, pausing to look in the river for the partly submerged boulders that give the East Falls of the Schuylkill its name. The boulders mark the Fall Line, the zone where the continental shelf collides with the Piedmont foothills. This is the easternmost falls on the river.

Leaving the bridge, turn left into West Fairmount Park. This side of the route is less urban and usually less crowded. On weekend days April through October, West River Drive (Martin Luther King Jr. Drive) is closed to vehicles. Hidden inlets along the river attract fish and anglers, birds sing among the trees that throng the riverbanks, and water spills from the bluffs on the far side of the road. On the west side too are grassy lawns and picnic areas. In other ways the west bank mirrors the east, albeit on a smaller scale: a few sculptures, a smaller grove of cherry trees. Regularly placed signposts show mileage to the art museum.

About two and a half miles from the museum, past the Belmont Water Intake, West River Drive merges with Montgomery Drive, and the Schuylkill Expressway emerges from above. Traffic noise increases measurably, unless the drive is closed. A fine distraction comes into view at just this moment: the classic view of Boathouse Row and the Fairmount Water Works. Lines are strung over the Water Works dam to help stop runaway boats. Cormorants—big, dark diving birds—often sit atop the lines, drying their wings.

Cross back over the river on the pedestrian Spring Garden Street Bridge. Bear right, and follow the walkway up the rock to one of several viewing gazebos atop Fair Mount; the coastal plain, stretching to the Atlantic Ocean, is to the east of this rock knob. This is a good place to sit and have a snack, as the bird's-eye view of the Schuylkill here is dramatically different from the view you've just left behind.

MORE INFORMATION

The Schuylkill River Trail (SRT) is open 24 hours a day and lit at night; however, the west side of the trail is not. Restrooms are located in Lloyd Hall, the only public athletic facility on Boathouse Row, open from 7 A.M. to 9 P.M. The Philadelphia Museum of Art's collections are world-renowned; the Fairmount Water Works also houses a water museum. The SRT continues past East Falls to Valley Forge and Phoenixville, and also below the museum to the Schuylkill Banks on the Delaware. Fairmount Park, One Parkway, 10th Floor, 1515 Arch Street, Philadelphia, PA 19102; 215-683-0200; www.fairmountpark.org.

TRIP 2
WISSAHICKON VALLEY PARK

Location: Philadelphia, PA
Rating: Moderate–Difficult
Distance: 7.0 miles
Elevation Gain: 250 feet
Estimated Time: 3.5 hours
Maps: USGS Germantown; trail map available at the Valley Green Inn, some local map stores and bookstores, and online from the Friends of the Wissahickon

This is a strenuous, varied hike through a rugged stream-studded creek gorge within the city of Philadelphia. It also features old-growth forests, meadows, rock formations, and historic stone structures.

DIRECTIONS

Take Germantown Avenue to Chestnut Hill Avenue; turn right onto Crefeld Street. The Fairmount Park entrance is on the left behind an unlocked gate. Park on the street, where you will find room for eight to ten cars. *GPS coordinates*: 40° 04.614′ N, 75° 12.990′ W.

To get to the trailhead by public transportation, take the SEPTA R8 Regional Rail to the Chestnut Hill West Station or bus route 23; walk downhill from Germantown Avenue and along Chestnut Hill Avenue to Crefeld Street.

TRAIL DESCRIPTION

That there is a place within the city of Philadelphia that has 57 miles of hiking trails—and that many of these miles are as challenging and scenic as any trails in the mountains hours away—may amaze the casual visitor and surprise even the most well-informed area hiker. The place is a rugged gorge surrounding the Wissahickon Creek: the 1,800-acre Wissahickon Valley Park.

The circuit hike described here is deliberately challenging, to satisfy the hiker who desires a strenuous workout over a rugged landscape within reach of public transportation. It provides encounters with the valley's history, the creek (its central feature), and the many shapes of Wissahickon schist.

People have been enjoying the Wissahickon's resources for centuries. The Lenape Indians fished, hunted, and built villages here. The eighteenth and

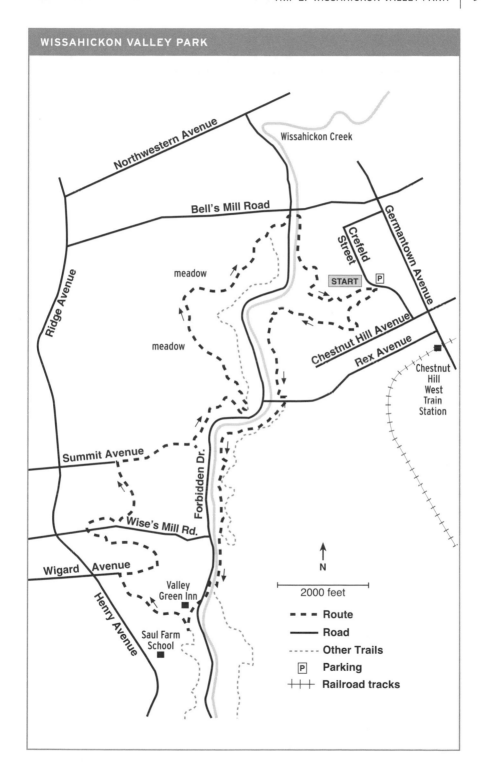

WISSAHICKON VALLEY PARK

Northwestern Avenue

Wissahickon Creek

Bell's Mill Road

Germantown Avenue

Crefeld Street

meadow

START

P

Ridge Avenue

Chestnut Hill Avenue

meadow

Rex Avenue

Chestnut Hill West Train Station

Summit Avenue

Forbidden Dr.

Wise's Mill Rd.

Wigard Avenue

Valley Green Inn

Henry Avenue

Saul Farm School

N

2000 feet

- - - Route
—— Road
---- Other Trails
P Parking
+++ Railroad tracks

nineteenth centuries brought industry: water-powered mills were built, and the hillsides were logged. Roads were laid for commerce, then for recreation, bringing tourists to the scenic gorge. Inns and taverns sprang up to serve travelers.

The city acquired much of the parkland in the late nineteenth century to safeguard drinking-water sources. Protected now for more than a century, the valley is rich in wildlife habitat.

The hike begins on the Lavender Trail, blazed lavender. (Signage is often, but not always, informative at trail crossings. Blazing is inconsistent; it is often excellent, but some trails—marked "other" on the map produced by the Friends of the Wissahickon—are not blazed at all.) Note that the hike can be shortened by stopping at any point prior to crossing the creek at Valley Green Inn and backtracking to the start.

From the gated entrance on Crefeld Street, take the left-hand trail fork, heading into an imposing forest of huge old oaks, beeches, tulip trees, and walnuts. This is one of many areas of old-growth forest in the Wissahickon valley, trees that grew up in the 150 years after the valley was last logged.

Head downhill, crossing a stream over a stone bridge. At the next intersection, continue straight onto the unblazed trail, which heads uphill; turn right onto the White Trail, a gravel road here. Head downhill to a fork, where there is a park bench. Take the left fork (the right fork drops off sharply to the creek) and the next sharp left, staying on the White Trail, which merges with the Green Trail and becomes a rocky footpath, going uphill.

The rocks here are crumbling into sand from the impact of so much traffic (foot, bike, and horse). Throughout the park, erosion has created difficult footing and overloaded the creek with sediment-borne storm water. (Some Wissahickon trails—though none on this hike—are being restored and the trail bed rebuilt.)

Go downhill, cross a stream, and turn uphill, passing by massive schist outcrops to the left. Stone steps make the path easier. About a fifth of a mile after the stream, look right; the "Indian statue" gazes out over the creek from a slab of schist known as Council Rock, where natives supposedly conducted powwows. John Massey Rhind's 1902 sculpture commemorates the passing of the Lenape from this region; the chief looks westward toward his departing people.

The trail descends the hill to a four-way intersection. Continue straight on the White/Green Trail, crossing the gravel road and a stream, then head uphill; bear right at the next fork away from the White/Green Trail onto the unmarked trail. Follow this along the creek, merging onto the Orange Trail.

Wissahickon meadows in winter display the stark beauty of tree forms and standing native grasses.

Stay on the Orange Trail, which crosses the creek via an 1832 stone bridge, at Valley Green Inn. Built in 1850, the inn is still in operation.

Turn left onto Forbidden Drive, an early-nineteenth-century turnpike that is now closed to motor vehicles. Immediately after the inn, turn sharp right and head uphill on the steep, rocky footpath. Turn right at a T onto the flatter, but still rocky, Yellow Trail. Keep straight at the next intersection, then make the second left onto an unblazed trail heading toward Henry Avenue. The trail comes out to a pasture and a T intersection. Turn right, going along fields of the Saul Farm School, a Philadelphia public high school for agriculture.

Turn right at the end of the field at Wigard Avenue past a metal gate onto an unblazed trail, once again coming into an old-growth woods of very big trees. You'll see many umbrella magnolias, which are uncommon in this region. Turn sharp left onto the Yellow Trail, heading downhill. Cross Wise's Mill Road (one of several old roads named for the creekside mills they led to). Continue on the Yellow Trail, crossing a stream, then uphill to residential Summit Avenue. Make a right; where the street takes a sharp left, continue straight, returning to the park through a gate into thick woods. Follow the trail to a T intersection. Turn left, continue up the ridge, and then head down to

Forbidden Drive. Immediately turn left over a bridge, make another immediate left, and ascend the ridge. At the next intersection with an unblazed trail, turn left. The trail is full of loose rocks.

Head uphill, bearing left at the next fork, passing through meadows. These meadows are being restored. The trees are being cleared, and grasses and wildflowers planted; the fields will be managed to prevent the woods from taking over. The trail briefly passes out of the park through a playground area, returns to meadows bordered by stands of aspens, and then reenters the woods. Go all the way downhill via the unblazed trail (bearing left at the first two forks and right on the third), turn left onto the Yellow Trail, and head to Forbidden Drive. Turn left and cross Bell's Mill Road via the stone arch bridge, built in 1820. Note mile marker 0 here (Forbidden Drive's terminus). Turn right on the Orange Trail, go uphill into woods, and bear left onto the Lavender Trail. This is the last leg. Follow this trail back to the Crefeld Street gate (bear left at the fork).

MORE INFORMATION

There are restrooms adjacent to Valley Green Inn, about the halfway point of the hike. The park is open for hiking 24 hours a day, 7 days a week. With the exception of the Lavender Trail and certain other trail segments, bikes and horses are permitted. Dogs must be on a leash no longer than 12 feet. The trails are maintained by Friends of the Wissahickon, 8708 Germantown Avenue, Philadelphia, PA 19118-2717; 215-247-0417; www.fow.org.

TRIP 3
PENNYPACK PARK

Location: Philadelphia, PA
Rating: Moderate
Distance: 8.0 miles
Elevation Gain: 50 feet
Estimated Time: 3.0 hours
Maps: USGS Frankford

Smaller, and under less stress from human impact than Wissahickon Gorge, Pennypack Park is an underutilized natural area within the city's borders. This hike takes you on trails that wind through a forested valley and alongside the wide, picturesque Pennypack Creek.

DIRECTIONS
Take Route 1 north (which becomes Roosevelt Boulevard), and turn left onto Bustleton Avenue. Go 3.2 miles and turn left onto Benton Street; the Pennypack Park entrance is immediately on the right. Make a U-turn and park across the street, where there is space for ten cars. *GPS coordinates*: 40° 04.525′ N, 75° 02.798′ W.

To reach Pennypack Park via public transportation, take SEPTA bus route 58 or 67.

TRAIL DESCRIPTION
Tucked into the far northeast section of Philadelphia, Pennypack Park doesn't get the same attention as Wissahickon Valley Park, its larger city park sibling. Pennypack deserves to be better known, as it boasts everything a hiker could ask for: rich woods, a scenic creek, a variety of terrain, and wildlife.

Pennypack Creek begins in Horsham, Pennsylvania, and empties into the Delaware River in Philadelphia's Holmesburg neighborhood under a stone bridge that was built in 1697. The creek, whose name derives from the Lenape word meaning "slow-flowing creek," is no longer so slow; its densely developed 57-square-mile watershed deluges the creek with storm water. But watershed restoration initiatives abound: planting meadows and trees (including at Pennypack Ecological Restoration Trust, Trip 9), removing dams, and installing fish passages.

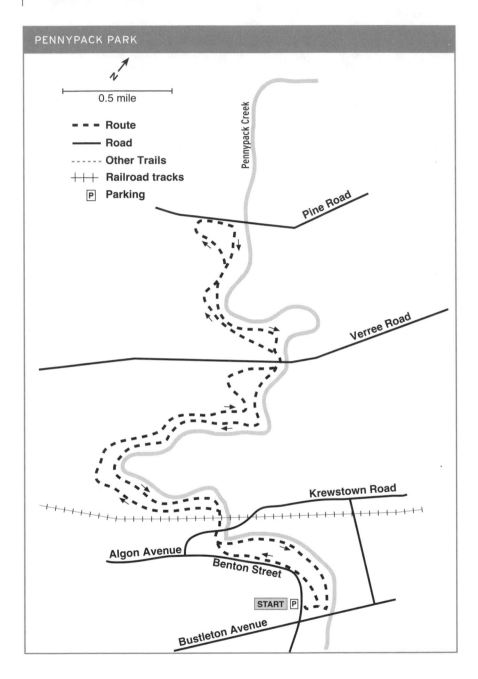

Pennypack Park's 1,334 acres run 9.0 miles along the creek valley from the Montgomery County line to the Delaware River. This hike focuses on trails in the northernmost, and prettiest, section. The circuit goes out on a natural-surface trail in the hills and returns on a paved multiuse path along the creek; you can also hike it in the opposite direction if you prefer.

Begin at the Benton Avenue entrance, heading downhill on the paved path. Take a left after 0.2 mile, onto the dirt path into the woods (i.e., don't go all the way down to the creek). This is a moist woods with big old trees (ash, maple, tulip tree) and a dense understory. There are deer in the park, but controlled hunting is reducing the damage they have caused, with the result that the condition of the woods in this northern section is as good as that in more remote areas. In winter, there are good views of the creek below, but in other seasons the forest envelops the trails in green. Horses use this trail, so it gets muddy, but their tracks make it easier to follow. After about half a mile, the trail approaches Krewstown Road. Cross the road by going downhill to pass under the stone bridge along the paved creekside path; continue on the paved path under the railroad bridge and take the next left to return to the dirt path going uphill.

The trail is rocky; underfoot are crumbled bits of the bedrock Wissahickon schist that underlies the valley and outcrops occasionally along the creek (see "Wissahickon Schist" on page 17). Cross a trail going to the left to the power line that parallels the railroad tracks; stay on the main (horse) trail, going gently right at the next four-way intersection. The trail is *not* marked, but at all crossings the horse trail can be identified by heavy square wooden beams placed across it to protect it from water damage. Stay straight at the next intersection, heading downhill to the creek and crossing the multiuse trail. Cross a stream on an iron bridge. Black walnut trees thrive in this section on the moist rocky soil. Go straight at the next two intersections, with a stream crossing in between, keeping the creek below and to your right. You'll enter a steep gorge with tall canopy trees above, ferns and moist-soil-loving wildflowers such as jack-in-the-pulpit below.

The trail bears left and up the hill, then back down toward the multiuse path. At about three miles, you'll reach Verree Road. At the intersection with the paved multiuse path is a wetlands area near the Pennypack Environmental Center (to the right on Verree Road); this area was created in 2007, when a former parking lot was planted with native scrub-shrub vegetation.

Cross Verree Road by following the multiuse trail under the bridge. You may see some aerobatic blue-brown, fork-tailed birds zipping out from under the bridge and back to catch insects on the wing; these are barn swallows, which build nests under the span.

Again bear left up the hill along the dirt path. This wooded area, closer to major parking areas, is more disturbed and not quite as rich or healthy as the

With its thick forest and network of streams, Pennypack Park is a hidden gem in the Northeast section of Philadelphia.

forest to the south, but it affords creek views even during the height of summer. There are extremely large old trees in this section, one of which, at 4 feet in diameter and about 200 years old, used to be a prominent landmark for a turn and now, fallen, still marks it. Head downhill alongside the remains of the tree, cross a stream, take the macadam path across a wide lawn area with a sunflower meadow, and at 4.0 miles, you'll reach Pine Road. There is a U.S. Geological Survey (USGS) gauging station here to measure the stream flow.

Turn around and follow the multiuse trail back along the creek. There are no turns to worry about. The path does have ups and downs, given the schist upwellings and outcrops in the terrain. At outcrops, you can look closely at the rock in cross-section to see its flat, platelike structure and the multiple color variations. The creekside trail also allows an intimate appreciation for the flow of the creek, which is in fact a recent development; between 2005 and 2009, four of the seven major dams on the Pennypack Creek were removed and two fish passages were installed in the lower reaches, eliminating sediment-trapping stagnant pools and creating healthier habitat for fish and aquatic life. You will pass under the same five bridges as on the outward leg; at the fifth bridge immediately after the railroad bridge, turn right to go uphill and make a right onto the dirt path to exit the park at Benton Avenue.

MORE INFORMATION

A portable toilet is located at Pine Road, the turnaround point. Pennypack Park is open 24 hours a day, 7 days a week. Trail maintenance organization: Friends of Pennypack Park (www.balford.com/fopp/). Pennypack Park, One Parkway, 10th Floor, 1515 Arch Street, Philadelphia, PA 19102; 215-685-0470; www.fairmountpark.org/PennypackPark.asp.

WISSAHICKON SCHIST

If a rock could be said to define Philadelphia, it is Wissahickon schist. It was first studied along the Wissahickon Creek in Philadelphia (see Trip 2). From a distance it appears dark gray-black, like the garments worn by Quaker settlers. On closer inspection, it is composed of multiple layers of colors and textures, like the diverse community that Philadelphia's founder, William Penn, sought to create: silvery mica, ruby-colored garnet, black tourmaline, ribbons of white quartzite, and splotches of gold, umber, gray, green, and tan. It is the bedrock that underlies the city's skyscrapers as well as much of southeastern Pennsylvania, southern New Jersey, and Delaware. Schist is a metamorphosed sedimentary rock, with layers of minerals originally deposited by inland seas. The minerals were transformed and recrystallized by heating and cooling, resulting in a hard rock that flakes into flat plates. The beauty and variety of Wissahickon schist, as well as its strength, made it a favorite building stone in the masonry era of the nineteenth and early twentieth centuries. In situ, the rock resists erosion from wind and water, forming vertical cliffs and ravines; its tendency to fracture into plates creates horizontal outcrops, like Council Rock, the slab on which the Wissahickon Indian statue sits, and wide, flat boulder debris from rocks that break off cliffs.

TRIP 4
JOHN HEINZ NATIONAL
WILDLIFE REFUGE AT TINICUM

Location: Philadelphia and Folcroft, PA (Delaware County)
Rating: Easy
Distance: 5.0 miles
Elevation Gain: Minimal
Estimated Time: 2.0 hours
Maps: USGS Lansdowne; trail map available online at the website for
the John Heinz National Wildlife Refuge

**Transport yourself to Pennsylvania's coastline without leaving the
city. This level walk winds around a pond and through a freshwater
tidal marsh.**

DIRECTIONS
From I-95 south, take Exit 14 (Bartram Avenue), and at the fifth light turn
right onto 84th Street. At the second light, turn left onto Lindbergh Boulevard
and follow it until you reach the first stop sign. The refuge entrance is on the
right, where you will find ample parking.

From I-95 north, take Exit 10 (Route 291) and at first light, turn left onto
Bartram Avenue. At the fifth light, turn left onto 84th Street and follow the
directions above to the refuge entrance. GPS coordinates: 39° 53.491′ N, 75°
15.450′ W.

To reach the refuge via public transportation, take SEPTA R1 Regional Rail
to Eastwick Station, or bus routes 37 or 108.

TRAIL DESCRIPTION
In the center of a triangle formed by I-95, Philadelphia International Airport,
and dense residential neighborhoods, a pair of bald eagles soars silently over
the placid waters of Tinicum Marsh. They glide beneath electric lines and
above a pipeline, wheel slowly with wings spread flat, then drop onto a tree.
They gaze north toward downtown Philadelphia, the city whose football team
is their namesake.

The John Heinz National Wildlife Refuge at Tinicum is the nation's most
urbanized national wildlife refuge (and was the first federal urban refuge).

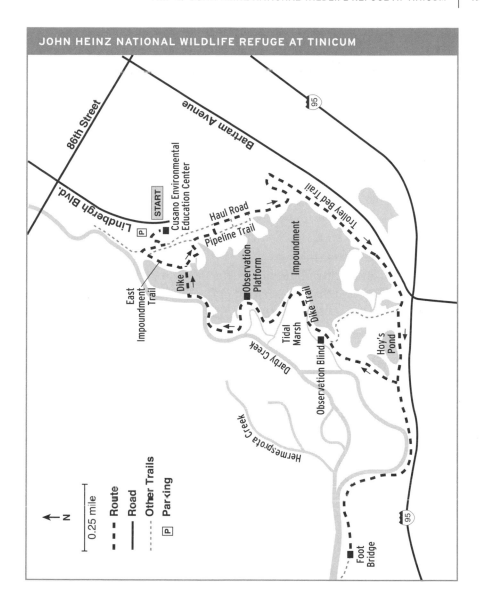

JOHN HEINZ NATIONAL WILDLIFE REFUGE AT TINICUM

Despite its location, it is a haven for wildlife, especially birds, because of its varied habitat.

Within the refuge lies Tinicum Marsh, Pennsylvania's largest freshwater tidal marsh. Though the state has no coastline, it does have creeks and rivers that receive an influx of tidal-influenced freshwater twice a day from Delaware Bay, creating a unique habitat of mudflats and aquatic vegetation. Tinicum's marshes were drained and filled over 300 years, reducing the 6,000 acres the marsh covered in the seventeenth century to a mere 200 today. In the early 1970s, concerned citizens, working with U.S. Representative (later Senator) John Heinz, succeeded in establishing a federal refuge to protect and restore 1,200 acres around the marsh.

The Cusano Environmental Education Center is certainly worth visiting. Not only does it boast outstanding exhibits detailing the nature and history of Tinicum Marsh, but the building itself, made of renewable materials and designed to be energy efficient (geothermal and solar-powered), is an award-winning example of green construction.

Hiking trails begin behind the Cusano Center. The short hike detailed here traverses the refuge's three main habitats: tidal marshland, woods, and nontidal diked impoundment. You can stretch it out by stopping at wildlife observation points along the way.

From the parking lot, follow the paved path around the center to the rear, where it winds toward the woods, crossing Haul Road, a gravel multiuse trail. The entrance to the woods is marked by a large metal sign indicating a 0.6-mile accessible trail. Follow this paved trail about an eighth of a mile, passing the impoundment, until it meets the long boardwalk over the impoundment. Do not go onto the boardwalk, but instead turn left into the woods and onto a natural-surface trail.

This trail winds through Warbler Woods, a low-lying, often flooded area of densely growing young trees and shrubs called an early-succession floodplain forest; it is thick with sweet-gum trees. The trail is unmarked but easy to follow as it passes in and out of woods and thickets; keep the impoundment on your right. After 500 feet the trail crosses a small bridge over an inlet. Turn right and continue a few hundred feet until the trail ends; turn left onto a wide grassy swath. Cross the petroleum pipeline "trail" (a wide area marked by upright metal posts) and turn right shortly, when it dead-ends at Haul Road. From here on, watch for blazed posts placed at trail intersections. Blue triangles indicate that you are heading toward the visitor center; yellow circles indicate that you are heading toward Route 420 (away from the center). You are heading away at this point.

Haul Road continues in a straight line for about three-eighths of a mile, enters an aspen grove, and turns sharply right where the surface becomes dirt. The trail bends right almost immediately and intersects with the Trolley Bed Trail. Look for excellent views to the north up the length of the impoundment. The reed domes that dot the water near the shore are the roofs of muskrat dens.

The trail approaches I-95 above and to the right; as the views of the impoundment become more dramatic, the road noise increases. After about

The John Heinz National Wildlife Refuge at Tinicum is a haven for birds of marshes, woods, and shores.

three-quarters of a mile, the trail comes close to the highway. A Y intersection is here. Bear left on the Y to go around the shallow Hoy's Pond.

After 0.25 mile, there is another Y intersection, this one next to a bench. Continue with the highway to your left, about another quarter of a mile to the next intersection. Turn right. Now you are in the midst of the tidal marsh area. With its low mudflats, shallow trickling streams, and open areas of reeds and grass, the marsh is dramatically different from the woodsy impoundment area. Whereas the nontidal impoundment attracts birds that dive for fish, such as cormorants, kingfishers, or gulls, this section is habitat for shorebirds that probe the mudflats and shallow waters. The refuge managers are gradually restoring the marshland by removing dredge spoil and breaching dikes to let in the tidewater and are planting native vegetation such as wild rice, which can be seen in the marshland to your right.

Continue for another 0.25 mile until you reach a small footbridge. This is an ideal spot to peer across the marsh in all directions. Darby Creek and its tributaries form an intricate network of channels, perhaps even as complex as the flight paths of the jets taking off next door.

Although the trail continues for another 1.5 miles through the marsh and to the parking area at Route 420, turn around here. Retrace your steps to the second Y intersection and turn left (toward the visitor center), away from the highway, and continue past Hoy's Pond on your right.

After 0.2 mile, rejoin the Impoundment Trail and bear left. The tidal marsh is on your left and the impoundment on your right, offering continuous contrast, with low water-loving trees, such as box elders, lining the pathway. The trail hugs the shoreline of the impoundment and goes around several shallow coves. This is good habitat for frogs of various species, including wood frogs, which can be heard in great numbers in early spring "quacking" like ducks (which also abound here).

A two-level observation tower provides long-distance views of the impoundment after 0.3 mile. After another 0.25 mile, turn right onto the long boardwalk over the impoundment. Numerous resting spots and interpretive signs describe the birds you are likely to see, encouraging you to walk slowly and stop along the way. The boardwalk meets the paved accessible trail on the other side of the impoundment; follow it out of the woods and past the center to the parking lot.

MORE INFORMATION

The refuge is open from sunrise to sunset every day of the year. Bikes are permitted. Restrooms are located at Cusano Environmental Education Center. Dogs are permitted, and must be leashed at all times. There are over 10 miles of trails. The trails are maintained by Friends of Heinz Refuge at Tinicum. John Heinz National Wildlife Refuge, 8601 Lindbergh Boulevard, Philadelphia, PA 19153; 215-365-3118; www.fws.gov/heinz.

TRIP 5
RIDLEY CREEK STATE PARK

Location: Newtown Square, PA (Delaware County)
Rating: Moderate
Distance: 5.5 miles
Elevation Gain: 225 feet
Estimated Time: 2.75 hrs
Maps: USGS Media; trail map available online

Ridley Creek is a hidden gem with four-season surprises. With its steep, forested hills and rocky streams, this hike demonstrates that you don't have to go far to get away.

DIRECTIONS

From the north, take West Chester Pike (Route 3) to Bishop Hollow Road and turn right onto Gradyville Road. Turn right onto Sandy Flash Drive South to enter the park; follow signs to Picnic Area 9. From the south, take Route 352 to Gradyville Road and proceed as directed above. You will find ample parking. *GPS coordinates*: 39° 57.228′ N, 75° 26.479′ W.

TRAIL DESCRIPTION

Ridley Creek State Park is a testament to the power of terrain. Driving along West Chester Pike through densely developed Delaware County, you'd never guess that this gem of a hiking park, with miles of wooded hillside trails and picturesque creeks, lies just off the road. Even many park users, walking or biking on the paved paths that wind through the park, are unaware that trails traverse the hills above and below.

The hilltops of the park are at the same elevation as the surrounding roads, hiding the internal topography. Ridley Creek itself lies at the bottom of a steep valley, while smaller tributary streams meander through shallower valleys. From any of these it is difficult to get a sense of the whole park. Hiking Ridley Creek is an experience of coming upon surprise after surprise.

Although the hike described here can be done in an afternoon, it provides beauty, challenge, and interest at almost every step along the way. This is a four-season hike; in spring, wildflowers carpet the woods and stream banks; cool shaded woods relieve summer's heat; autumn's leaves burnish the treetops in brilliant colors; and winter provides icy-clear views of hills, creek, and sky.

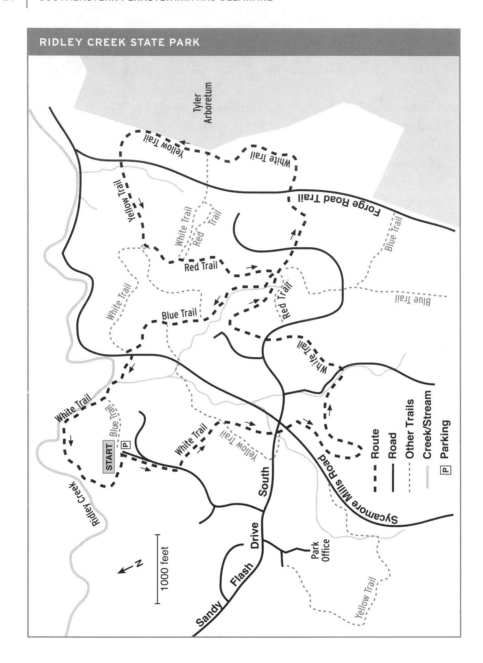

RIDLEY CREEK STATE PARK

The hike starts at Picnic Area 9. To get to the trailhead, walk along the roadway 750 feet to the White Trail entrance, marked on the left with a post. After a short open section, the trail enters a successional woods—trees and shrubs that have grown up in formerly open areas. When the state bought it, the land that became the 2,606-acre park was the Hunting Hill estate of the wealthy Jeffords family, with many cleared farm fields, pastures, and drives. The extensive grounds of Hunting Hill included not only a historic gristmill and associated structures but also a 1918 mansion designed by the noted architect Wilson Eyre (built around a 1773 farmhouse). Today, a wing of the mansion houses the park's main office. The mansion is worth a peek; in addition to its architectural interest, and formal gardens in season, there is a huge wall-mounted relief map of the park on display.

Watch for trail blazes that consist of white paint splotches on trees and occasional painted arrows where the trail turns. Other trails—Red, Yellow, and Blue—are marked by blazes and arrows in those colors; when two or more trails coincide, there are blazes in both colors. The trail is a natural-surface footpath that starts out relatively flat, climbs up the side of the hill, then descends steeply into a ravine.

The rock that creates most of the park's hills and ravines is gneiss— billion-year-old metamorphic rock created when colliding plates of Earth's crust crushed and heated existing sedimentary rocks, causing them to be deformed and recrystallized like taffy. Although the gneiss is hidden here, outcrops can be seen along the creek later in the hike.

At 0.25 mile, the White Trail bends right to cross the Yellow Trail; continue on the White Trail as the hill steepens even more. This section can be slippery. As the trail descends, it dodges large old oak trees. Steeper hills were more difficult to log, so larger, more mature forests occur on ravine slopes. At the bottom of the hill, the trail bends left to cross a small stream, which can be wet in spring and icy in winter. Follow the White Trail as it goes into a round-arched culvert that passes under Sandy Flash Drive.

On the other side, the White Trail crosses a paved multiuse trail and then ducks back into the woods, ascending a steep hill by fits and starts: up, down, and around. The woods are oak, hickory, and tulip tree. Look for the dark, blocky bark of the persimmon tree, too. Descend the hill, cross Sandy Flash Drive again, and then climb up the hill on the other side. As the trail descends, it crosses a pipeline section; follow the trail diagonally down where it reenters the woods. At the bottom, it crosses the drive again, skirts the rear of the restroom facilities at Area 16, and winds back around the hill. After a stream crossing, the White Trail meets up with the Blue Trail, then the Red Trail. This patriotic section can be confusing; follow the white blazes as the Red and Blue trails each peel off (you'll return to this point).

As you cross Sandy Flash Drive again, note the high banks on either side of the trail and the honey locusts at the corners. The White Trail is following a centuries-old, long-abandoned roadbed, wide enough for an oxcart. Near the

Rugged, rocky Ridley Creek is gorgeous any time of year.

top of the hill (the highest point on the hike) the trail bends around a ruins. Within the park are the remains of 25 eighteenth-century farmsteads and four roads; the process of historical succession (farm community to estate to park) is a counterpoint to natural succession (mature woods to cleared land to young woods) that can also be observed here. Head into a weedy thicket where succession by young woods has yet to take hold. The blazes end abruptly; watch for an arrow and follow the White Trail left. After 0.25 mile, there is a junction with the Yellow Trail. Say goodbye to the White Trail for a while and follow the yellow blazes. This section borders the Tyler Arboretum on the right; former trail access is, however, now closed. To your left is a white-pine plantation (i.e., not a naturally occurring woods, although the eastern white pine is native to the area). The sounds of the wind, the fragrance of trees, and the soft needle-covered footpath are sweeter and quieter in the pine forest than in the hardwood forest you've been walking through.

After another 0.25 mile, the trail turns left and descends into the pines. After it crosses the road 500 feet later, you're back in the deciduous forest. The Yellow Trail climbs a long, steep hill that falls away to Ridley Creek; at the top turn left onto the White Trail, then after about 500 feet turn sharp right onto the Red Trail. (This can be confusing: the Red Trail joins with the White Trail here; if you start off in the wrong direction, you'll shortly end up at Picnic Area 17, where the White Trail ends.) The Red Trail winds back down the hill to the Red-White-Blue intersection; this time, turn right to follow the Blue Trail heading downhill (conjoined with the White Trail for about 200 feet), then bear right to follow the Blue Trail as the White Trail splits off. Continue to follow the Blue Trail down the hill, as it joins and loses the Yellow Trail. As the trail skirts a stream bank, it narrows; the footing can be treacherous in mud or snow. The trail descends down to the multiuse trail, where it joins up with the White Trail again.

This section along Ridley Creek is one of the loveliest trails in the book, with the wide, rushing creek on one side and craggy boulders on the other. The terrain flattens out into a floodplain forest that is rife with wildflowers in spring, lush green in summer, and as wild as southeastern Pennsylvania gets any time of year. Gneiss outcrops, with their distinctive light-and-dark alternating bands, occur along the creek. Follow the White Trail along the creek as the Blue Trail turns up the hill. After about 1,500 feet the White Trail turns and ascends. The sounds of the creek gradually fade, and the trail ends at the parking lot where you started.

MORE INFORMATION

Restrooms are located at the main office parking area, none at the trailhead. The trails are maintained by Friends of Ridley Creek State Park (www.friendsofrcsp.org). Ridley Creek State Park, 1023 Sycamore Mills Road, Media, PA 19063 (for online mapping directions use 351 Gradyville Road, Newtown Square, PA 19073); 610-892-3900; www.dcnr.state.pa.us/stateParks/parks/ridleycreek.aspx.

Bowhunting is permitted in some areas; check with park office during deer season.

HERE TODAY, GONE TOMORROW

Spring comes to deciduous woodlands from the ground up. Even before the vernal equinox, small flowers appear on the forest floor. Hepatica, with bright blue or white blooms; spring beauties, with delicate pink-lined white flowers; nodding yellow trout lilies; bloodroot; trailing arbutus; wild ginger; dutchman's breeches; bluebells; toothwort—all these and dozens more have charmed woods walkers as long as there have been woods to walk in.

Wildflowers take advantage of the sunlight that reaches through the forest canopy before tree leaves appear. Some, such as spring beauties, bloom for a month or more; others, such as bloodroot, last only a day. Spotting these spring ephemerals is one of the joys of an early spring hike. Once you get to know where they grow, you can go back every year to greet them.

The plants time their blossoming to ensure that the sun has warmed the air enough for pollinators (flies, gnats, and bees) to emerge and forage. Ephemerals also need sunlight to grow leaf, stem, and root cells, and to produce flowers, pollen, and seeds. They've evolved differing strategies to meet the challenge of gathering enough energy to both survive and reproduce. The grasslike leaves of spring beauties appear first, collect energy, and then fade as the blooms appear. Hepatica doesn't bother growing leaves until after its flowers wither; its round, liver-colored leaves persist over the winter, collecting energy over a long time and storing it for spring.

Spring wildflowers bloom reliably year after year. But the timing of flowering in general has been advancing with climate change: 5 to 6 days earlier in North America over the last 35 years. If flowers continue to blossom earlier and earlier, plant-animal interactions could be affected; for example, if the timing of pollinator activity doesn't change at the same rate that flowering changes, insects won't be able to gather nectar and flowers won't go to seed.

Phenology is the study of periodic biological phenomena (e.g., bird migration or plant flowering) and their relation to climate. Local data can benefit phenologists, and individual "citizen scientists" can help by recording their observations of flowering times. Many conservation organizations have programs, such as the Appalachian Mountain Club's Mountain Watch program, to collect and analyze such data, with the goal of understanding how climate change may affect natural cycles. The National Phenology Network (www.usanpn.org) lists scores of opportunities. Whether for science or pleasure, observing spring ephemerals is one of the timeless activities of a woodland spring.

TRIP 6
VALLEY FORGE NATIONAL
HISTORICAL PARK–MOUNT MISERY AND MOUNT JOY

Location: King of Prussia, PA (Chester and Montgomery counties)
Rating: Moderate
Distance: 5.0 miles
Elevation Gain: 450 feet
Estimated Time: 3.0 hours
Maps: USGS Valley Forge trail map available at welcome center and online

Climb rocky hills and traverse old fields alongside a meandering creek in a rural landscape imbued with American history.

DIRECTIONS
Take I-76 (Schuylkill Expressway) west to Exit 328A; stay right and merge onto U.S. 422 west to the Valley Forge exit (Route 23 west). Turn left at the exit ramp. If you are stopping first at the welcome center (visitor center), stay in the center lane and, at the traffic light at the intersection of North Gulph Road, go straight into the park. If you are going to the trailhead, get into the right lane, turn right at the traffic light, and follow Route 23 west approximately 2.0 miles to the Washington's Headquarters parking area on the right. There is ample parking. *GPS coordinates*: 40° 06.083′ N, 75° 27.717′ W.

To use public transportation, take SEPTA bus route 125 to the welcome center; from May through September, there are free shuttle buses in the park, with a stop at Washington's Headquarters. (At other times, though, you will have to walk the 2.0 miles from the welcome center to the trailhead.)

TRAIL DESCRIPTION
Valley Forge hiking? Philadelphians often think of Valley Forge as a vast, open grassy area where paved drives circumnavigate scattered stone memorials and clusters of log huts—not as a hiking destination.

But Valley Forge contains two essential Philadelphia-area hikes: a pleasant riverside walk along the Schuylkill (the River Trail, see Trip 7) and this hike, a trek through a part of Valley Forge that retains a sense of the countryside in which the Continental Army endured a winter of privation during the Encampment of 1777–78.

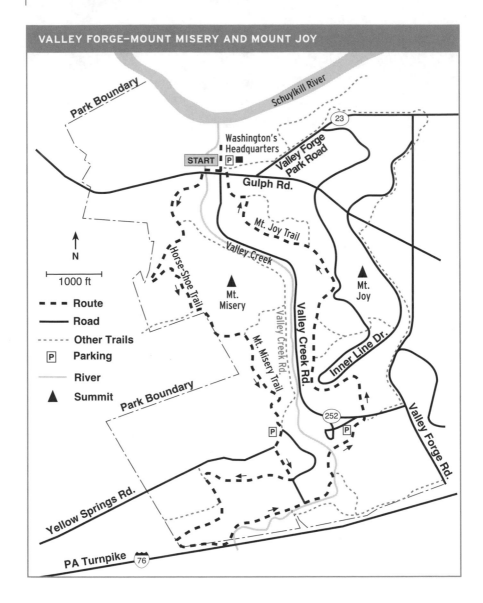

VALLEY FORGE–MOUNT MISERY AND MOUNT JOY

The northwest corner of the park, surrounding Valley Creek, preserves a landscape similar to that in the Delaware Valley during the Revolutionary War: stone farmsteads with small fields checkering the steep, wooded stream valleys. (Ironically, though, the Encampment devastated much of the landscape, as soldiers tore up fields and felled trees.) Muddy farm fields—not emerald lawns—provided the grounds for the Encampment. To travel any distance was either to go on foot over rugged, unlit dirt traces or to navigate through thick, forbidding woods.

This hike, a circuit between two summits with a level walk in between, can be done in either direction; the counterclockwise version described here climbs the steeper summit first.

Start at Washington's Headquarters. During the Encampment, George Washington lodged in this house of the Isaac Potts family, owners of the iron forges that gave Valley Forge its name. From the parking lot, head downhill about a third of a mile to cross Gulph Road (Route 23), then go west across Valley Creek Road (Route 252). A bronze plaque at the bridge marks the trailhead of the Horse-Shoe Trail, which heads northwest 140 miles to the Appalachian Trail at Stony Mountain. Follow its yellow blazes over Valley Creek, then left along a gravel road past a small complex of old stone buildings, to a gate with trail maps. The trail begins to climb Mount Misery.

Mount Misery (elevation 577 feet) on the west and Mount Joy (elevation 402 feet) on the east flank Valley Creek, which has cut a gorge through the sedimentary quartzite rock of the hills. The "mountains" loom over a plateau to the east composed of dolostone, a soft rock similar to limestone that dissolves easily in water. Quartzite, easily recognizable by its large, white crystals, weathers slowly but fractures easily when water freezes in crevices. Boulders split from exposed surfaces slide downhill, creating slopes of rock debris.

Tradition offers several explanations for the mountains' names (first mentioned in a seventeenth-century deed from William Penn). In Governor Samuel Whitaker Pennypacker's colorful 1872 version, two settlers wandered lost overnight on one mountain, bruising themselves on the numerous rocks and "in continual dread of being devoured by . . . wild beasts"; the next morning, they crossed the creek to climb the opposite peak and discovered their settlement below—thus the "misery" of the first mountain and the "joy" of the other.

About 1,500 feet from the start, you'll cross a wide road with signs marking the Valley Creek Trail to the left. The Horse-Shoe Trail becomes a rocky footpath, following a stream; it passes a ruined mill, then turns left and continues up the hill. As you pass through these dry, open oak woods, it is possible to imagine those lost settlers wandering at night among the boulders, hearing—instead of the noise from Route 23 below—the cries of wolves and bobcats, unable to see the stars through the thick canopy overhead.

After another 0.6 mile, the Horse-Shoe Trail meets the white-blazed Mount Misery Trail. Turn left (the Horse-Shoe Trail turns sharp right) and follow the white blazes along the ridge. After 0.25 mile, the trail reaches a junction with the Valley Creek Trail. Continue along the Mount Misery Trail and hike along the hillside, descending for 0.5 mile until it reaches a small parking lot near a covered bridge.

Fields, wooded hills, and history: the Mount Misery trail is quintessential Valley Forge. The trail winds past reconstructed soldiers' huts.

Exit the parking lot; turn right onto Yellow Springs Road, then left onto Wilson Road (closed to traffic). Follow Wilson Road for about 30 feet, and then take the footpath that leads diagonally to your right across the field. The trail approaches a cluster of old stone farm buildings identified as Lord Stirling's Quarters.

The trail bends sharp left (before you get to Yellow Springs Road, visible ahead), then right, and goes along the edge of a meadow of native grasses and wildflowers. This part of the trail is an abandoned roadway. The next turn, a sharp hairpin to the left, brings you to a modern roadway—the Pennsylvania Turnpike. The road noise here may drive you to walk faster and faster so that you can leave modernity and return to the eighteenth-century landscape. After less than 0.25 mile, the trail turns left to follow Valley Creek and becomes a footpath again; after a few hundred feet, you can see on the bluff above the house that served as the quarters for the 23-year-old Marquis de Lafayette, the French officer who became Washington's assistant at Valley Forge.

Go around a metal gate. To your right is an old pedestrian bridge over the creek; do not cross here. Instead, cross the old road and follow the trail along the left side of the creek. The banks are being restored with native trees and shrubs to reduce erosion and increase the shade that aquatic wildlife need.

To your left, the beautiful view across a field past the nineteenth-century P. C. Knox estate, with Mount Misery and Mount Joy in the background and the creek in the middle, is worth a long pause. Go along the stream and over a wooden footbridge. Pass between several buildings of the estate that served as General Henry Knox's quarters, and head over the grass toward a large parking area. Skirt the lot, heading left, where there is an asphalt path along Route 252 that takes you to a pedestrian crosswalk.

One you've crossed Route 252, a footpath through the field begins the ascent of Mount Joy. Ahead is a rocky woods; to your right are replica huts. Feel free to climb slowly; the view on this approach embodies the essence of Valley Forge.

Past the huts, the trail enters the oak woods and soon intersects with the Mount Joy Trail; turn left. From here the trail continues along the hillside, alternately ascending and descending with occasional views back along the valley. (Ignore all options that go off to the right, as none of them offer superior views. Do not be fooled by the "Observatory" trail marker; that structure was long ago dismantled.) Outcrops of the exposed quartzite along the trail also provide fine viewing platforms. The trees through which you peer are primarily drought-tolerant chestnut oak, black oak, and black gum. The trail briefly skirts the Inner Line Drive then returns to the woods. On its final half-mile, it descends into a floodplain forest with sweet gum, box elder, silver maple, red maple, and spicebush shrubs. The trail becomes a gravel road, then ends at Route 252; cross and return to the parking area.

MORE INFORMATION

The park is open year-round 6 A.M. to 10 P.M. The welcome center, which has extensive exhibits and information on the history of Valley Forge as well as on the American Revolution, is open 9 A.M. to 5 P.M. daily. Restrooms are at the Washington's Headquarters trailhead. Under a policy enacted in late 2009, hunting may be permitted; check in at the welcome center during hunting season. Dogs are permitted, and must be on leash at all times. There are about 20 miles of hiking trails in the park. The Mount Misery trails are maintained by the Appalachian Mountain Club's Delaware Valley Chapter (www.amcdv .org). Valley Forge National Historical Park, 1400 North Outerline Drive, King of Prussia, PA 19406; 610-783-1077; www.nps.gov/vafo/. Listen to a short narration of historical information about individual sites and monuments throughout the park by dialing 484-396-1018.

TRIP 7
VALLEY FORGE NATIONAL
HISTORICAL PARK–RIVER TRAIL

Location: King of Prussia, PA (Chester and Montgomery counties)
Rating: Easy
Distance: 6.0 miles
Elevation Gain: 25 feet
Estimated Time: 2.75 hours
Maps: USGS Valley Forge; trail map available at welcome center and online at the website for the Valley Forge National Historical Park (North Side Trails)

Follow a placid greenway along the Schuylkill River through a historic landscape.

DIRECTIONS
Take Route 76 west (Schuylkill Expressway) to Route 202 south. Follow Route 422 west to the Audubon/Trooper exit immediately after the bridge over the Schuylkill River. At the bottom of the exit ramp turn left onto Trooper Road; follow over Route 422 to the end of the roadway. The entrance to the Betzwood parking area is on the right; there is ample parking. *GPS coordinates*: 40° 06.596′ N, 75° 25.628′ W.

To reach Valley Forge via public transportation, take SEPTA bus route 125 to the welcome center and walk down the pedestrian walkway over Route 422, bearing left after the hill to the parking area.

TRAIL DESCRIPTION
A delightful benefit of the preservation of Valley Forge National Historical Park is that several miles of the lower Schuylkill River are largely undeveloped or have been restored to green space. Within 10 miles of Philadelphia, this river—so much a part of the early history of the city and its countryside—can be enjoyed for its natural scenery and placid qualities, characteristics that were fast disappearing even during the Encampment of 1777–78. (See "Valley Forge: The Encampment of 1777–78" on page 38.)

The Schuylkill River here is 105 miles from its headwaters in Schuylkill County and 28.5 miles from its mouth at the Delaware River. Although the river generally flows southeast, there is a great bend where it joins the Perkiomen Creek (just north of the trail's terminus) and arcs westward briefly

VALLEY FORGE NATIONAL HISTORICAL PARK–RIVER TRAIL

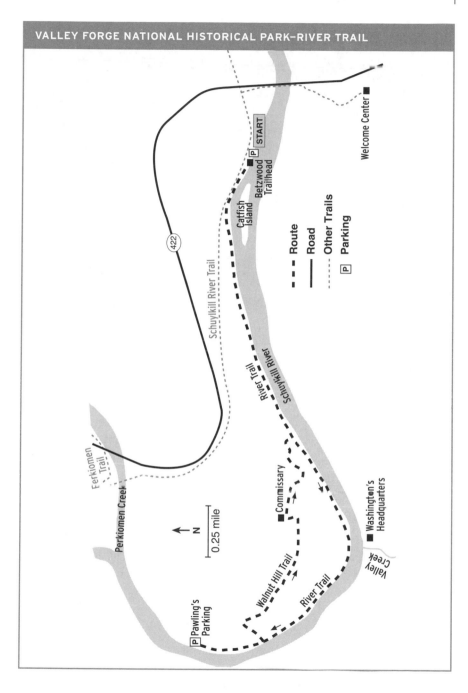

Welcome Center

START

Betzwood Trailhead

Catfish Island

Schuylkill River Trail

422

River Trail

Schuylkill River

Ferkiomen Trail

Perkiomen Creek

Commissary

Washington's Headquarters

Valley Creek

Walnut Hill Trail

River Trail

Pawling's Parking

N

0.25 mile

Route
Road
Other Trails
P Parking

at the erosion-resistant rocks that form Mount Misery and Mount Joy on its southwestern banks. The river again curves east where Valley Creek comes in on the opposite bank at Washington's Headquarters. The point of land encompassed by the bend is known as the Perkiomen Peninsula.

The delicate bell-like spring flowers of the unfortunately-named bladdernut tree turn into three-sided seed pods by summer's end.

This hike is an easy walk among riverside woods, with a foray into the surrounding fields and wetlands. It follows the park's River Trail from the Betzwood parking area to the Pawling parking area. The River Trail is also locally referred to as the Betzwood Trail to distinguish it from the Schuylkill River Trail (SRT), the paved multiuse trail that parallels it for a short distance (see Trip 1).

Begin the hike at the Betzwood parking area. You will see kiosks and trail information posts for the SRT at the eastern end of the parking area, but head west and upstream away from the SRT trailhead, through the parking lots, past the restrooms, to the park's River Trail entrance. The packed-dirt River Trail is usually a quiet haven for pedestrians, since most bikers are happier on the paved SRT. From the entrance, the wide, flat trail follows the river upstream for about three miles. Side trails (including a connection with the SRT) branch off to the right; keep left at these intersections.

The trees and other vegetation are typical of a southeast Pennsylvania floodplain forest. Tall silver maples and sycamores arch over the river and shade the trail, and basswoods and slippery elm populate the understory. Look for the beautiful (albeit unflatteringly named) bladdernut tree, with its three compound leaves of three leaflets each, dainty white flowers, and distinctive three-sided seed cases. The seed cases hang like miniature lanterns from the branches from spring through winter; they darken from light green to brown as they dry, with the seeds free inside to form rattles.

After about 1,000 feet you will pass the long, narrow Catfish Island, although bottom-dwelling catfish are seldom seen here. After another 0.25 mile, you will pass an oxbow, where a small tributary stream winds toward the river's banks; a footbridge crosses this stream.

At about a mile, the trail passes the site of Sullivan's Bridge, marked by a sign on a large boulder. During the Encampment, food and supplies were stored on the north bank of the river, and this bridge built by Major General John Sullivan enabled goods to be transported to the soldiers on the other side. Constructed from timber, it was the only bridge built by the Continental Army during the American Revolution. Primarily a natural area today, the peninsula formed by the bend in the Schuylkill was the center of activity for soldiers who loaded and unloaded the horse-drawn wagons that carried supplies and livestock to and from Pawling's Farm.

At about the three-mile mark, the trail passes opposite the site of Washington's Headquarters, clearly visible across the river through the trees. Here, Valley Creek meets the Schuylkill River. Just beyond this point, the river rushes over an obstacle course of large rocks. A short distance past these rapids, the trail terminates at the Pawling parking area.

Turn around and head back, bearing left at the fork at 0.3 mile. This trail heads uphill through a grassy area; after about 1,000 feet, at the intersection with a gravel road, turn right and continue heading east on this road; numerous trail turnoffs head over the network of berms. The upland forest here contrasts with the floodplain woods along the riverbank. At 0.5 mile the trail bends left to enter the historic commissary site. This was one of the main structures used during the Encampment.

Watch the trail carefully here, as it veers off sharply to the right just past an information kiosk. It heads across a meadow, then down into a moist woods dotted with pools and seeps. Soon the trail bends left and uphill a short way, turns right onto a rutted road, then bears right and downhill to meet the River Trail again. Turn left and follow the riverbank another 1.5 miles to the parking lot.

MORE INFORMATION

Restrooms can be found at the trailhead and at the welcome center. Bikes are permitted. Valley Forge National Historical Park, 1400 North Outer Line Drive, King of Prussia, PA 19406; 610-783-1077; www.nps.gov/vafo/.

VALLEY FORGE: THE ENCAMPMENT OF 1777-78

In late December 1777, the Continental Army, under the command of General George Washington, had just suffered defeats at the battles of Brandywine, Paoli, and Germantown; the British had captured the capital, Philadelphia. As was customary at the time, Washington decided to establish a winter camp for his 12,000 soldiers. He selected a site at Valley Forge, along the Schuylkill River 20 miles northwest of the city, at an easily defensible location high in the hills with a view of the valley.

Ill shod, poorly fed, sick, and weary, the citizens-turned-patriots marched into Valley Forge in an icy wind over snowy ground. The thriving ironworks settlement was situated on a creek, surrounded by farmland. Washington's soldiers felled trees and dragged them out of the woods to construct shelters, dug forts and trenches into the frozen earth, built a bridge over the Schuylkill, and laid out roads. Food was constantly in short supply, illness rampant. During the Encampment, 2,000 died, most from disease.

The seasonal hiatus became a transformative experience with the arrival of Prussian army officer Baron Friedrich von Steuben in February 1778. Von Steuben trained the encamped soldiers and organized them into a mature fighting force. In June 1778, the troops marched out of Valley Forge to Monmouth, New Jersey, where they crushed the British army and began the long road to decisive victory in the War for Independence.

A movement to protect what was viewed as sacred ground began in the late nineteenth century. The area around Washington's Headquarters was established as the first Pennsylvania state park in 1893. Efforts over the next 100-plus years preserved much of the land where the soldiers were encamped; the site became a national park in 1976. Historic buildings—some dating to the Encampment—have been preserved as well, and some (including Washington's Headquarters) restored. Scattered around the grounds are reconstructed log huts similar to those built by the soldiers.

The park has preserved neither the industry that occupied the valley at the time of the Encampment nor the community it sustained, although visitors can still see ruins of the two forges along Valley Creek, along with remnants of other industries that occupied the site over the years since. The expanse of open space invites visitors to contemplate history from the vantage point of those who made it and to ponder how choices made in the present may profoundly affect the future.

TRIP 8
GREEN RIBBON TRAIL

Location: Lower Gwynedd, PA (Montgomery County)
Rating: Easy–Moderate
Distance: 7.5 miles
Elevation Gain: Minimal
Estimated Time: 3.0 hours
Maps: USGS Ambler and Lansdale

**Take the train to the hike! Walk along (and over) the Wissahickon
Creek in quiet woods and in sunny thickets, and leave the driving
to SEPTA.**

DIRECTIONS

Take I-276 (Pennsylvania Turnpike) to Exit 339 (Fort Washington). Follow
Route 309 north to Norristown Road (Spring House); make a left at the bottom of the ramp. Take Norristown Road west to Bethlehem Pike, turn left,
and immediately turn right onto Penllyn-Blue Bell Pike. After 0.2 miles, turn
left onto Old Penllyn Pike; bear left and park on the street. Penllyn Station is
ahead (station parking is limited to commuters). Other street parking in the
neighborhood is available at Penllyn Woods. *GPS coordinates*: 40° 10.178′ N,
75° 14.624′ W.

To get to the trailhead by public transportation, take the SEPTA R5 Regional Rail to the Penllyn stop.

TRAIL DESCRIPTION

A model of sustainable thinking, the 20-mile-long Green Ribbon Trail winds
between Regional Rail stations from Fort Washington to North Wales along
the upper Wissahickon Creek (whose lower reach, through a gorge, can be
hiked in Philadelphia; see Trip 2). The Delaware Valley is served by an extensive hub-and-spoke network of commuter rail stations that connect neighborhoods and suburbs to Center City, but to connect a great day hike in a natural
area directly to public transportation is extremely difficult. From its begin-
nings in the late nineteenth century, the Regional Rail network has been used
for economic development, not its capacity to bring people closer to nature.
The Wissahickon Valley Watershed Association's Green Ribbon Trail is a vi-
sionary effort to change this approach.

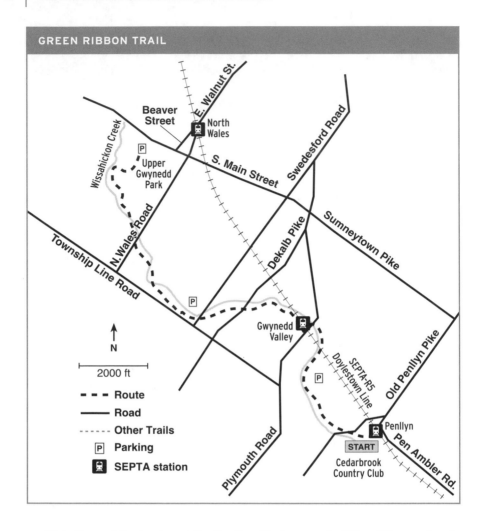

This linear hike begins at the Penllyn Station on the R5 rail line and ends at the R5's North Wales Station. Thus you can take the train, hike, and take another train home. The hike can also be shortened by taking the intermediate stop (Gwynedd Valley).

To reach the Green Ribbon Trail, exit from the southbound side of the Penllyn Station (signs say "To Center City") and walk down Old Penllyn Pike. (The street sign may be absent, but the pike is the middle of the three residential streets that intersect at the station.) You can see the Wissahickon Creek through the woods on the left.

After about 600 feet, you'll pass a sign next to an opening in the woods where the southbound Green Ribbon Trail (GRT) goes into the woods. You are now on the northbound GRT. Continue on the road to the intersection

The R5 Regional Rail line passes over the Wissahickon Creek and the Green Ribbon Trail on this bridge.

with Penllyn-Blue Bell Pike, turn left, and walk alongside the road another 1,000 feet to Township Line Road; turn right and cross the street to enter the Wissahickon Valley Watershed Association's Penllyn Natural Area. Note the stub of a stone bridge that used to cross the creek, next to an old one-room schoolhouse (converted to a water-quality station). Note the GRT sign, facing north. Signs facing both directions are planned, but even GRT signs facing the opposite direction will reassure you that you're on the trail.

After about 50 feet, the trail ducks left into the woods along the creek, becoming a natural footpath. This is a typical Philadelphia-area flat, wet suburban floodplain woods—mostly old or middle-aged trees (oak, beech, hickory) and a spicebush/multiflora rose understory. The woods are heavily deer-browsed. While it is no wilderness, it a pleasant natural area, and the sight and sound of the flowing creek are quite peaceful.

Note the green blazes here; they are not consistently placed along the trail but are useful where they do occur.

The trail leaves the woods, follows the street briefly, and returns over a footbridge, entering a very wet area with pools and braided channels, with some boardwalks over the swampy spots; black walnut trees thrive here. A sign indicates "GRT mile 5" (meaning 5.0 miles to the terminus from here). The

GRT then exits at a power-line clearing, becoming a gravel path, then a grassy path. Continue past a well maintenance shed to a Y intersection with the right fork being a cleared open area that goes up to a residential street. Take the far (left-hand) fork closer to the creek. As you enter the far fork, note the blue blazes and signs indicating this is a horse trail. Green blazes appear occasionally in this section, but continue to follow the wide grassy trail with the horse tracks in the middle and do not veer off to other blue-blazed (horse) trails. This wet thicket, with the creek unseen to the left and woods to the right, is a good birding area. After another 0.75 mile, the trail reaches the creek and follows its banks under a stone railroad bridge (quite rocky and slippery).

Bear right at the next Y, following the horse track. After about another 500 feet, at the 4.0-mile mark, the trail crosses the creek, which is quite wide here, fording it via concrete stepping-stones. Continue straight uphill to Plymouth Road, cross the road, turn left, and cross the grade-level tracks to the Gwynedd Valley train station parking lot. Note the GRT directional signs here. Turn right and go to the rear of the parking lot, where the trail parallels the tracks for a few hundred feet, then skirts tree-lined backyards, coming down to follow the creek's wooded banks, passing by a dam and old foundations for a skating hut (note the fireplace). Just 50 feet past mile marker 3, you'll cross Route 202. (Be careful. This is a very busy road.)

You'll enter a swampy, open thicket area with occasional boardwalks; the creek is below and to the right. After a little less than a mile, there is an unmarked Y intersection; take the left fork going away from the creek and, after another 750 feet, you'll reach the intersection of Swedesford Road and Township Line. (The Wissahickon Valley Watershed Association's historic Evans-Mumbower Mill, being restored to operation, is over the stone-arched bridge.)

Cross Swedesford Road and enter a lightly wooded area next to a tree-planting and restoration project; huge old specimen sycamore trees tower over the newly planted saplings. The trail goes behind houses for a while; cross the road at mile marker 2, then follow the thicket diagonally right to the creek. The trail continues to traverse an open wet area replete with thickets. Cross the creek several times (on concrete stepping-stones). Just after a pipeline clearing, you'll come to a four-way intersection; turn left (note the opposite-facing sign).

At North Wales Road, the trail angles 45 degrees to the right along the thickets. (To shorten the hike by about 1.5 miles, turn right instead and follow the road to the train station.) Now the trail wends through an open freshwater marsh and ponds, where unusual birds such as bitterns may be seen. Watch for stinging nettles along the trail.

After another stream crossing, turn left at the next Y; at the power-line clearing turn right and follow the meadow's edge to a paved path behind a housing development; turn right and follow the path to the terminus of the GRT in the Upper Gwynedd Township Parkside Place Park.

To get to the North Wales Station, continue along the paved path to right on Sumneytown Pike, then take a left on Walnut Street to the station (about a mile from the GRT terminus). Return to Penllyn via the southbound ("To Center City") side.

Station-to-station, the hike takes about 3 hours; on the train, it takes about 5 minutes. Through the speeding train window, the green ribbon is a green blur.

MORE INFORMATION

Restrooms are at the trail's end at Upper Gwynedd Township Park and at Penllyn Woods; there are portable toilets at Evans-Mumbower Mill. Dogs must be leashed. Hunting is not permitted in these largely residential areas. The Green Ribbon Trail is maintained by the Wissahickon Valley Watershed Association, 12 Morris Road, Ambler, PA 19002; 215-646-8866; www .wvwa.org.

TRIP 9
PENNYPACK ECOLOGICAL RESTORATION TRUST

Location: Huntingdon Valley, PA (Montgomery County)
Rating: Easy–Moderate
Distance: 7.0 miles
Elevation Gain: 225 feet
Estimated Time: 3.5 hours
Maps: USGS Hatboro; trail map available at Pennypack Ecological Restoration Trust

This hike provides a rare opportunity to experience extraordinary expanses of meadowland in a dense suburban area. These meadows, along with upland and floodplain forests, continue to be restored and managed to provide habitat and improve the Pennypack Creek watershed. The trust lands also include an old-growth forest, riparian areas along the creek, and farm fields.

DIRECTIONS
From the Pennsylvania Turnpike, take Route 611 south to Route 63 east (Moreland Road). At the first stop sign, turn left onto Edge Hill Road; at the next stop sign, continue straight. The Pennypack Ecological Restoration Trust entrance is 0.3 miles farther on the right. You will find ample parking at the lot. *GPS coordinates:* 40° 01.991′ N, 75° 11.273′ W.

TRAIL DESCRIPTION
A meadow is the botanical equivalent of a photograph. Both are the products of human efforts to stop time. Left to its own devices, a cleared site in the Delaware Valley will turn into a forest. It will quickly be colonized by sun-loving grasses, flowers, and small trees. Then shrubs and larger trees will take root in the field, eventually shading out the grasses and wildflowers. But if disturbed regularly, as by mowing or controlled burning, a meadow will stay a meadow. Preserving grasslands has become a high priority among the region's conservationists. One of the largest publicly accessible meadow habitats in the area is at the Pennypack Preserve of the Pennypack Ecological Restoration Trust. Of the trust's 771 protected acres, 160 are meadows, many planted since the organization began acquiring land in 1976. The trust keeps woody plants from taking over by periodically mowing the fields.

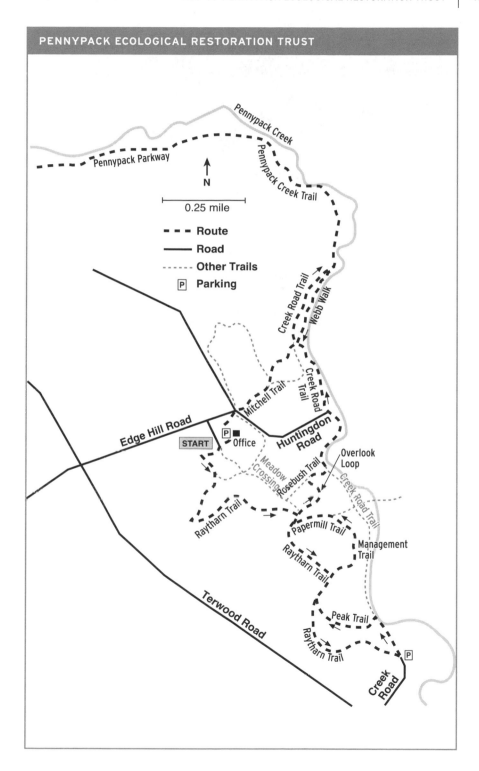

PENNYPACK ECOLOGICAL RESTORATION TRUST

Several varieties of milkweed are common in the Philadelphia region; most thrive in meadows and other sunny open areas. The pods burst open to reveal seeds with silken filaments that float on the wind.

This hike goes around many meadows, offering expansive landscape views, with distinct colors and textures during every season. But the preserve is more than meadows—it also contains streams, creeks, and wetlands; farmhouses and historic structures; and hundreds of forested acres that are being restored to improve wildlife habitat. The trails are well marked with signs that bear the trail names; take care, though, not to confuse maintenance paths cleared around field edges for the groomed trails.

From the northwest corner of the visitor center parking area, take the trail marked "To the Pond." The wood-chip path leads down through trees about 500 feet to the Raytharn Trail, marked by a large sign at the edge of a field (the old Raytharn Farm). Turn right, crossing the meadow of milkweed and summer-blooming wildflowers. Sweeping views include the Bryn Athyn Cathedral peeking over the hilltops to the east.

Follow the trail downhill, bending left and then right. Pass through a fence-row, and continue uphill through more grassland. When you enter a small woodlot, the Meadow Crossing Trail will intersect from the left, turn right and cross the Paper Mill Trail, continuing straight as the Raytharn Trail passes between meadows of native grasses. Where the Management Trail intersects from the left, turn right (uphill) into the woods. Climb gradually uphill, and emerge from the woods at a hilltop between two magnificent grass meadows with 360-degree vistas. The trail winds through the hilltop meadows, then goes downhill, skirting the woods at the bottom. Pass through a gap in the fence at Creek Road.

Turn left onto Creek Road Trail, an old road along the wide, rocky Pennypack Creek. After 0.2 mile turn left up the Peak Trail, a narrow footpath steeply ascending a rocky knoll under a canopy of towering, centuries-old oak and tulip trees. After beginning to descend, backtrack along the Raytharn Trail about 1,000 feet, turning right onto Management Trail. Pass through a very young woods.

At a three-way H intersection, pass by the first left (Paper Mill Woods Trail). Go under the gate, down steps, taking the next left to ascend via a shady old unpaved road, the Paper Mill Road Trail. (Downhill to the right, a historic stone bridge, built in 1817, crosses the creek.) At the top of the hill, turn right onto Raytharn Trail briefly; follow Meadow Crossing for 75 feet, then turn right onto Overlook Trail, which winds around the top of the ridge and offers good winter views of the Pennypack valley. Turn right at the T, taking Rose-bush Trail back down to the Creek Road Trail.

Remain on Creek Road Trail, traversing a floodplain forest of river birch, sweet gum, and sycamore, passing by old stone foundations—they are remnants of the mill and farming community that was centered here. The trail, which remains generally flat along old roads, passes through four gates, by a small but active Swedenborgian stone church, and through a small residential area by a rocky waterfall. The trail can be muddy after rain. The trail's name changes to Pennypack Creek Trail and, after Mason's Mill Road, Pennypack Parkway. At the end of the trail is the fifth gate and a five-car parking lot.

Turn around and retrace your steps, but when you return to the Creek Road Trail, cross it and go down by the bridge abutment to the creek via the Webb Walk. Pass through wetlands marked by skunk cabbage colonies, by an eighteenth-century stone springhouse, and along beautiful boulder outcrops. Rhododendrons crowd the trail. Root-clogged, it can be muddy and slippery; boardwalks cover some of the worst muddy spots.

The meadows at Pennypack Ecological Restoration Trust are a great place to get to know the beautiful native grasses that have all but disappeared from the Delaware Valley.

The Webb Walk rejoins the Creek Road Trail; turn left then just 50 feet later, turn right to take the Mitchell Trail steeply up a rocky hill, then into a mixed woods. At the top of the hill, cross Huntingdon Road (opposite the June Fete fairgrounds). Pass through a gap in the post-and-rail fencing. Bear left just inside the fence, then walk straight, between a double row of alternating silver maples and red cedars. Turn right at the bird blind and maintenance garage to return to the visitor center.

MORE INFORMATION

Restrooms are located at the visitor center and are open during business hours (Monday through Friday, 9 A.M. to 5 P.M.; Saturday 10 A.M. to 2 P.M.; Sunday, occasionally). Pennypack Preserve is open from 8 A.M. until dusk 7 days a week. Other than the Creek Road Trail, Pennypack Creek Trail, and Pennypack Parkway, trails are for hikers only (no bikes, dogs, or horses). Where permitted, dogs must be leashed. Pennypack Ecological Restoration Trust, 2955 Edgehill Road, Huntington Valley, PA 19006; 215-657-0830; www.pennypacktrust.org.

SPLENDOR IN THE GRASS: MEADOWS AND GRASSLANDS

If you have experienced the rattle of wind coursing through a canopy of dried grass stems; gotten dizzy looking out at waves rippling a sea of amber seedheads; watched a kestrel hover high in the sky and plunge straight down to snare a vole; followed a monarch butterfly as it flits from milkweed flower to milkweed flower, and later in the year chased the fluffy seeds from the milkweed pod; or breathed in the sweet magical fragrance of goldenrod . . . then count your blessings. If you have never done any of the above, then you have been missing meadows from your life.

Fields of native grasses and wildflowers are among the rarest of habitats in the Delaware Valley, as they are throughout the Northeast. The reason for their rarity is trees, which thrive in the Northeast because of the region's abundant rainfall, the moderate temperatures afforded by the Gulf Stream (the warm current of the Atlantic Ocean), and the shelter from winds afforded by Piedmont foothills.

But trees do fall, do burn, or are cut down. Any area cleared of trees is a potential meadow. Grass and wildflower seeds buried in the forest floor that have never had a chance to sprout in the shade suddenly have an opportunity to do so. Seeds blow in from nearby meadows, or are carried in on animal fur or human clothing. In the new opening, plants quickly sprout and drink in the unaccustomed sunlight. Native grasses appear, and their roots stabilize the soil and prevent other plants from proliferating. Suddenly, the opening is a field.

Meadows do not last long, though. Trees and woody shrubs colonize the fields, their tough roots breaking through those of the grass. Eventually the trees shade out the sun-loving meadow plants, and the meadow disappears.

Aside from its beauty, the meadow is an important habitat for vulnerable pollinators such as bees and butterflies, grassland birds such as the kestrel and meadowlark, and other wildlife. Grasslands provide food, shelter, and cover for distinct species year-round. Birds hide their nests and fledglings under dense grass clumps. In spring and summer, they eat the insects that are attracted to flowers; in fall, they eat the flower seeds. In late winter and early spring, the meadows warm up more quickly than woods and therefore can be a critical source of food for hibernating wildlife. In the larger sense, diversity of habitat is critical to the long-term sustainability of the web of life.

Prior to extensive human settlement in the Delaware Valley and surrounding region, the landscape was a mosaic of habitats: meadows were created naturally, usually by wildfire, and reverted back to forest over time. With the rise of agriculture, meadows were created by farmers as a side effect of the common practices of rotating crops and leaving fields fallow. As cities and suburbs replaced farms, and fires were suppressed, meadows vanished.

Today, therefore, meadows are rare in the wooded Piedmont. (In the coastal plain of New Jersey and Delaware, meadows are more common, especially on the coast, because the dry, sandy soil and wind are conditions unsuited for trees.) Wildlife conservation managers in the region target the restoration and preservation of grasslands as a high priority. Meadows need disturbance to be established, and regular disturbance to persist. To establish a meadow as a habitat, the land manager must first clear woody vegetation from a field, or clear a woods. To ensure that the meadow gets started with native plants and not weeds, the land manager will plant grasses or wildflowers, using specialized machinery that plants the seeds at just the right depth. After a meadow is established, it must regularly be mowed (or, less often, burned in a controlled manner) to keep trees from coming in to the field. Keeping a meadow going is an intensive operation, which is another reason that grasslands are so rare—nature's services are free, but human labor is not.

Meadows have been extensively restored and protected at the Pennypack Ecological Restoration Trust (Trip 9). Smaller meadow restoration areas can be seen, for example, in Wissahickon Valley Park (Trip 2), along the Green Ribbon Trail (Trip 8), in Green Lane Park (Trip 17), at the Peace Valley Nature Center (Trip 18), and at the Jacobsburg Environmental Education Center (Trip 39).

Almost anyone can create a meadow in a backyard, even a tiny one. Many grassland birds require at least several acres, but bees and butterflies can benefit from small meadow areas. The more small meadows there are in a landscape, the less the pollinators need to roam. Ask your county agricultural extension agent for specific planting guidance for your yard. Whether you go out and find a meadow or make your own, there is no excuse for missing out on the grasslands experience.

TRIP 10
ALAPOCAS RUN STATE PARK

Location: Wilmington, DE
Rating: Easy
Distance: 4.5 miles
Elevation Gain: 100 feet
Estimated Time: 2.0 hours
Maps: USGS Wilmington North; trail maps available at Blue Ball Barn
and online at website for Alapocas Run State Park

**Take an easy walk through lush woods along the Brandywine Creek
and through a huge pawpaw patch, right next to historic mills and
the remains of a quarry.**

DIRECTIONS

Take I-95 south to Exit 8, U.S. 202 north. Stay to the right. Take the first exit for
DE 141 south/61 north. On the exit ramp, stay to the left for Route 141 south.
At the light, turn left to go under U.S. 202. At the next light, turn left onto West
Park Drive. The entrance to the Blue Ball Barn will be on the left, just before
the traffic circle. *GPS coordinates*: 39° 46.617′ N, 75° 32.735′ W.

To reach the park via public transportation, take SEPTA R2 Regional Rail
or Amtrak to Wilmington; take bus route 2, 11, 12, 21, or 35 to the Brandywine
Zoo; and walk 1.0 mile along the Northern Delaware Greenway to an informa
tional sign complex. You will do the hike in the opposite direction.

TRAIL DESCRIPTION

The small city of Wilmington, Delaware, boasts an impressive and growing
network of trails connecting numerous parks, centered on the Northern Delaware Greenway. Offering a short, pleasant hike that combines waterside walks
with views of a historically significant quarry and mills, and a plunge into a
lush Piedmont woods, the 145-acre Alapocas Run State Park is, as the promo-
tional material says, an urban oasis.

Like Brandywine Creek State Park (see Trip 13), Alapocas Run is in part a
legacy of the wealthy families of the Brandywine Valley, the Du Ponts and the
Bancrofts; structures related to each bookend the hike. The Blue Ball Barn,
built in 1914 by Alfred I. du Pont, has been adapted into a stellar example
of environmentally friendly architecture, Delaware's first public building to

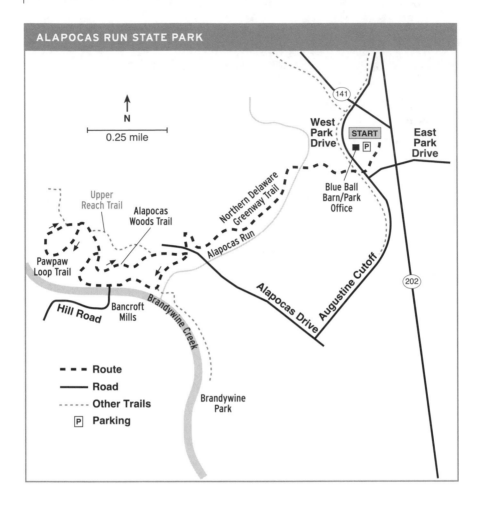

ALAPOCAS RUN STATE PARK

receive a Leadership in Energy and Environmental Design (LEED) certification. The barn houses the Delaware Folk Art Collection and is worth a stop.

Begin the hike at the entrance to the Northern Delaware Greenway trailhead by taking the short trail that goes downhill below the parking lot. The Greenway is a wide, paved, well-marked trail. Turn right; cross over Route 141, cross an open area, and after another 0.1 mile, enter the woods.

The trail bridges the Alapocas Run—a rocky, wild-looking stream—and continues through an oak-hickory woods with the stream to the left. After a hairpin turn, it crosses Alapocas Drive and shortly intersects with the Alapocas Woods Trail. Take this trail, which goes off to the right. Trail intersections are well posted in this park, as they are in all Delaware state parks, but this park seems to suffer more vandalism and loss of trail markers than others. Nonetheless, the trails are short enough that getting lost is quite unlikely.

Follow the narrow natural footpath as it descends the wooded, rocky hillside. The predominant tree in this woods—the main natural attraction in this park—is the pawpaw, a bottomland understory tree that grows up to 30 feet high and has large, dark green, teardrop-shaped leaves (glossy when wet) that fan out around the end of the branch. There is a huge, dense colony of these trees covering the hillsides here. The pawpaw is a member of the tropical custard-apple family, which includes the breadfruit—the only such member, in fact, native to North America. The leaves are the only food for the caterpillars of the dramatically striped zebra swallowtail (also a tropical butterfly). The trees' branches bear cup-shaped dark purple flowers. Mango-shaped fruits arrive in early fall, ripening on the tree. Although you may see fruits here, leave them alone; picking pawpaws is illegal in Delaware state parks and would endanger the plant's continued survival in the state (in Delaware the trees grow naturally only in the tiny Piedmont section north of the Fall Line).

The trail winds up and down through the woods, and after about half a mile the PawPaw Loop branches off to the left. Take this trail downhill into a virtual forest of pawpaws; they seem to have taken over every square inch of ground. Or perhaps "they" should be "it"—pawpaws spread, in part, by cloning themselves, so what seems like many trees are, genetically, one and the same tree.

The Alapocas Run is very close here; an unofficial spur trail takes you down to its rushing waters. Follow the PawPaw Trail (0.3 mile) to its intersection with the Alapocas Woods Trail, and turn right.

The Alapocas Woods Trail passes the PawPaw Loop on the right and a left-hand turnoff for the Upper Reach Trail; at the next right, turn onto the unnamed connector trail that heads straight downhill to the Brandywine Creek, then heads left along its banks to the paved Greenway Trail, opposite the Bancroft Mills. Built on the site of an eighteenth-century paper mill, the Bancroft Mills began operating in 1831 and by 1930 had become the world's largest textile finishing complex. Although the complex was the longest-running one on the Brandywine, successor owners of the Bancroft Mills went bankrupt. The old mill buildings are now, in part, condominiums. Alapocas Run State Park was opened in 2007, 97 years after William Poole Bancroft (of the mill-owning family) donated 123 acres to the city of Wilmington for parkland.

Continue on the Greenway, passing through yet another historic site: an old quarry. High sheer cliffs of "blue rock" (570 million-year-old gneiss) tower over the trail, seemingly carved out of the ground, and indeed they have been. The trail goes along the back wall of a quarry that operated from the 1870s through 1938. Brandywine blue gneiss, Wilmington's bedrock, is royal blue when freshly broken and turns dark gray after weathering. This hard rock forms a 4-mile-long gorge through which the creek flows, dropping 120 feet and generating enormous energy as it does—the power source for much of the Wilmington area's early industry.

Past the complex of informative signs, the Greenway forks left and right. The right fork continues along the creek to Brandywine Park (site of the zoo); turn left to return to the Blue Ball Barn.

MORE INFORMATION

Restrooms are located at the Blue Ball Barn, which is open daily 8 A.M. to sunset, as are the trails. Dogs must be on a leash no more than 6 feet long. Hunting is not permitted. The trails are maintained by Delaware State Parks with support from the Northern Delaware Trail Stewards (www.delawaregreenways .org/sections/programs/steward.shtml). Alapocas Run State Park, 1914 West Park Drive, Wilmington, DE 19803; 302-577-1164; www.destateparks.com/ park/alapocas-run/index.asp.

TRIP 11
LUMS POND STATE PARK

Location: Bear, DE (New Castle County)
Rating: Easy–Moderate
Distance: 7.5 miles
Elevation Gain: Minimal
Estimated Time: 3.0 hours
Maps: USGS Saint Georges; trail map available online at Lums Pond
State Park website

Walk along a level path through rich, cool, moist forests and wetlands, taking in scenic pond views throughout the hike.

DIRECTIONS

From I-95, take Exit 1A (Middletown) to Route 896 south. Go 6.0 miles and take a left onto Howell School Road. The park entrance will be on your right. From Route 1, take Exit 152 to Wrangle Hill Road and drive 2.2 miles until you reach Porter Station Road. Take a left, go 2.2 miles, and take another left onto Route 896/301. Go 1.2 miles to Howell School Road and take a left. The park entrance will be on your right, where you will find ample parking. *GPS coordinates*: 39° 33.739′ N, 75° 43.256′ W.

TRAIL DESCRIPTION

A hike around Lums Pond, which at 200 acres is the largest freshwater pond in Delaware, is an easy, level walk in diverse woods and wetlands, with views of the pond at many points. The route recommended here adds a loop through fields for variety.

Much of the park's 1,790 acres is wooded. The pond was created in the early 1800s when the Chesapeake & Delaware Canal was built to connect the Delaware River and Chesapeake Bay. The St. George's Creek was dammed, creating the pond, and water from the pond was used to fill the locks of the canal just to the south. Today, the canal has been transformed into a sea-level waterway, carrying 40 percent of all shipping traffic to and from the Port of Baltimore. The locks were removed, but the pond remains.

The combination of woods and water draws a variety of wildlife, including beavers and birds. Waterfowl such as herons and egrets fish along its shores; songbirds populate the surrounding woods and fields.

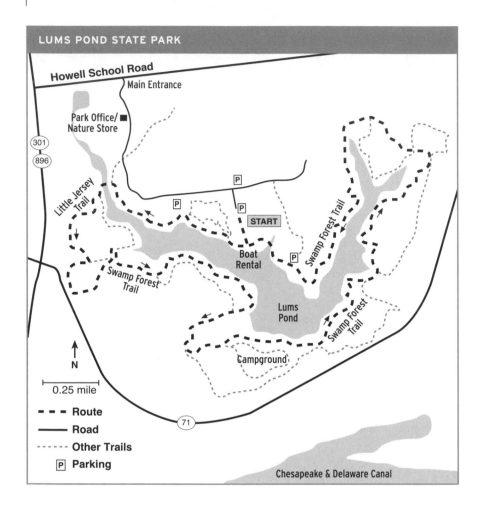

LUMS POND STATE PARK

Howell School Road

Main Entrance

Park Office/■
Nature Store

301
896

Little Jersey Trail

Swamp Forest Trail

Swamp Forest Trail

Swamp Forest Trail

P

P

P

START

Boat
Rental

P

Lums
Pond

Campground

N

0.25 mile

- - - Route
——— Road
----- Other Trails
P Parking

71

Chesapeake & Delaware Canal

The state of Delaware acquired the land around Lums Pond and created the park in 1963. There are many parking areas, picnic tables, and campgrounds as well as a boat rental and even a dog run. Two main trail systems are in place, with connectors between them: an outer loop (the blue-blazed Little Jersey Trail) and an inner shoreline loop (the yellow-blazed Swamp Forest Trail). Both trails are easy, but Swamp Forest, fittingly, can be muddy in spots, so wear either waterproof shoes or hiking boots. The trails are well-maintained natural paths with good footing, though not all intersections are marked.

Begin at Parking Area 2. Head for the boat rental, and find the sidewalk at the water's edge. Turn right, and follow the shoreline. The sidewalk gives way to a natural trail surface, which can get muddy. Oaks and willows shade the pond, ferns and wildflowers spread on either side, and bluebells abound here in early spring. Just past the entrance to the Life Course (a fitness course), cross a bridge and find your way along the gravel trail, skirting the parking

The pink lady's slipper, a native orchid, appears in occasional colonies along decaying wood in acidic soil.

lot to the woods where a trail marker indicates the yellow-blazed Swamp Forest Trail.

The trail continues along the shoreline for about one-quarter of a mile, then turns inland toward Parking Area 5. Immediately after the parking lot the Swamp Forest and Little Jersey trails intersect and cross a bridge. Once over the pond, the trails diverge. Bear right. You will be following the blue-blazed Little Jersey Trail for a short distance; note that horses and bikes are permitted on the Little Jersey Trail, but not on the Swamp Forest Trail. The Little Jersey Trail moves out of the willow/sweet-gum floodplain forest to a pine/cherry successional woods (an area where young trees are colonizing a cleared area), then into a grassy open area; turn right at the T to go around a meadow and farm field, following a grass-lined path (which might be full of ticks, especially in summer and fall). In this "edge" area in spring and summer, look for blue-birds and flycatchers flying back and forth from woods to field.

Three-quarters of the way around the field, the trail intersects unobtru-sively with the purple Swamp Forest Connector Trail off to the right past a gap in the split-rail fence. Take this trail about 1,000 feet to the Swamp Forest Trail, which enters a moist hardwood forest. Note the abundant wide leaves of skunk cabbage that indicate this is a wetlands.

At the next two unblazed intersections, bear left, keeping the pond to your left. For 0.5 mile, the trail hugs the shore beneath a deep woods, shaded by large oaks and tulip trees. The scarred and fallen trees provide evidence of former beaver activity here.

The trail turns inland, joins with the Little Jersey Trail for another 0.25 mile, then bears left after a footbridge. The blazing in this area may be absent.

Bear left at the next two intersections. These woods are especially rich with warblers in spring and fall.

Cross a bridge over a muddy stream and turn left, following the yellow blaze; a campground is to your right up the hill. After 0.25 mile, you pass a pier on the left. These woods are acidic and full of blueberries and fragrant native azaleas, which bloom in spring. Pass along the parking lot for the boat launch after another 0.3 mile, then across the ramp. Red-winged blackbirds call *conk-a-ree* in the reeds; watch for the bright red-and-orange epaulets of the male. The drab female is harder to spot as she quietly goes about the business of building and provisioning their nest.

The trail bends inland again into woods; here look for fresh beaver activity: chewed tree trunks with V-shaped gouges at the base, piles of shavings, and perhaps a dome-shaped lodge at the pond edge.

At the next three junctions with the Little Jersey Connector Trail, continue to follow the yellow blazes. The trail climbs slightly uphill and inland. At the last junction, note the sign for the parking area. The trail becomes a flat gravel tunnel between two narrow, claustrophobia-inducing rows of tall autumn olive shrubs. Fortunately, after 0.25 mile this path ends at the parking area for the dog run and reenters the woods as a natural trail.

This moist woods has many small streams and footbridges, and one very deep ravine. Look for colonies of pink lady's slipper; this native orchid, with a single sack-shaped flower, likes acid soil and decayed wood. Savor the sighting—each plant expends so much capital producing a flower that it may be four years before another one appears.

The trail continues close to the shoreline, passes a tiny viewing pier with half-log benches, then turns right and inland again; just over a bridge it skirts the disc golf course.

After 0.25 mile you pass below Parking Area 1 and, shortly, go over a large bridge. Turn left (the trail is unmarked) and follow the trail another 0.125 mile to Parking Area 2, where you began, a great spot for an end-of-hike picnic by the pond.

MORE INFORMATION

Restrooms can be found at the park office and at the trailheads for all parking areas. The fee is $5/car March through November. The trail is maintained by Delaware State Parks with support from the Friends of Lums Pond (www .destateparks.com/park/lums-pond/friends.asp). Lums Pond State Park, 1068 Howell School Road, Bear, DE 19701; 302-368-6989; www.destateparks.com/park/lums-pond/park-office.asp.

SIGNS WITHOUT WORDS

The signs are everywhere. Some serve as labels, indicating wet ground or deer country. Others give advice, such as "Breathe deep." These are not the numbered or lettered signs on a nature walk. They're plants. They tell you about the landscape, because they thrive under specific conditions. They're called indicator plants.

Skunk cabbage, for example—which grows only in marshes, swamps, and bogs—says "Wetlands." Its enormous, thick-stemmed, bright green leaves (1-2 feet in diameter) appear in spring and last all summer. They smell "skunky" when bruised. Moreover, skunk cabbage can live for a century or more, so in particular it says "old wetlands."

Both sycamore and Atlantic white cedar indicate that water is present. With its striking white bark (mottled brown-green at the base), the graceful sycamore stands out in a deciduous woods. It grows in floodplains, the area by a waterway that fills up during the rainy season. A line of sycamores tells you that a stream or river flows along that same line. The sycamore's seeds float downstream on spring floods, land in mud, and grow to become the next floodplain sycamore. The Atlantic white cedar grows in the Pine Barrens and on the coastal plain. Tall and straight with a dark blue-green foliage crown and reddish shredded bark, it is an instantly recognizable tree. Cedars, too, thrive near water. A cedar line indicates a stream; a stand indicates a bog.

The white-tailed deer has become the forest's nemesis; deer eat too many young plants for the woods to regenerate. But plants that deer find distasteful flourish. A healthy forest may contain both these plants and many others; by contrast, a deer-damaged forest is not diverse. Extensive patches of beech trees with few other trees, a shrub layer mostly of spice-bush or multiflora rose, and groundcovers primarily of hay-scented fern are signs of deer overbrowsing.

Lichens—fungi-algae partnerships—can say "Clean air." Certain species are sensitive to specific pollutants such as sulfur and nitrogen. If you see many tree trunks covered with patches of scaly, leaflike lichens, for example, you know the air is relatively clean. In the Philadelphia area, you're more likely to see these indicators in lowlands, because air pollutants blown east are deposited on the windward side of mountain ridges.

TRIP 12
WHITE CLAY CREEK PRESERVE/
WHITE CLAY CREEK STATE PARK

Location: Landenberg, PA (Chester County), and Newark, DE (New Castle County)
Rating: Moderate
Distance: 10.0 miles
Elevation Gain: 200 feet
Estimated Time: 4.5 hours
Maps: USGS Newark West and Newark East; trail maps available at park offices and online at websites for White Clay Creek Preserve and White Clay Creek State Park

Two states, one creek. This hike begins and ends in a lovely wooded creek valley; in the middle it goes up, down, and around the surrounding hills, through woods and across meadows, with nice hilltop views.

DIRECTIONS
To get to the Pennsylvania-side entrance (no fee is charged here), take Route 1 to the Forrestville exit; go south on Route 896 and turn left onto Indiantown Road. Pass the park office and park in the lot just beyond Yeatman Station Road, where you will find ample parking. Note that parking at any Delaware lot incurs a per-vehicle fee, although walking into the park from the Delaware side is free. *GPS coordinates*: 39° 44.813′ N, 75° 46.442′ W.

TRAIL DESCRIPTION
White Clay Creek winds through the hills of southern Chester County, Pennsylvania, and New Castle County, Delaware. It has been designated a National Wild and Scenic River for the high quality of its scenery and natural resources throughout its 107-square-mile watershed. The White Clay Creek Preserve in Pennsylvania and White Clay Creek State Park in Delaware protect the main stem from encroaching development and provide access to the creek and the surrounding land. Trails on the Pennsylvania side go alongside the creek, while on the Delaware side they spiral up and down hills overlooking the valley. Together the two parks encompass more than 5,000 acres.

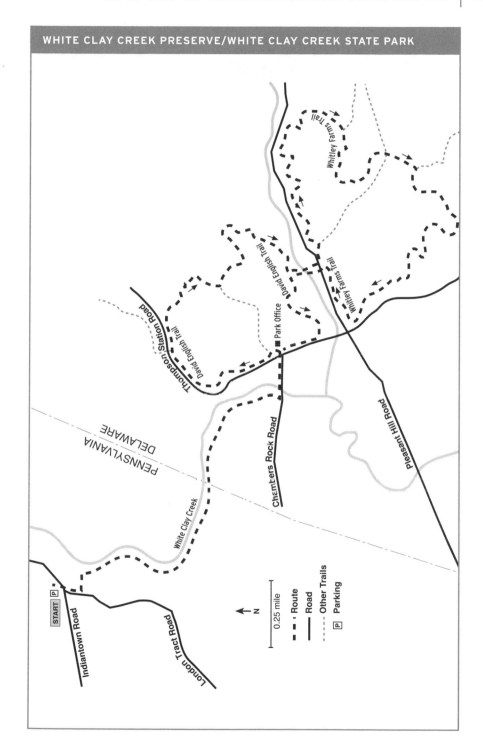

WHITE CLAY CREEK PRESERVE/WHITE CLAY CREEK STATE PARK

The hike begins on the Pennsylvania side, at the parking lot for the main office. Head south along Indiantown Road, turn left onto South Bank Road, and cross the bridge, turning left at the sign for the hiking trail, to go along an old gravel road. Shortly, you'll reach an intersection with the Mason-Dixon and PennDel trails. Continue straight, following the blue blaze of the Mason-Dixon Trail (MDT). The MDT, which despite its name does not follow the Mason-Dixon Line, is a long-distance trail through Delaware, Pennsylvania, and Maryland (see Trip 26). The Mason-Dixon Line itself terminates in the preserve at the Tri-State Marker; its would-be intersection with the Delaware arc border is in the state park at Arc Corner.

The flat, wide trail runs along the right bank of the White Clay Creek, which is broad, clear, and swift-running at this point. The lovely surrounding woods are lush with tall old oak, beech, and sycamore trees as well as various ferns and shrubs. Birds—notably wood warblers and forest-interior-dwelling birds such as veery, scarlet tanager, and pewee—are abundant along this corridor. As the trail rises and falls, it passes through wet patches with skunk cabbage, wood nettle, and jewelweed.

After 1.0 mile, the trail crosses into Delaware. Follow the MDT as it heads left around a bridge ruins, into the woods. The creek is quieter here: slow, wide, and stately.

After another 0.6 mile, you'll reach a parking lot; continue to Chambers Rock Road and turn left. (Be careful: this is an actively traveled road.) Go over the creek via a bridge, and head across Thompson Station Road (closed weekends) into the parking lot for the park office. Here, pick up a map for the Delaware section. At the far end of the lot, enter the David English Trail, blazed yellow. In the Delaware section, all the trails have names and colors; the signage is excellent. Follow this trail, bearing left at the next Y. It is a narrow footpath through more rich woods, rife with songbirds; in summer they sing even during the heat of the day, happy to be in such a cool, moist, shady forest.

The trail goes around the base of the hill, climbing it slowly, emerging from the woods intermittently to traverse meadows. Pass by the Twin Ponds Cutoff Trail, then through a meadows with views of the ponds. Returning to the woods, the trail follows along an old farm road marked by a line of Osage orange trees. These "living fences" were planted along boundaries by rural landowners all over the Delaware Valley because of their resistance to rot. The track of the old road, lined with the trees, can be seen continuing where the trail turns left.

Continue following the David English Trail to its intersection with the Tri-Valley Trail; turn left. The trail goes through bottomland forest, crosses a road, and connects to the Whitely Farms Trail about 300 feet later. Turn left

The White Clay Creek cuts a channel into surrounding banks as it winds through southern Chester County, Pennsylvania, and New Castle County in Delaware.

on this trail and then make another sharp left, going clockwise around the hill. Similar to the David English Trail, this trail passes alternately through shady woods and sunny meadows as it ascends and descends the hill, crossing many streams as it does so.

Continue following this trail to the intersection with the Tri-Valley Trail, and follow that trail north to its intersection with the David English Trail. Bear left to follow this trail clockwise around the hill, until it reaches the Delaware Park Office. Return to the Pennsylvania Park Office by backtracking from here, through the parking lot, along the road over the creek, into the Pennsylvania parking lot, and back along the creek via the MDT and the roads to the parking lot where you started.

MORE INFORMATION

There are no restrooms. White Clay Creek Preserve in Pennsylvania is open from sunrise until sunset. White Clay Creek State Park in Delaware is open from 8 A.M. until sunset. Trails are maintained by the respective state parks with assistance from Friends of White Clay State Park (www.whiteclayfriends. org). White Clay Creek Preserve, P.O. Box 172, Landenberg, PA 19350-0172; 610-274-2900; www.dcnr.state.pa.us/stateparks/parks/whiteclaycreek.aspx. White Clay Creek State Park, 425 Wedgewood Road, Newark, DE 19711-2123; 302-368-6900; www.destateparks.com/park/white-clay-creek.

TRIP 13
BRANDYWINE CREEK STATE PARK

Location: Greenville, DE (New Castle County)
Rating: Moderate
Distance: 8.0 miles
Elevation Gain: 275 feet
Estimated Time: 3.5 hours
Maps: USGS Wilmington North; trail maps are also available at the park office and at the website for Brandywine Creek State Park

Enjoy the legacies of two of Delaware's more prominent families, the du Ponts and the Bancrofts; hike through the steep, forested blue-rock valley of the Brandywine Creek.

DIRECTIONS

Take I-95 south to Exit 11, then I-495 south to Exit 6, Naamans Road. Proceed west on Route 92 for 5.0 miles; turn left onto Route 202 south. Go 1.6 miles and turn right onto Mount Lebanon Road. Go 1.4 miles and turn right onto Rockland Road. Go 0.3 miles to Adams Dam Road; the park entrance is on the right. There is ample parking. *GPS coordinates*: 39° 48.463′ N, 75° 34.757′ W.

TRAIL DESCRIPTION

Brandywine Creek was the source of great wealth before it became the center-piece of a great hiking area. Prior to being acquired for parkland in 1965, the 933-acre Brandywine Creek State Park was a dairy farm owned by the wealthy Du Pont family. The Du Ponts, virtually synonymous with Delaware, trace the origins of their vast fortune to an eighteenth-century gunpowder mill on the Brandywine. The park abuts 2,000 acres of publicly accessible lands of the Woodlawn Trustees in Delaware and Pennsylvania. William Poole Bancroft, a prominent Delawarean whose family wealth came from cotton mills on the Brandywine, founded the Woodlawn Trustees in 1901 to preserve natural open space in the Brandywine Valley. Trails connect the state park and the Woodlawn Trustees land, which blend seamlessly into one another. Trail inter-sections are clearly marked, and trails are blazed with paint splotches.

Begin the hike behind the park office, taking the yellow-blazed Indian Springs Trail (which at the start coincides with the red-blazed Hidden Pond Trail) to enter the Tulip Tree Woods. This nature preserve includes many

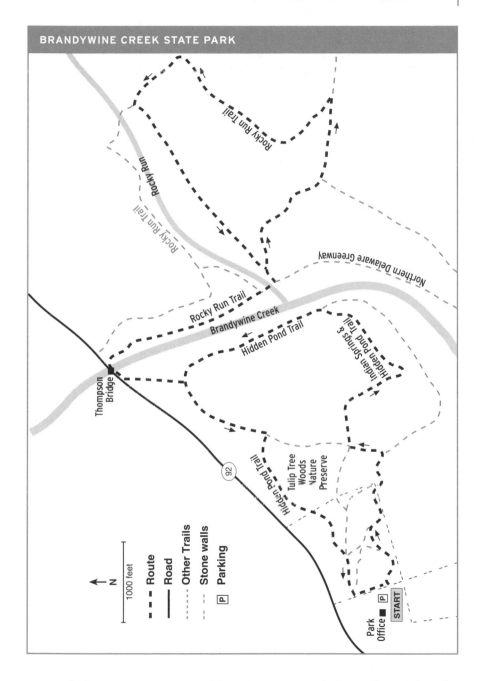

extremely large trees—some as old as 225 years—including tall, straight tulip trees and majestic oaks. Stone walls made of dark gray, fine-grained gneiss (locally referred to as "blue rock") snake through the woods; when this area was farmland, the walls marked boundaries between landholdings or between fields and pastures. Some of the largest of the old trees grow along the walls and at corners; property-marking trees (especially those mentioned on surveys) were typically not logged even when forests were clear-cut.

The trail—a wide, rocky path—sneaks through a gap in a corner of the wall and continues downhill, out of the old-growth woods and into an oak-beech woods. About a third of a mile from the start, the red and yellow trails split; take the red-blazed trail to the left. After about 1,000 feet, it merges again with the yellow-blazed trail; turn right downhill to the Brandywine. The trail follows the creek's banks through a moist (occasionally muddy) floodplain forest. The creek is quite wide and swift here; indeed, local residents often refer to it as a river.

After 0.3 mile, the trail curves left away from the creek and comes to a T. Turn right to take the unblazed trail. This is one of several unnamed, unblazed park trails that appear on the official maps but may not be maintained as regularly as the named trails. After about 50 feet, it bridges a small stream, which empties into Hidden Pond. The trail climbs uphill and leaves the woods at Thompson Bridge Road (Route 92), turning right and going alongside the road, crossing the bridge over Brandywine, and then turning right into the creekside parking area.

Pick up another red-blazed trail at the far end of the parking lot. This flat, wide trail goes along the creek in a narrow forested floodplain. To the left are sheer blue-rock cliffs 150 feet high; across the creek are high forested hills. This trail is part of the Northern Delaware Greenway, a many-branched multiuse trail under development that will eventually connect Brandywine Creek, Christina River (in downtown Wilmington), and Delaware River (see Trip 10).

After about half a mile, the trail crosses Rocky Run on a footbridge. This creek lives up to its name, leaping and frolicking over big rocks, cascading in falls and pools. In the park, the courses of the Brandywine and the Rocky Run follow boundaries between different types of bedrock, running along faults—fractures where two sides of the earth's crust have shifted past each other—resulting in dramatic topography and boulders that litter the hillsides.

The blue-blazed Rocky Run Trail goes up the slope after the footbridge. Unofficial trails have created a three-way fork after the bridge; take the middle or right fork—they soon merge. The trail, though wide, becomes steep and rocky. It is an old road; you'll see evidence of former human habitation, including white pines planted in lines and a patch of hosta plants by the road.

The pine plantation turns into a beech-oak woods shortly; the trail passes through a meadow, reenters the woods, and crests the ridge to continue down the other side, where the forest thickens. At a T intersection, one branch of the blue-blazed trail continues straight downhill; instead, turn left and follow the ridge. Although not marked, this trail passes into Woodlawn Trustees lands. After a flat section, the trail bears left and descends steeply. You'll pass numerous gneiss outcrops; rock steps improve footing in this section.

At the bottom, continue straight (look for blue blazes on rocks) until you reach the Rocky Run. Although the trail fords the stream, the crossing stones are often underwater; passage may be difficult or even impossible, so, after enjoying the view, backtrack about 400 feet to pick up the trail that leads to the right and is marked by a brown-blazed post. This unmapped trail parallels the stream, reenters the park, and comes to a T at the Rocky Run Trail.

Turn right to backtrack over the Rocky Run; go through the parking area, across the Brandywine, and into the woods along the unmarked trail past Hidden Pond. At the T intersection with the red-blazed Hidden Pond Trail after the bridge, turn right. The trail goes uphill (steeply at times) through the woods, bearing left at a Y marked with a post with a punch for the Delaware Trail Challenge. You'll reach an open meadow with a Y intersection; take the right fork along the edge of the meadow, and reenter the woods. Bear right at the next Y intersection as well, continuing in the woods along a small stream; the trail leaves the stream and joins the yellow-blazed trail. Continue until you reach a stone wall dividing the woods from a meadow; turn left and follow the wall to the park office and the parking area.

MORE INFORMATION

Restrooms are located at the main office; you will also find composting toilets at the Route 92 parking area. Dogs must be on a leash no more than 6 feet long. The park is open daily 8 A.M. to sunset. The parking fee is $3 for Delaware residents, $6 for nonresidents from March through November. Hunting is permitted in designated areas in season in the state park; there is no hunting on Woodlawn Trustees lands. The park office has a small store and a helpful interpretive staff. Many other trails in the park traverse different habitat, including meadows, a freshwater marsh, and a hawk watch. Visitors to Delaware state parks can take part in the Delaware Trail Challenge, a program in which hikers can get prizes for hiking certain trails. Brandywine Creek State Park, Routes 100 and 92, Greenville, DE 19807; 302-577-3534; www.destateparks .com/park/brandywine-creek.

TRIP 14
HIBERNIA COUNTY PARK

Location: Wagontown, PA (Chester County)
Rating: Easy
Distance: 3.0 miles
Elevation Gain: 90 feet
Estimated Time: 1.25 hours
Maps: USGS Wagontown; trail map available at park office and at website for Hibernia County Park

Hike along an old railroad bed and an upland trail portion with rocky but gently rolling hills in a woodland setting. Historical remnants along the trail reveal the park's past as an iron forge.

DIRECTIONS

From Route 82 south, turn right onto Cedar Knoll Road. Follow signs for the park. The first right onto Park Road is the back entrance to the park. The second right onto Park Road is the main entrance leading to the park office. To reach the Hatfield House parking lot and the Rim Trail trailhead, continue on Cedar Knoll Road past the main entrance. Turn right onto Hibernia Road. Go 1.4 miles to a stop sign intersecting with Wagontown Road. Continue straight and over a one-lane bridge leading to a Y in the road. Veer to the right at the Y. The Hatfield House is immediately to the right of the road. Go past the Hatfield House and turn right onto Camp Stewart Road. There is a No Outlet sign. Follow this road 150 feet and turn right into the parking lot. The parking lot can accommodate 40 cars. *GPS coordinates*: 40° 00.865′ N, 75° 50.724′ W.

TRAIL DESCRIPTION

From busy industrial site to country estate to a peaceful natural area, Hibernia encapsulates the history of many of the area's best suburban hiking spots. Hibernia County Park encompasses more than 900 acres of diverse habitats, including the West Branch of the Brandywine Creek. From 1793 to 1876, Hibernia was the site of an iron works. The centerpiece of the park is Hibernia Mansion, which was originally the residence of the ironmaster and was expanded by subsequent owners. By 1850, Hibernia had become a self-sustaining community, with two iron forges, two heating furnaces, a rolling mill, a grist mill, the ironmaster's residence, houses for employees, a farm, gardens,

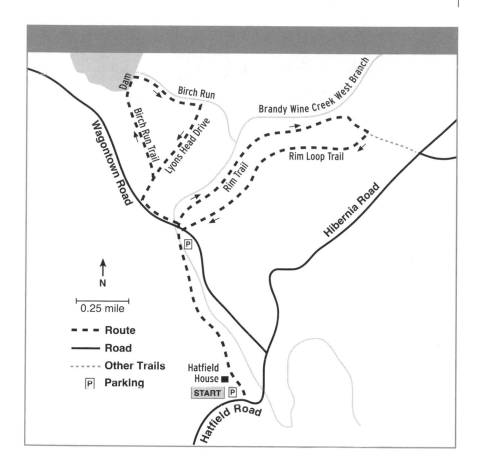

and orchards. Many buildings of the era are still standing and in use; the area is part of the Hatfield-Hibernia Historic District.

The hike begins at the parking lot for the Hatfield House, which was used as a convalescent home from 1920 until it was acquired by the county in 1980. From the porch, follow the steps down to the yellow gate at the road's edge. The Rim Trail, which begins here, has a stone-dust surface covering a stretch of old railroad bed. In the mid-1800s, the railroad brought both soft and hard coal to the iron forge. It also transported ice to surrounding cities.

The trail parallels the West Branch of the Brandywine Creek for 0.6 mile. The blue-blazed trail is flat and smooth and provides many ways to access the scenic creek. Along this section of the Rim Trail, jewelweed appears in abundance from May through October. Growing on the edge of creek beds and moist woods, jewelweed typically reaches heights of 3 to 5 feet. It has oval, round-toothed leaves and trumpet-shaped orange or yellow flowers that attract ruby-throated hummingbirds in the summer. In late summer and

A century ago, the scenic West Branch of the Brandywine Creek provided power for a thriving iron forge at Hibernia.

fall, its hair-trigger loaded seed pods jump off from the plant at the slightest provocation.

Cross over the creek on the remains of the Wilmington and Northern Railroad Bridge. In less than 25 feet, the trail intersects with busy Wagontown Road. Use caution when crossing. Pass through the yellow gate, and continue on the Rim Trail into the woods. Brandywine Creek is now to the left of the trail; after about a quarter-mile it bends away from the trail. After another half-mile, look for the remains of ice houses to the left of the trail—trenches, stone foundations, and a sign that reads "Ice Houses." The ice houses were used to store harvested blocks that were to be delivered by railroad. In the days before refrigerators, ice blocks were used to preserve food.

After passing the ice houses, the Rim Trail ends at the yellow gate. Turn right before the gate to take the Rim Trail Loop. A blue diamond-shaped sign with an arrow indicates this right-hand turn onto a natural-surface trail. Head uphill for 200 feet, where the trail forms a Y. Bear right to head back in the direction you came.

The Rim Trail Loop traverses the rocky woods above the Rim Trail and Brandywine Creek. This is a young woods of tulip tree and beech, which has re-grown since a gypsy moth infestation in the 1980s.

Follow the blue blazes that are marked on trees and rocks. The trail is wide and straight, albeit rocky. After 0.75 miles, bear right at a Y intersection, go another 150 feet, and turn right again. The trail descends steeply to Wagontown Road. Use caution; there are many loose rocks. At Wagontown Road, turn right. For a shorter hike (total 1.75 miles), cross the road and backtrack down the Rim Trail. Otherwise, proceed about 500 feet and turn right onto Lyons Head Drive (marked by two white gateposts with lions' heads).

After another 400 feet, turn left onto Birch Run Trail at the yellow gate opposite a private residence (cottage #1). This grassy path winds uphill along meadows of wildflowers and native grasses. At a T intersection with an unpaved maintenance road, turn sharp right, cross a mowed field for about 25 feet, and veer right into an opening at the edge of the woods. Follow the footpath beside two pipes downhill through the woods to a paved path below the Hibernia Dam. Turn right and follow the paved path along the pretty Birch Run stream to the next yellow gate at cottage #3 and continue onto Lyons Head Drive. To the left next to the historic millers' house is a pond that makes for a nice place to have a snack. Turn right onto Lyons Head Drive, a paved but lightly traveled road. After about 1,200 feet, make a left at Wagontown Road, cross the bridge, and take the first right onto the Rim Trail to return to Hatfield House.

MORE INFORMATION

In the park are picnic sites, multiuse trails (hiking, biking, horseback riding, and cross-country skiing), campgrounds, and a lake. Fishing and boating are allowed. Dogs are allowed on a leash. Hunting is permitted in season. There are no restrooms on the trail but you will find some at the campgrounds in the park. Hibernia County Park is managed by Chester County Parks and Recreation, P.O. Box 124, Wagontown, PA 19376; 610-383-3812; http://dsf.chesco .org/ccparks/site/default.asp.

TRIP 15
MARSH CREEK STATE PARK

Location: Downingtown, PA (Chester County)
Rating: Easy
Distance: 2.0 miles
Elevation Gain: 200 feet
Approximate Time: 1.0 hour
Maps: USGS Downington; trail map available at park office and online at website for Marsh Creek State Park

Marsh Creek State Park is especially notable for hundreds of acres of open fields as well as a 500-acre lake with superb fishing and quiet-water boating, and miles of forested trails.

DIRECTIONS

From the Pennsylvania Turnpike, take Exit 312 and head north on Route 100 toward Pottstown. After 2.0 miles, turn left onto Little Conestoga Road and take a right again to stay on it. (Do not follow signs to Marsh Creek via Park Road.) After 2.4 miles, Little Conestoga Road makes a sharp left turn. In another 0.6 mile, turn left on Chalfant Road. At 2.1 miles, Chalfant Road dead-ends in a parking lot with space for about a dozen cars. *GPS coordinates*: 40° 04.182′ N, 75° 43.831′ W.

TRAIL DESCRIPTION

Marsh Creek State Park is one of many green spaces that help protect the Brandywine Creek watershed (see also Trips 10, 13, and 14). The centerpiece of the park is a 535-acre lake, constructed in the 1970s in the headwaters of the East Branch of the Brandywine, to help manage water resources in the watershed. The park also includes about 1,200 acres of fields and woods.

Recreation at the park centers on fishing and quiet-water boating on the lake, which has several bays and miles of shoreline. There are informal trails around the lakeshore, but these tend to be muddy and rich in poison ivy. A well-used trail system occupies the southwest corner of the park, away from the shore of the lake, and the hike described here explores this area. Note: The trail system at Marsh Creek State Park is heavily used by bikes and horses, so be careful where you step.

The trailhead is obvious at the southeast corner of the parking lot by a signboard. Take the right-hand path. In late summer this trail is a tunnel of

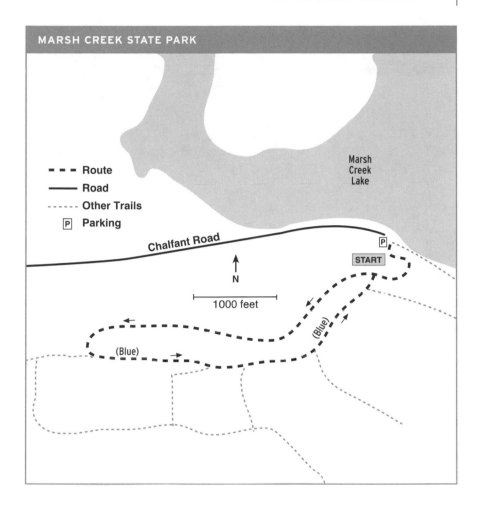

jewelweed, which thrives in sunny, moist openings. The trail goes back and forth between sun and shade, through light-filled clearings and under trees heavily draped in Asiatic bittersweet vine and wild grape, and through intermittent clearings. In about 150 feet, pass an obscure trail junction, where a path branches off to the left. You are following blue blazes here, but the trail is obvious as it snakes its way gently uphill. In places you'll pass through stands of young Norway maple, in whose dense shade nothing can grow. Note a trail marker on a flat pole that says, "B1."

In about a quarter-mile, approach the edge of an open field; the blue-blazed trail leads up to the edge of the meadow. There is a "Share the Trail" sign on a tree as well as a trail marker, saying "B2." Here is a junction; turn off the blue-blazed trail and head out into the edge of the meadow on an obvious trail. The view will draw you anyway. The trail turns left and follows the edge of the woods; look right down a slope toward the lake, which is mostly hidden by

Fleabanes, daisy-like common wildflowers found in fields and by roadsides, derived their common name from their purported ability to repel insects.

trees, and outward toward more wooded hills in the distance, with only a few housetops to be seen in the middle distance.

The level path proceeds through orchard grass and timothy—indicators that you are in a hay meadow. In early summer, the grasses here are quite tall. Dogbane, a native colonizer of fields, has bean-like dark seed pods from which, in late summer, float wispy silken-haired seeds similar to those of milkweed. Where the trail branches left, continue straight. Head toward a gap in the hedgerow under a tall walnut tree on the left, then pass through a second meadow, triangular in shape, heading slightly downhill.

The trail leads back into woods, becomes a wide lane, and curves uphill and to the left, into another stand of second-growth trees struggling under the weight of vines. Soon walk through a grove of tall ash and walnut trees, free of vines. After about 300 feet, enter a third meadow, even larger than the first two. The trail heads diagonally across the meadow toward the right, dropping slightly.

At this point you have come 0.7 mile from the trailhead, as you pass through yet another hedgerow of trees and enter into the fourth meadow, which is the largest yet. This vast field, spreading to the west, encompasses at least 100 acres;

the hills and trees that surround it, with nary a sign of humanity, evoke a remote landscape. This is Chester County's big-sky country.

The trail you are following is a clearly defined farm lane, and it leads along the left side of a hedgerow that divides the field. Head down the lane toward the distant treeline, where the lane takes a sharp turn to the right, but go straight through the hedgerow about 10 feet to a hard-packed trail that is the official blue-blazed path. Note that this path has paralleled the farm lane across the meadow. Turn left.

In about 300 feet, you come to a series of trail junctions, offering connections that enable you to extend the hike for several miles. (See the park's trail guide.)

To return, follow the blue-blazed trail back across meadow number 4. Pass a yellow-blazed trail junction, then another trail junction as you reenter the forest with an orange-blazed trail leading off to the right. The blue trail becomes a woods road through large oak and poplar trees. After 0.5 miles from the turnaround, a red-blazed trail, heads off to the right.

Proceed along the woods road. Note the meadow that you can see to the left through the trees; you walked through it on your outbound route. Where the road makes a sharp right turn and descends, look for a double blue blaze on a tree and turn left.

Proceed on the narrower blue-blazed path, which curves to the left; after 100 yards you pass the "B2" sign where you entered the first meadow. Retrace your steps to the parking lot.

MORE INFORMATION

Restrooms are located near the park office, accessible from the Park Road side of the park. Hunting is permitted in certain areas in season, including the location of the trails described here. There are other trails in the park and the long-distance Brandywine Trail passes nearby. Marsh Creek State Park, 675 Park Road, Downingtown, PA 19335-1898; 610-458-5119; www.dcnr.state .pa.us/stateParks/parks/marshcreek.aspx.

TRIP 16
FRENCH CREEK STATE PARK

Location: Elverson, PA (Berks County)
Rating: Moderate
Distance: 6.75 miles
Elevation Gain: 500 feet
Estimated Time: 3.0 hours
Maps: USGS Elverson and Pottstown; trail map also available at park office and at French Creek State Park website.

Explore the hills and forests where Daniel Boone learned to become a frontiersman; French Creek's beauty is new and old at the same time.

DIRECTIONS
Take I-76 west to Route 100 north (Exit 312). Turn left onto Route 401 and go 6.5 miles, then turn right onto Route 345; go 3.4 miles to South Entrance Road, then 1.4 miles to Park Road, at the park office entrance. To get to the trailhead, continue on Park Road, make the first left, and go 0.25 mile to first parking lot on left. *GPS coordinates*: 40° 11.859′ N, 75° 47.467′ W.

TRAIL DESCRIPTION
French Creek State Park is in Daniel Boone country. The explorer was born in 1734 in a log cabin in the Oley Valley (about 5 miles away), and he spent his childhood roaming the Berks County forests, which at that time were on the western edge of the Pennsylvania frontier. Although the park's deep, rich forests are in many ways far different from those that shaped the boy who would discover the Cumberland Gap, they still have the power to draw visitors back into a time when the wooded frontier seemed to stretch endlessly into the future.

French Creek State Park's 7,475 acres include 35 miles of trails and two artificial lakes (not here in Boone's day); adjacent to the park is the Hopewell Furnace National Historic Site, a restored iron-making village. The furnace operated from 1771 to 1883. The fact that iron making was a thriving industry here is a dead giveaway that the woods in this area were, a century or so ago, clear-cut and logged to make charcoal to feed the furnace. Old-growth chestnut-dominated forests with gigantic trees segued to treeless hillsides, which now host middle-aged oak-hickory woods.

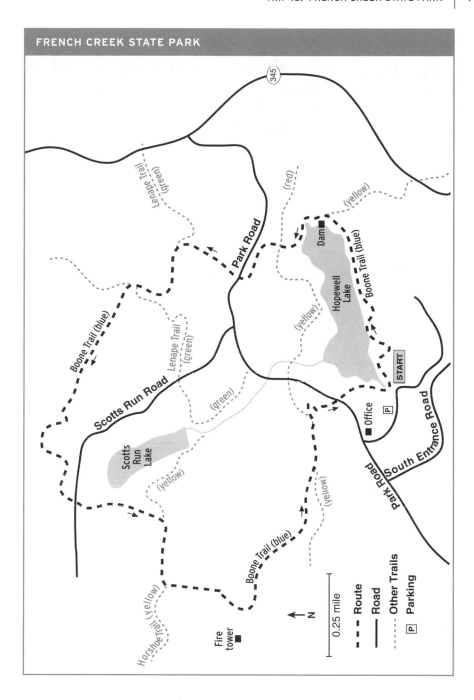

FRENCH CREEK STATE PARK

The Boone Trail, one of many loops throughout the park, makes a wide circle that encompasses a variety of habitats. French Creek State Park also, appropriately enough, offers an orienteering (map-and-compass navigation) course so that you can practice finding your way in the woods.

The modern-day explorer in French Creek State Park can be excused for dreaming of discovering new worlds deep within the thick forest.

Enter the Boone Trail at the south end of the Hopewell Lake boat launch parking lot, near the orienteering course. The trail is blue-blazed, and the blazes are well maintained and consistent. Follow the blue blazes at all forks and intersections; note double blazes indicating turns.

Go over a metal bridge; turn left onto a paved drive just after the bridge, bear left into the woods, and continue on a gravel/paved path paralleling the Hopewell Lake shore to the left and continuing through a grassy picnic area. The pretty, tree-lined 68-acre lake is popular with paddlers and sailors. After about half a mile, the path becomes a dirt trail along a natural lakeshore amid woods of maple, oak, hickory, beech, and dogwood; abundant fungi indicate that this is a forest with a healthy cycle of decay and regeneration.

The trail bears left below the Hopewell Lake dam, a pretty area with a lovely stepped spillway. Go uphill past the dam, bearing left at the Y after the helpful steps. (To the right is the path to Hopewell Furnace.)

Yellow blazes shortly join the blue, then quickly disappear. These mark the Horse-Shoe Trail, a 140-mile-long trail connecting Valley Forge (see Trips 6 and 7) to the Appalachian Trail. The Horse-Shoe Trail joins and leaves the Boone Trail at many points along the route.

At about the 2.0-mile point, the trail veers right to cross Park Road and enters a wet woods. On warm, rainy spring evenings, Entrance Road and Park

Road may be closed by park managers because this woods is full of vernal pools—small seasonal ponds that attract masses of frogs, toads, and salamanders to breed every year. The amphibians come down by the thousands from the ridges high above and far away to mate and lay eggs in the hidden pools; they are heedless of roads and cars, as they have been making this journey for far longer than humans have been driving. After the eggs hatch and the young mature, the ponds dry up and the amphibians quietly return to the hills, where they spend most of the year.

The Boone Trail joins briefly with the green-blazed Lenape Trail and becomes very rocky. Continue on the Boone Trail when the Lenape Trail goes left down to Scotts Run Lake at about the 2.5-mile point.

Cross Firetower Road at about the 3.5-mile mark, and enter a young, wet woods on recently disturbed ground; here you'll see cherry trees, dogwood, grapevines, and bittersweet. The trail crosses several streams, some sandy-bottomed, others rocky; the bridges may be slippery. This moist area supports a particularly lush woods, with many varied fungi as well as patches of mountain laurel (Pennsylvania's state flower) in the rockier sections.

At about the 4.5-mile mark, the trail begins going uphill. The woods becomes noticeably drier as the trail climbs Williams Hill, with chestnut oak predominating in the canopy and blueberry bushes on the forest floor. At about the 5.0-mile mark, the trail reaches its highest point, almost 1,000 feet. The Hopewell Fire Tower is just above the trail, on the summit.

The trail then begins to descend. Pink lady's slippers, a native spring-blooming orchid, are common in this section. The trail continues downhill, passing through an area of very large conglomerate boulders. At the bottom of the hill, it terminates at Park Road. To return to the parking lot, cross the road and bear right around the shores of Hopewell Lake on the left.

MORE INFORMATION

Restrooms are located at the park office and at the trailhead. Dogs must be leashed. Boating (paddling, sailing and electric motors) and fishing are permitted on Hopewell Lake and boats may be rented. Hunting is permitted in designated areas in season (see trail map). Hopewell Furnace National Historic Site (www.nps.gov/hofu), adjacent to French Creek, has been restored to depict an early American ironworking community. French Creek State Park, 843 Park Road, Elverson, PA 19520-9523; 610-582-9680; www.dcnr.state.pa.us/stateparks/parks/frenchcreek.aspx.

JUMP IN THE POOL

The late-winter sun rises higher and higher in the sky. In the woods, slowly warming air thaws the frozen soil; water trickles into troughs, carves out a path downhill, and collects in a low spot where a tree once stood. Frogs and salamanders arrive at these vernal pools to mate and lay eggs. The pools shrink over the course of the spring, giving the eggs room to hatch and the newborn amphibians time to mature. Before predators such as fish, snakes, and turtles can move in on their prey, the summer's heat has dried up the pools, and the young frogs and salamanders have moved on.

Wood frogs are typically the first to arrive at vernal pools, sometimes as early as mid-February. Leaf brown, with a black mask, they are terrestrial during most of the year, hence their name. In winter, they burrow into the soil; their cells contain an antifreeze that enables them to survive cold temperatures. These frogs spend summer and fall hiding in leaf litter. Only in spring do they attract attention. The vernal pools seem alive with their distinctive calls. Following a chorus of strident quacks, hikers can find a pool alive not with ducks, but with frogs swimming frantically this way and that, with males searching for an available female. Once she has mated, a female wood frog lays thousands of eggs in a mass that floats just under the surface of the pool and is often tinged green from algae.

In mid-to-late March, the calls of spring peepers pierce the air. The tiny peeper, a thumbnail-sized frog, seems to be all voice. Its high-pitched *peep*—often mistaken for a bird call—seems to come out of nowhere and yet to be everywhere at once; when a chorus of peepers gets going, the noise can be deafening. A calling male perches on a waterside stem to attract a female. After he has succeeded, she lays hundreds of eggs underwater around the submerged vegetation.

Spotted salamanders remain silent in spring, as they do the rest of the year. Black with yellow spots, and 6 to 8 inches long, they hide during the day under leaves, rocks, or logs, or in underground burrows, emerging only at night. On warm spring nights, usually after a rain, scores of salamanders make their way to the vernal pools to mate, even traveling far from home (hundreds or even thousands of feet) and crossing roads to get there. They return to the same pool year after year, perhaps drawn by familiar smells. The salamanders' distinctive egg masses are gelatinous blobs that rise to the surface as the eggs grow. The young hatch, leave the pool, and find the woods, but they remember where they came from, and will return next spring.

TRIP 17
GREEN LANE PARK–PERKIOMEN TRAIL

Location: Green Lane Borough, PA (Montgomery County)
Rating: Moderate
Distance: 9.0 miles
Elevation Gain: 150 feet
Estimated Time: 4.0 hours
Maps: USGS Perkiomenvillle, Sassamansville, East Greenville, Milford Square; trail maps available at the park office were not accurate at the time of this book's printing

Hike through a diverse upper Montgomery County landscape of woods and meadows and deep ravines, around a forested lake reminiscent of New England.

DIRECTIONS
Take the Northeast Extension of the Pennsylvania Turnpike (I-476 north) 15 miles to Exit 31 (Lansdale). Take Route 63 north 10.0 miles to Green Lane Borough, and turn left onto Route 29 south. After 0.8 mile, turn right on Deep Creek Road; go 0.6 miles and turn right onto Snyder Road. Stay on Snyder Road until you reach the main office parking lot, where there is ample parking. *GPS coordinates*: 40° 19.937′ N, 75° 28.987′ W.

TRAIL DESCRIPTION
Green Lane Park sneaks up on you. Just when you think it's about the water, and you're admiring the herons and egrets fishing in the shallows, the hilltop meadows astound you with their shimmering beauty. Just when you think it's about the dramatic rock-bottomed creek ravines, the reservoir surprises you with its continuous tree-lined shores reflected in green water.

With water covering 870 of its 3,400 acres, the park, owned in part by Montgomery County and in part by a water company, attracts large fishing birds of prey, including ospreys and bald eagles, as well as birds that dabble along the shorelines. There are also 2,300 acres of forest—a quarter of which is interior (deep) forest—which host a huge diversity of bird species, both migrants and breeding birds. The park is part of the Upper Perkiomen Watershed, one of the Pennsylvania Highlands areas designated as Critical Treasures.

Green Lane Reservoir impounds the Perkiomen Creek and numerous streams, within a shallow but steep valley; the smaller Deep Creek Lake and

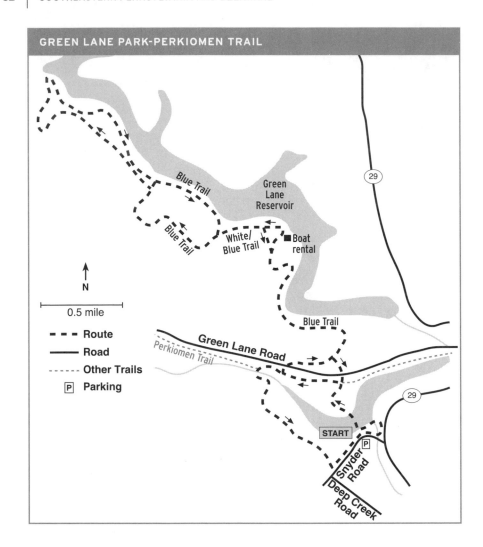

GREEN LANE PARK-PERKIOMEN TRAIL

Green Lane Reservoir

Blue Trail

Blue Trail

White/ Blue Trail

Boat rental

Blue Trail

N

0.5 mile

▪ ▪ ▪ Route

▬▬ Road

▭▭▭ Other Trails

P Parking

Green Lane Road

Perkiomen Trail

29

29

START

P

Snyder Road

Deep Creek Road

Knight Lake are adjacent. Parkland completely surrounds the water, much of it forest. The terrain on the north side is rugged and rocky, with many waterfalls; the southern side is hilly and pleasant.

The hike begins at the parking lot for the main office on Snyder Road, adjacent to Deep Creek Lake. Turn right (facing the lake) to go down the closed Snyder Road; proceed past the gate and to the 1903 iron bridge over Deep Creek. Cross to the center, where there are delightful views of the creek and the dam; turn around and go right to follow the lake past the dam. Turn right and cross at the bridge to a grassy area. Follow the trail across the lawn to where it meets the Perkiomen Trail just before Green Lane Road.

The 20-mile Perkiomen Trail (PT) begins about a mile from here, to the right at Route 29, and ends at Valley Forge, where it joins the Schuylkill River Trail, following the course of the Perkiomen Creek along an old rail bed. Turn left onto the PT, which generally parallels the road along this stretch but occasionally goes onto the road. Between the road and the creek, native wildflowers, grasses, trees, and shrubs are being planted to reduce erosion, sediment loss, and pollution in this riparian (streamside) area.

Just after crossing the bridge over Deep Creek, turn right onto the Equestrian Trail, which crosses the road and then becomes a gravel trail that goes uphill diagonally, to the edge of the woods; you'll have nice views of the park and hills beyond. The trail then turns left and goes up through the woods to a lovely grass-and-wildflower meadow overlooking the reservoir; a perfectly placed bench at the front edge of the meadow is a good place to sit and take in the view. This meadow is being restored.

Follow the trail through the woods to the Equestrian Campground. Take the first right turn off the gravel path to get onto the Blue Trail. Follow this trail—a narrow natural footpath—through the woods, crossing Hill Road and entering an oak-hickory forest with many ferns and wildflowers; the now-rocky trail goes up and down along the side of the hill, with views of the reservoir to the right. Eventually the trail goes down to the shore and follows it before heading steeply uphill to a T intersection with a sign indicating "upper" and "lower" sections of the trail; turn right onto the Lower Blue Trail. At the paved drive, make a right and go downhill to the boat rental parking lot. Picnic tables here make it a good place for a rest.

From the office, head uphill and to the right to reach the trailhead for the Whitetail Nature Trail, a gravel path that enters the woods and becomes a natural footpath. White blazes mark this interpretive trail as it enters the woods; it is coincident with the blue blazes for the Blue Trail. Just before the next footbridge over a creek, it turns sharply left and goes uphill along a rocky hemlock ravine, following a small stream. Turn right (note the double blaze), cross the stream (sign indicates Helen's Ravine), head down along extremely fractured rocks, and cross the stream again (sign indicates Hillside Ravine).

Follow the blue blazes (and signs for the Equestrian Trail) up and across the ridge to a dirt road, and across the ridge to a dirt road; turn left. At the residential Swinging Bridge Road, turn right and go downhill until this road changes to a dirt surface where the blue blazes indicate that the trail turns left into the woods. (Optionally, shorten the hike by continuing straight downhill to the Blue Trail and head right.) Continue uphill, crossing the stream on rocks, and

A hilltop meadow in Green Lane Park overlooks the Upper Perkiomen Creek valley.

then bear left away from the stream (with another optional shortcut down to the lake). The trail becomes noticeably less rocky and flatter as it traverses the ridge on brittle red sandstone, in a young woods of cherries and cedars, along a stone wall (this was a former farm that has been relatively recently overgrown).

This trail traverses a rich rocky woods, eventually crossing a spectacular small ravine with a dramatic rock-ledge outcrop (sign indicates Rock Falls). The trail goes down to the shore; turn right at the T. (The trail at first appears to head straight into the reservoir.) Follow the blue-blazed trail along the reservoir and enjoy beautiful views of the tree-lined shores; you'll cross several streams that you crossed before, as well as Swinging Bridge Road. Rock outcrops along the way provide scenic rest stops. Swimming is prohibited, and very limited boating is permitted on these waters; human intrusion into the natural scenery is minimal.

Return to the intersection with the Whitetail Trail just after the footbridge. Follow the blue trail blazes to the paved road, turn right, and make a left at the second crosswalk to backtrack along the Blue Trail to the Equestrian Campground.

Follow the Equestrian Trail, but after the meadow do not turn right to continue on that trail; instead, turn left down the hill along the woods to Green

Lane Road. Cross the road and pick up the Perkiomen Trail on the other side. Turn right and follow the Perkiomen Trail as it passes by the restored riparian area, then crosses Deep Creek on an old stone bridge and heads downhill via Deep Creek Road. Cross the parking lot diagonally and turn left at Snyder Road to return to the parking area.

MORE INFORMATION

Restrooms are located at the main office parking lot; there are portable toilets at Equestrian Campground and at the boat rental area (along the hike). Maps for the Whitetail Nature Trail are available at the nature center on Route 20 in Marlborough. Trails are open dawn to dusk. Hunting is prohibited. Dogs must be on a leash not more than 6 feet long. Green Lane Park, P.O. Box 249, 2144 Snyder Road, Routes 29/63, Green Lane, PA 18054; 215-234-4528; www2 .montcopa.org/parks/cwp/view,A,1516,Q,26377.asp.

TRIP 18
PEACE VALLEY NATURE CENTER

Location: New Britain, PA (Bucks County)
Rating: Easy–Moderate
Distance: 7.0 miles
Elevation Gain: 150 feet
Estimated Time: 3.0 hours
Maps: USGS Doylestown; trail map available at the main office and online

This hike offers a number of options for a pleasant walking tour of diverse habitats typical of rural Bucks County: fields, streams, and wooded hillsides.

DIRECTIONS

Take the Pennsylvania Turnpike to Exit 343. Continue on Route 611 north to Route 313 west and take a left onto New Galena Road. Then turn left onto Chapman Road to the parking lot on the left. From Quakertown, take Route 313 east, turn right onto New Galena Road, and go left onto Chapman Road. You will find ample parking. *GPS coordinates*: 40° 20.432′ N, 75° 10.285′ W.

TRAIL DESCRIPTION

When educator Carolyn "Corey" Jarin founded the Peace Valley Nature Center in 1975, she took as its motto "Who learns will love, and not destroy, the creature's life, the flower's joy." This statement adorns an outbuilding on the former estate of the nineteenth-century Doylestown iconoclast Henry Chapman Mercer. Like Mercer's three hand-crafted tile-and-concrete buildings (now Fonthill, Moravian Tile Works, and Mercer Museums), Peace Valley began as an expression of a personal vision and became a Bucks County cultural resource. Jarin's vision was to create an "outdoor living museum" to teach children about nature.

Peace Valley is a Bucks County park created out of farmland as a flood control/water supply project, with the North Branch Neshaminy Creek getting dammed to produce the 2-mile-long Lake Galena. The 750-acre nature center, with 14 miles of trails, occupies the northeastern portion of the park. Because of its diverse habitats—some natural, some designed—it hosts a wide variety of birds.

PEACE VALLEY NATURE CENTER

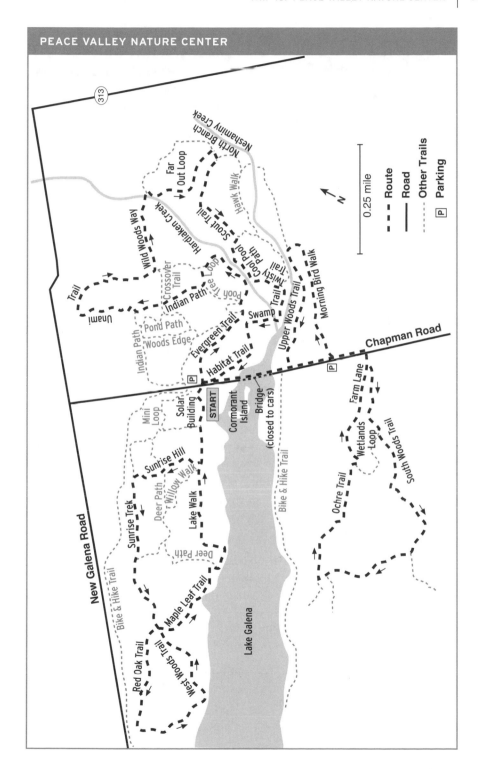

313

North Branch Neshaminy Creek

Far Out Loop

Hawk Walk

Scout Trail

Wild Woods Way

Hardiaken Creek

Crossover Trail

Pooh Tree Loop

Cool Pool

Twisty Trail

Morning Bird Walk

Unami Trail

Indian Path

Pond Path

Woods Edge

Indian Path

Evergreen Trail

Swamp Trail

Upper Woods Trail

Habitat Trail

Chapman Road

P

START

Solar Building

Cormorant Island

Bridge (closed to cars)

P

Farm Lane

Mini Loop

Wetlands Loop

South Woods Trail

Sunrise Hill

Willow Walk

Ochre Trail

Deer Path

Lake Walk

Sunrise Trek

Deer Path

New Galena Road

Bike & Hike Trail

Maple Leaf Trail

Bike & Hike Trail

Lake Galena

Red Oak Trail

West Woods Trail

0.25 mile

N

- - - Route
—— Road
······ Other Trails
P Parking

The guiding ethic behind Peace Valley Nature Center.

The trail system falls into four rough quadrants around the main parking lot. The trails are designed to accommodate busloads of schoolchildren and other large groups; visitors can start at the entrance, enter a single quadrant, walk through multiple habitats, and return. (Note that some trails, which are not used for education, are minimally maintained, including West Woods Trail, Red Oak Trail, South Woods Trail and Ochre Trail.) The hike described here passes through all four quadrants but can easily be shortened or done in a different order. Trails are inconsistently blazed, but most are marked with signs.

Northwest quadrant (2.5 miles): Begin at the main office (the "solar building") across Chapman Road. The Lake Walk begins opposite the birdseed shop. Turn right at the Sunrise Hill Trail, heading uphill. Like many of the trails, this one is a natural surface worn into the earth and is almost always wet, muddy, swampy, or puddled. The rock underlying the park (and much of Bucks County) is red shale and sandstone, which erodes to clay, yielding slow-draining soil. Where the red rock is close to the surface, the high water table creates the wetlands, seeps, pools, and muck typically found throughout the nature center. The woods are dominated by oak, ash, and hickory trees as well as spicebush and arrowwood shrubs. Wildflowers such as spring beauties, toothwort, bloodroot, and trout lilies are common in spring in the moister parts of the woods.

At the top of the ridge, turn left. You'll find good views of the lake along this section. The trail crosses a dry streambed and enters a woods after 0.25 mile, becoming the white-blazed West Woods Trail. There are numerous small stream crossings; the trail becomes a stream as it descends, and you'll have to rock-hop. After another 0.25 mile, turn right onto the yellow-blazed Red Oak Trail, which climbs uphill gradually then bends sharply downhill.

Throughout this woods walk and elsewhere on the hike, note that the understory is almost entirely composed of spicebush or invasive multiflora rose and that there is little ground cover. The ubiquitous deer have devastated the park's young trees and shrubs, with the exception of those they dislike. As a result, the woods are declining in diversity and quality; lack of vegetation leads also to erosion of the hillsides, exacerbating the trails' swampiness.

Follow the trail as it descends into one of these swampy areas, turns left, and then ascends again along the West Woods Trail until it comes to a T. Turn right onto the Maple Leaf Trail, hiking downhill and meeting the Lake Trail at the bottom. Turn left; the office is 0.25 mile away.

Southeast quadrant (0.5 mile): Continue to Chapman Road and turn right. Cross the bridge over the North Branch where it empties into Lake Galena, a natural place to pause and watch the ever-present cormorants as they fly, dive, or just sit and dry their wings. Great blue herons fish here in the shallows, painted turtles bask on logs, and water snakes may be seen sunning themselves on the rocks. Because the lake is a water supply reservoir, its level may change over the year. At times, it is drawn down enough to create mudflats, which attract great varieties of shorebirds such as sandpipers.

Continue up the road and make a left onto Morning Bird Walk. This trail skirts the edge of a meadow; in summer it is a sea of goldenrod and aster. After 0.25 mile the trail turns left into the woods and meets the Upper Woods Trail. Turn left and follow the Upper Woods Trail to the road.

Southwest quadrant (1.25 miles): Go left, uphill past the parking lot and a meadow; turn right at the gated former farm lane, and after 50 feet enter the woods via the South Woods Trail. On this trail you'll see several remnants of the farm buildings that were here before the park. The trail passes a springhouse, which was used to keep food cold before mechanical refrigeration. Springwater still flows through its base. This is a wetlands loop, a quiet open area with small flowing streams that is an ideal spot for viewing dragonflies in summer.

Instead of making the loop (unless you wish to shorten the hike), turn uphill onto the unmarked South Woods Trail. It turns right after 0.25 mile, heading downhill, where it meets a field. Go along the edge of the field, duck left into the woods, and head downhill to a T; turn right onto the unmarked Ochre Trail, which passes old ochre (iron oxide) pits. After ascending to a hedgerow between two fields, continue via this hedgerow to the Wetlands Loop;

bear left. As you head back through the wetlands, you pass several decaying outbuildings of the former farm, and a wolf tree—an oak that grew large when this was a clearing and now seems out of proportion with the surrounding young trees. Return via the farm lane to Chapman Road, turn left, and cross the bridge.

Northeast quadrant (2.75 miles): Just as you reach the parking lot there is a trail entrance to the right. This quadrant of the trail system is complicated, but trail intersections are generally well marked. It offers an enormous variety of habitat in a small area. You'll pass through evergreen stands, deciduous woods, streams, swamps, scrub-shrub fields, and meadows. Take the Evergreen Trail, pass the small Persimmon Pond, and turn right onto Pooh Tree Loop. The highlight of this trail along the Hardiaken Creek is a giant hollow sycamore that begs children of all ages to stand in it. Having pretended to be Pooh (or Piglet), continue on to the Indian Path, then to a T. Go straight onto the Unami Trail, which skirts a field in a 0.25-mile hairpin loop; note the deer exclusion/native planting area. Go left into the woods via the Wild Woods Way. When the Wild Woods Way meets the Far Out Loop, bear right, then go right again onto the Scout Trail. Bear right onto the Cool Pool Path, left onto Twisty Trail (don't cross the stream), right onto the Swamp Trail, and left onto Habitat Trail (where there is another deer exclusion/native planting area), and continue to the road. Turn right to reach the parking lot.

MORE INFORMATION

The Peace Valley Nature Center office is open Tuesday through Sunday from 9 A.M. to 5 P.M. All other areas are open dawn to dusk, 7 days a week. Restrooms are located at the nature center office. Boots are advised for any hike here due to the chronically wet trails. The small nature center offers exhibits relating to wildlife, including two spectacular murals by Taylor Oughton. It also has newly renovated solar panels. In the park section of Lake Galena (not the nature center), fishing and boating (but not swimming) are permitted, and boats may be rented on an hourly basis. Trails are maintained by the Friends of Peace Valley Nature Center. Peace Valley Nature Center, 170 Chapman Road, Doylestown, PA 18901; 215-345-7860; www.peacevalleynaturecenter.org.

BAMBI, KEEP OUT!

The white-tailed deer is both an iconic emblem of the woods and a threat to it. This gentle, graceful animal—a vegetarian whose "crime" is eating twigs—has become an object of enmity for Delaware Valley conservationists.

A century ago, deer had virtually disappeared from Pennsylvania and New Jersey. Unregulated hunting had decimated the population; forest clearances had eliminated their habitat. Game managers reintroduced deer, established management regimes, and supported restoration and protection of habitat.

The results of those good intentions have been either successful or disastrous, depending on one's perspective. Deer populations have rebounded—to 150,000 in New Jersey and 10 times that number in Pennsylvania. But now forests are being eaten to death. Deer eat plants. If left unchecked, they eat all the plants they can. Their numbers should ordinarily be limited by predation. However, humans long ago extirpated their natural predators (wolves, primarily); the only animals that regularly kill deer today are people.

As development has spread into deer-inhabited woods, deer have been feasting on suburban gardens and landscaping; this extra food supports a higher density than could subsist on forest vegetation alone. And in populated areas, hunting is limited or prohibited. As a result, deer density in certain areas has increased far beyond the forest's capacity to regenerate. Deer eat seedlings faster than new ones can sprout. Deer dislike multiflora rose, beech trees, spicebush, honeysuckle, and hay-scented fern—in some woods only these plants survive.

The contrast between a deer-browsed woods and a healthy forest is startling. A good rule of thumb is that a healthy forest is one you can't see through. At summer's height, a green curtain extends from the canopy to the floor: mature trees, young trees, shrubs, wildflowers, ground cover. A deer-browsed woods has no young trees, a sparse or absent shrub layer, bare ground, and an overall open look.

If left alone, deer-devastated forests will die. Mature trees will expire, and no young ones will replace them. And wildlife that depends on the woods will die off too. As the acres of healthy forests in Pennsylvania and New Jersey have declined, so too have the numbers of forest birds.

There are no easy answers. Managed hunting can't address influx from surrounding areas. Deer exclosures (fenced-in sites planted with native vegetation) support forest regeneration but are impractical over large areas. In the end, something will have to give: either the deer or the forest.

TRIP 19
RALPH STOVER STATE PARK
AND TOHICKON VALLEY PARK

Location: Point Pleasant, PA (Bucks County)
Rating: Moderate
Distance: 8.0 miles
Elevation Gain: 225 feet
Estimated Time: 4.0 hours
Maps: USGS Lumberville; trail map for a portion of this hike available at the trailhead, the state park office, and online

On this hike in the Tohickon Gorge, from the bottom to the top and back again, you can view rushing waters, rocky wooded hills, and— most marvelous of all—the spectacular High Rocks overlooks.

DIRECTIONS
Take Route 611 north to Route 413 north. Go 2.0 miles and turn right on Stump Road. Continue for 2.0 miles on Stump Road and turn left onto State Park Road, then turn right into the parking area. (To reach an alternative parking area, turn right on State Park Road and follow the signs.) Alternatively, take Route 32 to Point Pleasant, Plumstead Township (south) side; take State Park Road north 2.0 miles and keep straight to end at the parking area, where you will find space for about 60 cars. *GPS coordinates:* 40° 26.083′ N, 75° 05.876′ W.

TRAIL DESCRIPTION
Although Bucks County is known for gently rolling hills and a bucolic landscape, one of the most dramatic and beautiful gorges in eastern Pennsylvania can also be found here. Easily accessible, Tohickon Gorge in Ralph Stover State Park and Tohickon Valley Park centers on a 200-foot cliff called High Rocks. Adding to the beauty is the Tohickon Creek, which begins in northern Bucks County near Nockamixon State Park (Trip 20), is impounded by the Lake Nockamixon dam, and then flows southeast out of the lake for 11.5 miles to the Delaware River at Point Pleasant. The creek's course to the river is over gray sandstone and argillite and red shale. As the creek wore through the rock, it carved a meandering course amid sheer vertical cliffs.

RALPH STOVER STATE PARK AND TOHICKON VALLEY PARK

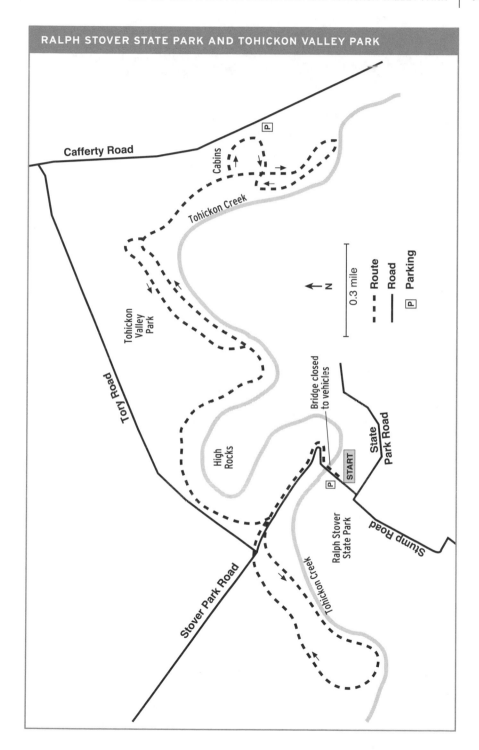

Seen from High Rocks cliffs, the Tohickon Creek winds through the gorge it continues to create.

The hike starts in Ralph Stover State Park. At the turn of the nineteenth century, the Stover family established gristmills and sawmills along the Tohickon Creek. The Stover-Myers mill just north of the park is the only structure that has been preserved; it operated continuously from 1800 to 1956. On the site of the state park was a gristmill, but the only remains of it now are the millrace (which channeled water from the creek to the mill) and the stub ends of a former dam. The dam was removed in 2007 to improve habitat for aquatic wildlife in the creek.

Walk down from the parking area to the creek to see the remains of the dam. Then continue along the creek—the trail parallels the millrace on the right for about 1,000 feet—to a footbridge that crosses the creek. On the other side, continue up Stover Park Road (infrequently used by cars) past several private residences.

About one-quarter of a mile from the bridge, enter an opening in the woods on your right, marked with yellow blazes. You are now in Tohickon Valley Park. The trail travels across a finger of land that forms one of the two portions of the great S-bend in the Tohickon, which sweeps southeast from Ralph Stover State Park, northwest toward High Rocks, then southeast again. (This portion of the park was donated by author James Michener.)

The park and the woods are much used, and this trail is crisscrossed by bike trails and "social trails" that go every which way, cut into the brush by visitors for whom the official routes are apparently inadequate. Proceed straight over a dry stream crossing for about 1,500 feet until you reach the series of fenced overlooks, named Argillite, Balcony, and Cedar.

No written description, or even a photograph, can do justice to the magnificent views of the gorge from the 200-foot High Rocks. There is something about the combination of the sheerness of the drop, the red rock cliffs, and the sinuous curve of the creek that sets off this vista as one of the wonders of the Delaware Valley.

Eventually, you must move on, so continue along the trail as it parallels the cliffs. Again, there are many crisscrossing trails. The one you want to take has white blazes with a red dot; these are old county blazes that are not well maintained. The yellow-blazed trail is above you and eventually intersects with the white/red trail. Bear right at the Y. You will bear right at the remainder of the Ys that you will encounter on this hike.

The woods become more rugged—chestnut oak, beech, hickory, hemlock, ash, and cinnamon fern are common—and rocks jut out above you. The narrow rocky trail crosses several very rocky streams that plunge down the hills; after rainstorms the streams may become impassable. After about a mile and a half, bear right at a Y where the white/red trail goes uphill to the left. This lower trail continues descending along the side of the hill for another 0.25 mile, goes behind a cabin, and meets a paved road. Follow the road down to the right, where you encounter the Tohickon Creek as it emerges from the gorge. You may want to rest on the flat rocks, listening to the rushing water and watching it flow.

Then return to the road and follow it all the way uphill, to a sign bearing the word "Trail" opposite the main parking lot. Enter here; when you reach the clearing, follow the tree line around to the left to another "Trail" sign. (There is a sign directly across the clearing for a different trail.)

Now follow the white/red trail all the way back to High Rocks and then to Stover Park Road, retracing a portion of the hike. Cross the road (though paved, it is lightly traveled) and turn right. After 200 feet, take the unmarked trail on your left heading down the hill. This trail, on county property, heads downhill gradually through pleasant woods and meets the creek after about 1,500 feet. Follow the trail another 1,500 feet along the creek; this is a quiet,

The American toad is well camouflaged to hide among the leaf litter of the woods.

flat portion with steep cliffs opposite, contrasting with the earlier dramatic creek-side experience.

The trail then heads steeply uphill to a stone wall. Follow the wall to the right; the trail then goes along a meadow and returns to the woods, proceeds along the ridge, and reenters Stover Park Road just 50 feet north of the entrance. Turn right to go downhill, crossing the bridge and returning via the millrace path to the parking lot.

MORE INFORMATION

The state park office is open when a park ranger is available. Restrooms are located at the trailhead. Trails are open sunrise to sunset, 7 days a week. As in other Pennsylvania state parks, pets must be on a leash. Rock climbers use the cliffs. Twice a year, at the end of March and the beginning of November, the state park releases water from Lake Nockamixon, which flows into the Tohickon Creek and creates whitewater conditions in the gorge. The cliffs are fenced for safety, but the High Rocks are extremely dangerous; children must be supervised. Ralph Stover State Park, c/o Delaware Canal State Park, Upper Black Eddy, PA 18972; 610-982-5560; www.dcnr.state.pa.us/stateParks/parks/ralphstover.aspx.

TRIP 20
NOCKAMIXON STATE PARK

Location: Quakertown, PA (Bucks County)
Rating: Moderate
Distance: 5.75 miles
Elevation Gain: 125 feet
Estimated Time: 3.0 hours
Maps: USGS Bedminster and Quakertown

Hide in plain sight in a thick rocky forest with groves of big old trees, views of Lake Nockamixon, and remnants of preindustrial-age rural Bucks County.

DIRECTIONS

Take Route 611 to 313 to 563 north, or Route 412 to 563 south. The entrance to the trail is on the south side of 563 just west of the park office entrance, on Deerwood Lane (the sign reads "Fishing Pier"). There is a large unpaved parking lot to the right, where you will find ample parking. *GPS coordinates*: 40° 27.612′ N, 75° 14.551′ W.

TRAIL DESCRIPTION

"Let's get lost!" That's what a person might exclaim before deciding to hike the Old Mill Trail in Nockamixon State Park. Between the heavily boated Lake Nockamixon and heavily driven Route 563 lies a tract of boulder-laden forest that has the secluded feel of a remote mountain camp. Trails wind across remnants of old settlements, under towering trees, and along narrow inlets.

The time-out-of-mind sense is compounded by the casual approach to trail maintenance here. There are many more trails than are shown on the official park map; the official trails are mostly unmarked, and those that are marked are occasionally discontinuous. Nonetheless, if you keep your wits about you, this is a straightforward loop—and even if you do get off the suggested route, just head downhill and you will eventually get to the lake, where you can easily find your way. A compass could be helpful as well.

The trailhead is at the north end of the parking lot at the edge of the woods, marked by a tiny sign for the Old Mill Trail. Enter the mixed pine-and-hardwoods forest, following the natural footpath. This trail is open to horses; their hooves keep the treadway clear but also cause it to be torn up and mucky in

NOCKAMIXON STATE PARK

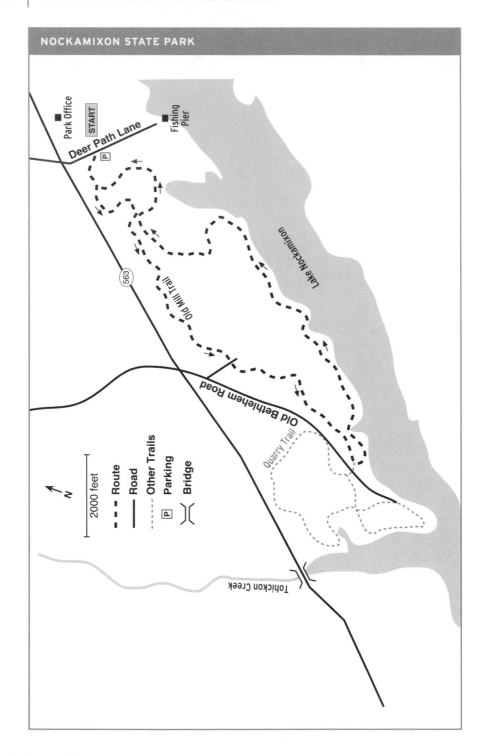

many places; wear boots. You may see occasional green ribbons, tied by equestrians to mark the trail.

You will soon come to a fork; bear right, heading southwest toward Route 563. Wildflowers abound here, especially in spring. At about four-tenths of a mile, the trail reaches a wide, mossy, boulder-filled stream and turns left. The boulders are made of diabase, the volcanic rock that underlies the ridge this forest occupies.

About a fifth of a mile farther on, you'll pass a horse crossing, go up a steep rise and down the bank, and then cross the stream on the boulders. Bear right at the T intersection, heading south-southwest. This low streamside area is open and marshy, but as the trail ascends gradually, the woods quickly close in. Ash, maple, tulip tree, and musclewood are common. In summer, look for ripe black raspberries. The understory is thick with shrubs and ferns. The presence of songbirds that favor deep woods, such as scarlet tanager and veery, indicate that this is a relatively healthy, not overly deer-browsed, forest.

Turn right when the trail reaches a T at an old woods road (0.9 mile), then left at the next Y intersection (1.0 mile). After 0.5 mile, the trail enters an area of very big trees, mostly oak and hickory, and shortly the woods becomes a pine forest. Cross Old Bethlehem Road at 1.6 miles and pass through a scrubby area. The trail now descends gradually. After crossing a gravel maintenance road, the trail traverses a wet meadow, a good place to spot woodland orchids.

Turn right at the next T (2.2 miles) and cross a small stream; the lake appears on the left. Take the next left into the scrubby woods. (If you miss this left, you will shortly reach Old Bethlehem Road again; turn around, backtrack, and take the first right.) Turn right at the next Y, turn immediately left at another Y, then bear left to follow the lakeshore on the right. Make a right and then a left to reach the water's edge. Turn right at the next Y and then right again, entering a muddy, grassy area; then turn right at the next T (2.8 miles). Here there are excellent views up the lake. Lake Nockamixon is created by a dam on the Tohickon Creek, about four miles east of this point.

The trail enters a cedar grove with good lake views in the winter. It then joins a gravel road that leads to a dock (3.3 miles); immediately veer right at the Y into the woods, cross a stream, and continue to follow the lake to the right. The woods here is once again primarily hardwoods characteristic of rich, moist soil (particularly hickory, silver maple, and walnut). In spring and summer, this area is rife with wild ramps, an edible member of the onion family whose leaves appear and die before the white spherical flower head appears.

At 4.1 miles, there is an excellent view down the lake. Another 0.2 mile ahead, the woods changes to conifers. Turn right at the next Y. The trail shortly crosses an old road; stay straight. Here the trail is also an old road, as indicated by the line of trees on either side. Now a shady trail in the woods, this spot was once a rural intersection, part of a vibrant community. Turn right at the next four-way intersection (4.8 miles). An old stone wall is further illustration that this site was once settled. Bear left at the wall, then cross it twice. Bear right at the next Y; the trail turns into a high stone berm made of local diabase rocks (this is an old mill dam). To the left is a wet meadow and remains of an impounded stream; to the right, water spills over the rocks. These ruins are remains of one of many grain mills in upper Bucks County owned and operated by the Stover family from the early nineteenth century through the middle of the twentieth century. All area roads led here, as farmers brought grain to the mill and the miller transported grain to city markets.

After crossing the dam, turn left to go uphill. (Down and to the right, past an interpretive sign, is a mile-long paved path that leads back to the parking lot.) Turn right at the next two forks to continue through the woods, ascending the hill and then going down to the stream. Turn right at the next three-way crossing, heading east, then left at the next T (also east). Go through a pine woods, and end at the parking lot.

MORE INFORMATION

Restrooms are located at Pavilion 1 near the park office. The park is open from sunrise to sunset. All dogs must be leashed. Boating is permitted on Lake Nockmixon and boats may be rented. The trail maintenance organization is AMC's Delaware Valley Chapter. Nockamixon State Park, 1542 Mountain View Drive, Quakertown, PA 18951; 215-529-7300; www.dcnr.state.pa.us/stateparks/parks/nockamixon.aspx.

TRIP 21
NEVERSINK MOUNTAIN PRESERVE

Location: Reading, PA (Berks County)
Rating: Moderate–Difficult
Distance: 4.0 miles
Elevation Gain: 525 feet
Estimated Time: 2.5 hours
Maps: USGS Reading; trail map available online

Neversink is a 900-acre mountain with a trail system hugged on the south by the Schuylkill River and on the north by the city of Reading. The preserve allows hikers to feel far from the city by exploring the 500 acres of protected land with scenic vistas of Mount Penn and Reading.

DIRECTIONS

From I-76 (partial toll road), take Exit 298 to merge onto I-176 north toward Reading/Morgantown. Take Exit 11A to merge onto Route 422 east for 1.0 mile. Take the Mount Penn exit. Turn left at East Neversink Road. Take the first left onto Hearthstone Drive for 0.7 mile. Turn left onto West Neversink Drive. Take an immediate first right onto Klapperthal Road. Follow the road 0.4 mile until it reaches a dead end at the trailhead for Klapperthal Trail. There is space for four to five cars. Alternative parking at Forest Hills Cemetery (adjacent to Klapperthal Road) at the back of the cemetery by Forest Hills Pond. *GPS coordinates*: 40° 18.882′ N, 75° 53.577′ W.

TRAIL DESCRIPTION

Although Neversink Mountain's name is derived from an American Indian word ("Navesink") meaning fishing ground, it is valued today for its forested slopes, the views from its summit, and abundant plants and wildlife that include diverse butterflies and moths. Of its 900 acres, 500 are owned by the Berks County Conservancy, which has established a 9-mile trail system. In the late nineteenth century a number of resort hotels on the mountain drew summer visitors from Philadelphia seeking cooler air. Railways ran on the mountain to serve the hotels. The hotels were razed and rail beds turned to trails, so the mountain is now a quiet natural haven within the urbanized Reading area.

This hike loops around the mountain to the Reading overlook and the Witch Hat Pavilion before returning to the Klapperthal parking area. As you hike the

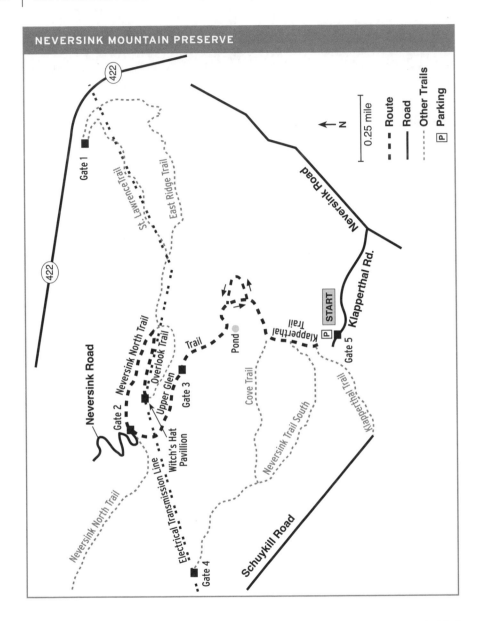

NEVERSINK MOUNTAIN PRESERVE

preserve, be sure to follow the map above or the preserve map. Almost half of the mountain is still privately owned. Some of the trails are on private property, permitted by the landowners. Be careful to respect the rights of property owners. Because it may be hard to tell where boundaries are, stay on marked trails. (At press time trails were being reblazed. The colors of the blazes may differ from those described here.)

From the Klapperthal parking area, walk right, onto the Klapperthal Trail, entering the forest. A gently trickling stream is on the right. (Ironically, "Klapperthal" means "booming valley," referring to an area where cannonballs were tested during the Civil War.) Shortly, cross a bridge; pass an intersection with Neversink Trail South to the left. Continue straight, at 0.15 mile cross a second bridge and three boardwalks then the intersection of Cove Trail and Upper Glen Trail (both blazed red); bear right onto Upper Glen Trail. This section of the trail runs through private property. It goes uphill, bends sharp left, continues up, then slightly downhill. At a fork, bear slightly right, passing a concrete walled "pond" on the right.

The trail climbs steeply to a gravel road. Turn left, passing Gate 3. This portion of the trail is sometimes used to access private landowners' driveways. Watch for vehicles. The trail crosses a transmission line and intersects a macadam road. Turn right and stay to the edge of the road, keeping an eye out for vehicles. Follow the road downhill to the pavilion parking area at Gate 2. Pass through the gate and continue straight onto Neversink Trail North.

In late May and early June mountain laurel (Pennsylvania's state flower) blooms abundantly on this section of the mountain. A member of the heath family, pink-flowered mountain laurel is an evergreen.

Neversink Trail North meets up with the transmission line. Note the wooden sign marked with a triangle, indicating Witch's Hat and "OL," indicating an overlook. Go to the right to Witch's Hat Pavilion, bearing left at the next four-way intersection. Local residents gave the pavilion its common name because of its conical shape. Built in 1892 as part of a mountain hotel, it was constructed as a memorial to foundry owner William McIlvain, for whom it was originally named. The view of the city of Reading and Mount Penn is spectacular. When you reach this spot, you may find yourself surprised that the city is so close to such a gem of a mountain. Mount Penn is identifiable by the 72-foot pagoda on its summit. William A. Witman, Sr., a local quarry owner, built the pagoda in 1908. Abandoning quarrying after years of public criticism of its scarifying effects on Mount Penn, Witman built the pagoda with the intention of making it a luxury hotel, but the venture failed. The structure was sold, eventually becoming city property in 1911.

From Witch's Hat Pavilion, backtrack along the transmission line, up through Gate 2, up the road, past Gate 3 and downhill along Upper Glen Trail. Just after passing the concrete walled pond on the left of the trail, you reach a fork. Turn right, following the trail to the next fork. Turn right. Backtrack to the parking lot, crossing three boardwalks and a bridge, you come to the intersection of Klapperthal Trail and Neversink Trail South. The parking lot is approximately 0.25 mile from this point.

To extend your hike, turn right onto Neversink Trail South from Klapperthal Trail. Within a half-mile, reach a view of the Schuylkill River, where you might hear or see a train passing along the river. Turn around once you reach Gate 4, where the transmission line runs perpendicular to the trail. This area has private property along the trail; if you accidentally take a nonpublic trail, you may end up trespassing. Follow Neversink Trail South back to Klapperthal Trail. At the intersection of the two trails, turn right to return to the Klapperthal parking lot.

MORE INFORMATION

There are no restrooms, drinking water, or telephones on the mountain. Limited hunting is permitted in season. Trails are maintained by Berks County Conservancy volunteers. Berks County Conservancy, 25 North 11th Street, Reading, PA 19601; 610-372-499; www.berks-conservancy.org.

THE HIGHLANDS CONSERVATION ACT AND AMC

From Connecticut, through New York and New Jersey, to Pennsylvania runs the Mid-Atlantic Highlands, a 3.5-million-acre rugged landscape of mountains, rivers, and forests that is home to millions of birds, fish, and mammals. Abundant rain replenishes the underground aquifers and the rivers and creeks that supply clean water to cities and suburbs. Forests, wetlands, and fields absorb storm water and prevent flooding. Trees cool and clean the air. Farms grow grain, vegetables, and fruit, and provide pastureland for livestock. Lakes, streams, woods, mountains, and meadows create diverse habitat for wildlife and diverse places to hike, bike, paddle, climb, fish, and camp—all within a short distance from the megalopolis.

This greenbelt is the easternmost ridge of the Appalachian Mountains and connects Shenandoah National Park to the Berkshires. However, the greenbelt keeps shrinking as the tide of human population continues to rise. According to the U.S. Forest Service, between 1997 and 2001 more than 44,930 acres of farmland were developed in the Highlands, and more than 5,000 acres a year are lost in the New Jersey/New York Highlands alone.

If current trends continue, irreplaceable lands in the Highlands will disappear. These lands provide essential services to the millions of people living in and around the Highlands: clean air and water, fresh food, and places to play, to learn, and to connect with the natural world.

For the Appalachian Mountain Club, the nation's oldest conservation and recreation organization, protecting the Highlands from development is a top priority. AMC works to conserve land using a unique integrated, multi-faceted approach appropriate to its distinctive status as a conservation *and* recreation organization. Researchers identify and map lands of high preservation value, policy advocates work to make funds available for preserving these areas, and recreation planners develop trails and public access opportunities. AMC's staff and chapter volunteers promote recreational opportunities by telling people about the special places close to home and taking them there.

In 2004, Congress passed the Highlands Conservation Act. AMC and the Highlands Coalition were instrumental in its passage through mapping, education, and advocacy. The act designates the 3.5-million-acre, four-state Highlands region as nationally significant. It provides funds for land conservation (up to $100 million over 10 years), and the study of ecological and recreational resources (up to $10 million over 10 years). The act works by providing federal matching funds for conservation projects in which a state entity acquires land or an interest in land from willing sellers in the mapped areas.

Even with funds available, preserving important lands in the Highlands is a daunting task. The Highlands has national, regional, and statewide value; however, local involvement is needed if this area is to be protected. Much of the land is owned in parcels of 50 acres or less; individual landowners must be contacted and engaged in the preservation process. Municipalities and local conservation organizations have both on-the-ground knowledge of local land use policy and the capacity to hold and manage conservation lands. Coordinating the many little things that have to be done by all the different people and organizations requires not only a commitment to partnership but also a view of both the big picture and the little pieces.

AMC continues to be involved in the implementation of the Highlands Conservation Act by working to help create partnerships among nonprofit, federal, state, and local entities. AMC plays a leadership role in the Highlands Coalition, a four-state alliance of nearly 200 organizations working collaboratively to preserve the region. AMC is also working to identify greenways for conservation and recreation. By putting together conservation and recreation, AMC staff and chapter volunteers are working to connect people to the Highlands, to help people understand their value, and to protect these valuable resources for future generations.

To learn more about the AMC's conservation efforts in the Highlands region, visit www.outdoors.org/conservation.

TRIP 22
NOLDE FOREST ENVIRONMENTAL
EDUCATION CENTER

Location: Reading, PA (Berks County)
Rating: Moderate
Distance: 8.0 miles
Elevation Gain: 500 feet
Estimated Time: 3.0 hours
Maps: USGS Reading; trail map at the trailhead, at the main office, and at the website for the Nolde Forest Environmental Education Center

Welcome to a tree-lover's heaven: meander up and down hills under an ever-changing canopy of thousands upon thousands of evergreen and deciduous trees.

DIRECTIONS
Take Route 422 west to Morgantown Expressway (I-276); after less than a mile take Exit 10 (Route 724 west) toward Shillington. Remain on Route 724 for 2.5 miles; turn left onto Route 625. The Nolde Forest trailhead is 1.7 miles ahead on the right. There is ample parking. *GPS coordinates*: 40° 16.869′ N, 75° 56.903′ W.

TRAIL DESCRIPTION
Nolde Forest's 665 acres are covered with trees; there are scores of species, and the specimens range from young to old, planted and nurtured by dedicated foresters. As the trees have grown, they've twisted their intertwined branches toward sunlight and snaked their enmeshed roots toward water. The forest has become a dense matrix of shapes. Hiking through it is like walking through a community whose members silently converse with and accommodate one another.

The thousands upon thousands of trees that grow here are the result of the efforts of one man: Jacob Nolde. A hosiery baron, Nolde acquired this property south of Reading in 1904. The site, like many others in southeastern Pennsylvania, had been cleared of trees, primarily to burn for charcoal production. Nolde came across a single white pine in a meadow and was inspired to plant a forest of conifers. Nolde and an Austrian forester named William

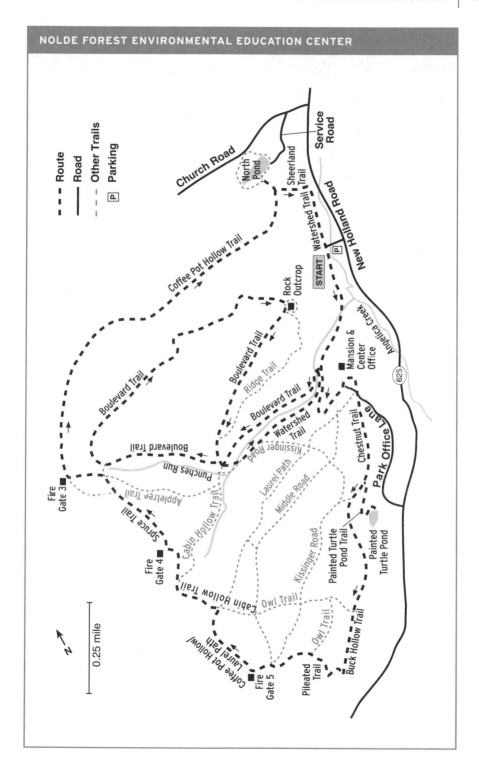

NOLDE FOREST ENVIRONMENTAL EDUCATION CENTER

On the Boulevard Trail in Nolde Forest, conifer needles and deciduous leaves touch each other.

Kohout planted more than a million pines, spruces, and firs. Deciduous trees also sprouted.

Pennsylvania acquired the site from the Nolde family in 1966 and established the state's first environmental education center here in 1971. More than 10 miles of trails, mostly on old forest or colliers' (charcoal-makers') roads, wind through the park. Because they were once roads, the trails are generally wide with good footing, and elevation gains are gradual. The trails are also well maintained, are in excellent shape, and stay dry even in wet weather. Trail intersections are, with few exceptions, well marked, with posts indicating the name of the trail.

This hike consists of a 3.0-mile inner loop and a 5.0-mile outer loop. If time is limited, select just one of the loops. Begin at the sawmill parking lot. Head up the steps and over the Angelica Creek, onto a red-gravel trail, turning left at a T after 50 yards, onto the Watershed Trail, then bear left onto Mansion Road. The road heads uphill, along a stream at the bottom of a steep-sided hemlock/yellow birch ravine. Bear right at the teaching station, onto the Boulevard Trail. Stay on the Boulevard Trail for the remainder of this inner loop. The trail ascends to the ridge top (winter views here), then descends about three-quarters of a mile.

The trail bends right, but straight ahead via a short spur is a 15-foot-high rock outcrop. In contrast to the crumbly red shale and sandstone that predominate in the park south of the main entrance, this rock is dark gray (almost black) and smooth. If this rock appears to have been squeezed up from the earth, that's because it has done exactly that. This is an exposed chunk of intruded diabase, a volcanic rock; 200 million years ago molten magma flowed into fractures in the sedimentary red shale and sandstone rocks around it, then hardened. Over eons the softer rock around the diabase eroded away, leaving the hard volcanic rock to stand alone. The diabase ridge falls off below the outcrop.

Shortly after the Boulevard Trail leaves the outcrop, it becomes an arboreal neutral zone, the dividing line between a conifer plantation uphill and hardwood forest below. When the Boulevard Trail crosses itself just past a restroom, bear left, then turn right onto the Cabin Hollow Trail; 50 yards later, turn left onto the Watershed Trail and head back down the ravine. The narrow Watershed Trail has a natural surface that parallels the wide Boulevard Trail, by which you ascended the ravine, and takes you into much more intimate contact with the trees, wildflowers, stream, and rocks. Continue to follow the Watershed Trail as it crosses back and forth over the Punches Run. Note the fine stone bridge that carries the Boulevard Trail over the stream; almost immediately, join the Boulevard Trail and then make a sharp right where a paved road intersects.

Follow the road as it approaches the old Nolde family home, which now serves as the park's main office. A good place for a lunch break, the stone Tudor-style mansion is worth a detour. Observe its architectural details, including the delightful nursery tower, the imposing oak entrance door, and the stained-glass plaque depicting the single white pine that inspired Jacob Nolde to create a forest.

Head away from the mansion and bear right onto the Chestnut Trail. There are quite a few American chestnut saplings on this trail, recognizable by their long, pointed leaves with jagged serrations. The early-twentieth-century chestnut blight killed off billions of chestnuts, which used to dominate eastern forests. The fungus culprit lives on—even though chestnut saplings still sprout from old stumps, they die before reaching nut-bearing age. (See "The King Is Dead; Long Live the King" on page 237.)

At 0.25 mile, take the spur about 800 feet downhill to the Painted Turtle Pond, a pretty little pool where basking turtles are common on sunny summer days. Return to Chestnut Trail; bear left onto Buck Hollow Trail. After 0.375 mile, turn right onto the Pileated Trail, which connects to the Owl Trail, and then turn left.

At Fire Gate 5, turn right onto the Coffee Pot Hollow Trail (depicted on the park map as Laurel Path). It's lined with glossy-leaved evergreen mountain laurels that are adorned in star-shaped white-and-pink flowers from late April to early May. Bear left onto Cabin Hollow Road, which descends through a lowbush blueberry patch, then left onto Spruce Trail. Continue past Fire Gates 4 and 3.

After Fire Gate 3, there is a Y with no trail markers; bear left. You are on Coffee Pot Hollow Trail. Continue on this trail for 1.25 miles, then bear left onto Beech Trail and take it downhill to the Pond Loop Trail. This trail goes to the large, lily-pad-covered North Pond. Backtrack to the Beech Trail; turn left onto the Sheerland Trail, which dead-ends at the Watershed Trail, and turn right to end at the sawmill parking lot.

MORE INFORMATION

The office and mansion parking lot are open from 8 A.M. to 4 P.M., Monday through Friday. All other areas are open sunrise to sunset, 7 days a week. As in other Pennsylvania state parks, pets must be on a leash. Full restroom facilities are located at the C. H. McConnell Environmental Education Hall; nonflush toilets are located at the trailhead for the Watershed Trail and at other locations along the route. Nolde Forest Environmental Education Center, 2910 New Holland Road, Reading, PA 19607; 610-796-3699; www.dcnr.state.pa.us/stateparks/parks/noldeforest.aspx.

TRIP 23
CLARENCE SCHOCK MEMORIAL PARK
AT GOVERNOR DICK

Location: Mount Gretna, PA (Lebanon County)
Rating: Moderate
Distance: 7.5 miles
Elevation Gain: 300 feet
Estimated Time: 3.0 hours
Maps: USGS Manheim; park map available onsite and online

Clarence Schock Memorial Park at Governor Dick is one of the largest woods in southeastern Pennsylvania. This forested loop hike leads to an observation tower with a 360-degree view.

DIRECTIONS

Take the Pennsylvania Turnpike (I-76) to Exit 266. Merge onto Lebanon Road/ Route 72 toward Lancaster for 1.4 miles. Turn right onto Cider Press Road; go 0.4 mile and turn right onto Pinch Road. The entrance to the park's environmental education center is on the right after 1.7 miles, across from State Game Lands 145 parking lot, which can accommodate up to twenty cars. *GPS coordinates:* 40° 14.652′ N, 76° 27.803′ W.

TRAIL DESCRIPTION

The 1,105-acre Clarence Schock Park constitutes one of the largest areas of contiguous woodlands in southeastern Pennsylvania. Because of their size and lack of fragmentation, the woods are important habitat for a wide variety of wildlife. These forests, though, are only a century old and are second-growth woods that grew up after the hills were logged to provide charcoal for iron forges. Flattened, circular areas of blackened soil are still-visible artifacts of charcoaling.

The name of the tract on which the park is located is therefore somewhat ironic; "Governor" Dick was a woodsman and collier who lived in the area and logged a large portion of it in the mid-1800s. The park is the legacy of Clarence Schock, a local industrialist and philanthropist, who acquired the tract in 1934; in 1953, he deeded the land in perpetuity to a local school district and it is now managed by a co-trusteeship of the Clarence Schock Foundation and Lebanon County.

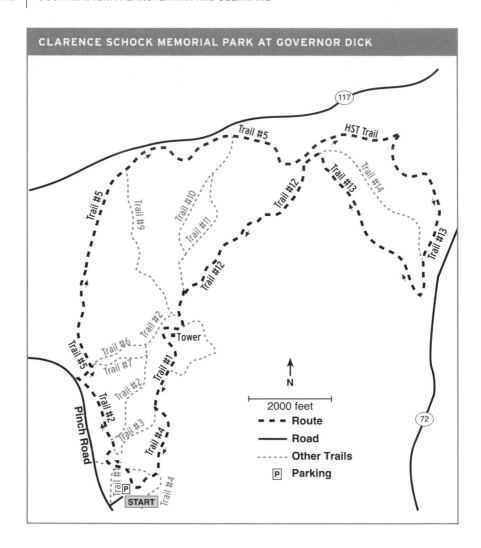

CLARENCE SCHOCK MEMORIAL PARK AT GOVERNOR DICK

From the parking lot, head away from the center to a trailhead marked with a sign saying, "To the Tower." Most trails in the park are numbered with markers placed at intersections and are blazed with distinct colors and shapes. Because of the rocky soil's high water table, the trails are wet in places. Bikes and horses that use many of the trails create muddy patches along the way.

Turn left at the next T, marked "To 1," and at the next T turn right onto Trail 1, a crushed-stone fire road. Note the yellow rectangular blazes, which indicate that this section of the trail coincides with the long-distance Horse-Shoe Trail (H-ST). After a quarter-mile, turn left at a double yellow blaze, as the H-ST diverges from the park trail. You will follow the easily visible H-ST blazes for the next several miles.

Clarence Schock Park contains one of the larges areas of contiguous woodlands in southeastern Pennsylvania.

The forest here, along Pinch Road, was defoliated by gypsy moth caterpillars in 2008. Dead and damaged trees have been cut and salvaged; the area will be reforested with 15,000 tree seedlings and deer-exclusion fencing (see "Bambi, Keep Out" on page 91).

Follow the H-ST as it bears right, away from the road at a parking area, after 0.6 mile. The woods here, and those along the remainder of this hike, are in good condition. Oaks, birches, white pines, and tulip trees predominate, with an understory including hophornbeam, dogwood, and redbud. After 0.1 mile the trail merges with Trail 5 (white rectangles), a rocky narrow footpath that becomes a gravel road that passes through a residential area before turning back into the forest onto an old woods road. These deep woods are quiet, except for the music of wind and birdsong. Continue on Trail 5/H-ST past Trail 9—at this point you have hiked 1.5 miles). At a yellow gate (1.8 miles) the trail bears right, away from Route 117, on a narrow rocky footpath. At 2.2 miles, pass a parking area and Trail 10. The trail becomes a woods road. Go through an area with many large boulders. Governor Dick Hill is a diabase ridge (see "Black Rock, Green Forests" on page 159); the rocks have broken off and toppled from above.

Cross Trail 12 (2.7 miles). You are now on the east side of the ridge. Take in a brief view of the hills through an opening at a residential site before the forest closes in again. At 3.2 miles, leave the H-ST and turn right onto Trail 13, a narrow footpath marked by green diamonds. The trail follows the contours of the hill. Pass an access trail to "old" Route 72 and Trail 14 (4.0 miles). Road noise from "new" Route 72 to the left briefly intrudes, and the trail bends away and passes Trail 15. At an unmarked Y, bear left. This area has many boulders; above are high dramatic outcrops where the boulders came from. It is so quiet here you can almost hear the rocks slowly fissuring at their geologic pace.

Turn left at a T onto Trail 14 (5.0 miles). After 0.2 mile turn left onto Trail 12 (blue diamonds) to traverse the ridge; the often muddy trail includes several boardwalks. Pass through an extensive patch of pawpaws, large-leaved understory trees occasionally found in moist, rich woods.

At 6.2 miles turn left at a T onto Trail 10. As the trail (a road to a former radar installation) crests the hill, you will see the observation tower. After another 0.1 mile turn left onto Trail 2 at a T, pass Trail 8, and reach the tower at 6.5 miles, at the summit of the 1,148-foot high ridge. The 66-foot high, 15-foot wide tower was built in 1954. A series of ladders lead to a circular platform, from which you can see the park's extensive contiguous woodlands, and on a clear day Lebanon, Dauphin, York, Lancaster, and Berks counties.

Continue around the tower, picking up Trail 1 (a wide gravel road) at the edge of the clearing. Turn left onto the red diamond-blazed Trail 4 (6.8 miles), which winds steeply downhill through boulders, and continue until you reach a T at Trail 15. Here, turn right onto the white-blazed trail marked with a sign that says "Controlled: foot travel only." This is the Interpretive Trail; a brochure is available at the Environmental Education Center. Follow it to the center, where you started. Trails around the center meander through meadows, planted to diversify habitat. In summer, it attracts abundant butterflies, bees, moths, and bee flies, as well as hummingbirds. In other seasons look for American goldfinches, common yellowthroats, sparrows, and other birds of open fields.

MORE INFORMATION

Trail maps and portable toilets are outside the environmental education center. The center is open Thursday to Saturday 10 A.M. to 4 P.M. and Sunday 1 to 4 P.M., April through October, as well as additional weekends in March and November. Bicycles and horses are allowed on the multiuse trails. Dogs are allowed on a leash. The park is managed by a co-trusteeship of representatives of the Clarence Schock Foundation and the Lebanon County Commissioners. Clarence Schock Memorial Park at Governor Dick, P.O. Box 161, Mount Gretna, PA 17064; 717-964-3808; www.parkatgovernordick.org.

TRIP 24
MONEY ROCKS PARK

Location: Narvon, PA (Lancaster County)
Rating: Moderate–difficult
Distance: 3.25 miles
Elevation Gain: 275 feet
Estimated Time: 2.0 hours
Maps: USGS Honey Brook; park map available online

This multi-loop hike includes an overlook of Lancaster County's farmland, impressive rock outcrop, and wooded hills of the Welsh Mountains.

DIRECTIONS

From the Pennsylvania Turnpike (I-76), take Exit 298. Go south on Route 10 for 0.9 mile to Route 23. Go west on Route 23 for 7.8 miles to Route 897. Go south on Route 897 for 0.6 miles to Route 322. Go east on Route 322 for 2.9 miles to Narvon Road. Go right on Narvon Road for 1.2 miles. The entrance is on the right across from Alexander Drive. The parking lot can accommodate twenty cars. *GPS coordinates*: 40° 05.734′ N, 75° 58.906′ W.

TRAIL DESCRIPTION

The name "Money Rocks" comes from a local legend. Supposedly, Pequea Valley farmers hid cash amongst the boulders along the ridge. You may not find any money cached in the dramatically situated rocks, but you will discover plenty of green: lichens, mosses, and ferns abound here. So too does the evergreen mountain laurel.

From the parking lot facing Narvon Road, turn left toward the beginning of the Overlook Trail. This trail is blazed white and has a rocky natural surface. The park trails are well blazed. You'll see a kiosk where the Overlook Trail enters into the woods. The trail goes to the left past the kiosk to an intersection with Cockscomb Trail. Stepping over a wooden beam, continue straight on Overlook Trail for 0.2 mile. The trail comes to a T. White double blazes indicate a turn; go left.

In less than 15 feet, you'll come to the beginning of the Overlook Trail loop. Turn right, following the white blazes downhill; you'll begin to see rock

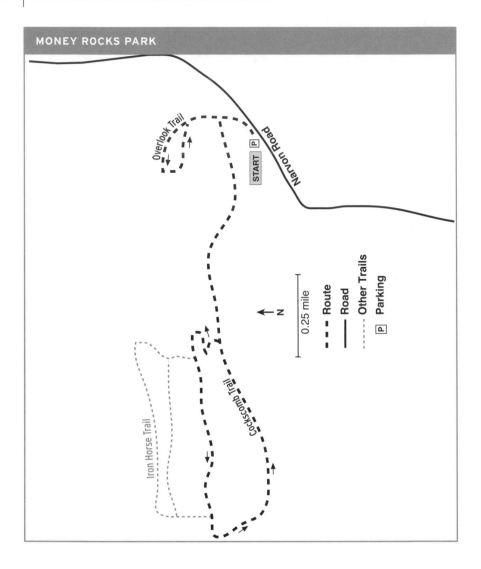

MONEY ROCKS PARK

Overlook Trail

Narvon Road

START

P

N

0.25 mile

Route
Road
Other Trails
P Parking

Cockscomb Trail

Iron Horse Trail

outcrops to the left of the trail. At the bottom of the hill, you'll see the Narvon Clay Mine below the trail, and the foot of impressively high rock above and to the left. Look at the rocks along the trail for skolithos, long straight tubes up to 12 inches long. These fossilized burrows of ancient worms lived on an ancient sand beach that was recrystallized into quartzite. To reach the top of these rocks, continue on the white-blazed trail as it follows the outer perimeter of the hillside. "No Trespassing" signs indicate the park's boundary with the Narvon Clay Mine. After 150 feet, the trail turns left, heading uphill toward the outcrops. Continue uphill on the Overlook Trail over three steps. The trail turns to the right over a wood beam and continues uphill for 30 feet. Go up a

Despite local legend, the prominent spine of boulders in Money Rocks Park does not hide any cash, but the park is rich in natural beauty for the hiker to discover.

series of six wooden steps. Here, mountain laurel, Pennsylvania's state flower, is abundant as an understory plant; pink-and-white flowers bloom in late May and June. After the sixth step, the trail turns left to go over the highlight of the park, the Money Rocks. The 1,000-foot-high rocks afford views of Lancaster County's farm towns, and distant wooded hills. The dominant tree species growing on and among the rocks is black birch.

Carefully climb along the top of the rocky spine, (scrambling is not required, but balance and patience are). Be on the lookout for graffiti said to date from the Civil War era. Immediately after passing a black metal railing at the end of the outcrop, bear right. Descend for 150 feet to the beginning of the loop. After 15 feet, turn right heading downhill to the red-blazed Cockscomb Trail.

Turn right onto wide, rocky Cockscomb Trail, which leads into the remainder of the park's 300 acres of woods. After 0.5 mile, come to a four-way intersection with a wood beam. Turn right; continue to follow the red blazes. The trail intersects with a trail to the right marked by a cairn (a pile of rocks used as a trail marker). Go straight to continue on the Cockscomb Trail. Along the next 200 feet of the trail are high rock outcrops called Cockscomb. You have to leave the trail to climb them. Look closely on the right for double red blazes and after about 30 feet an obscure opening. Turn right at the opening and follow the rocky trail downhill. This is the beginning of the Cockscomb Trail Loop.

Caution: The rocks are loose. After approximately 30 feet, the trail turns to the left, indicated by double red blazes. Continue winding downhill, passing a large hole to the right. It is a test pit; former owners explored the site for clay. The trail bottoms out at a T; turn left onto an old road. The trail becomes flat and wide but is still rocky. An old wellhead by the trail is another artifact of clay mine exploration. At 0.5 mile, you'll see a large tree with double red blazes in the middle of the trail. Bear to the left of the tree and go 50 feet, crossing a small stream. Turn left and climb slightly uphill. Turn left at the red double blazes and almost immediately cross a stream again; go uphill for 20 feet. Turn left at the double red blazes, and then turn right almost immediately to begin a steep uphill climb. Step up a series of wooden beam steps to reach the top of the hill.

Once uphill, the Cockscomb Trail turns left and then continues straight, at which point you return to the beginning of the loop. Backtrack, following the red blazes to the four-way intersection with a wood beam. Turn left and hike 0.5 mile to the intersection with the white-blazed Overlook Trail. Turn right and head back to the parking lot.

MORE INFORMATION

The park offers multiuse trails (hiking, mountain biking, horseback riding, and cross-country skiing). Dogs are allowed on a leash. Money Rocks Park has 3.5 miles of scenic trails. Hunting is permitted is many parts of the park in season. Trails are open sunrise to sunset. Money Rocks Park is managed by Lancaster County Department of Parks and Recreation, 1050 Rockford Road, Lancaster, PA 17602; 717-299-8215 or 717-299-8220; www.co.lancaster.pa.us/parks.

TRIP 25
KELLY'S RUN

Location: Holtwood, PA (Lancaster County)
Rating: Moderate–Difficult
Distance: 7.0 miles
Elevation Gain: 300 feet
Estimated Time: 3.5 hours
Maps: USGS Holtwood; trail map available at the website for the Holtwood Environmental Preserve

On this challenging but extremely rewarding hike, explore a rugged, wild gorge under cascading rhododendrons surrounded by an old-growth forest; take in sweeping views of the lower Susquehanna River.

DIRECTIONS
Take Route 1 south to Route 272 north to Buck. Turn left onto Route 372 west, turn right and go 6.0 miles on River Road, turn left and go 0.5 mile on Old Holtwood Road, and then turn left and go 0.5 miles on New Village Road. Continue to the second parking lot on the right, where you will find ample parking. *GPS coordinates:* 39° 50.451′ N, 76° 19.005′ W.

TRAIL DESCRIPTION
One of the region's most beautiful and challenging short hikes explores the Kelly's Run–Pinnacle Natural Area in PPL Corporation's Holtwood Environmental Preserve, along the lower Susquehanna River. A 2-hour drive from Philadelphia's Wissahickon Valley (see Trip 2), this scenic trek compresses the sublime beauty of the larger, more celebrated gorge into a 3.5-mile hike along a deep ravine and up to a high promontory. Flowing water here encounters Wissahickon schist, the rock that underlies much of the Philadelphia area, creating sheer cliffs and sculpted landforms.

The 5,000-acre preserve surrounds Lake Aldred, the stretch of the Susquehanna impounded by the Holtwood hydroelectric dam. The preserve, including 39 miles of trails, is open to the public for recreation. (See Trip 26, which covers the west side of the river.) The natural areas surrounding Kelly's Run comprise a lush valley of mosses, ferns, and cliff-hugging trees and shrubs, harboring abundant wildlife.

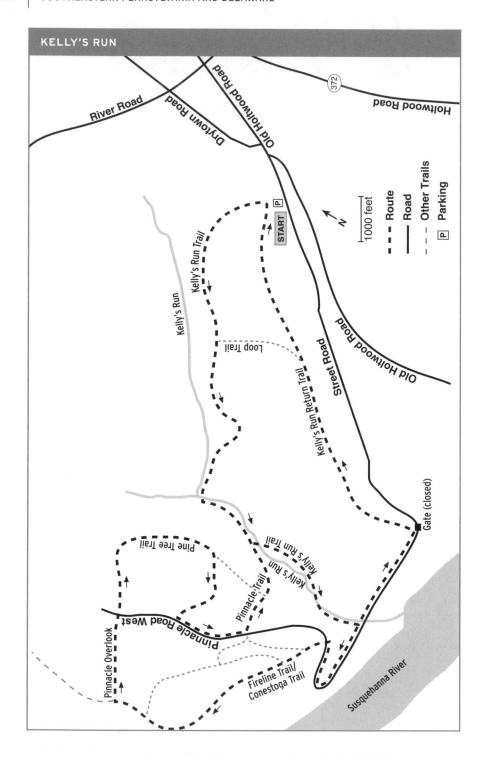

KELLY'S RUN

Bald eagles, once endangered, have made a strong comeback after the banning of the pesticide DDT, and now nest in substantial numbers along the Susquehanna River.

On this hike a trekking pole is advisable—almost essential—for traversing the slippery rocks along the stream.

Begin the hike by heading diagonally uphill to the woods' edge from the lower parking lot; the Kelly's Run trailhead is between the upper and lower parking areas. The trail is blue-blazed. It begins in a moist bottomland woods of yellow birch and silver maple and passes through an extensive pawpaw patch. The small, large-leafed understory pawpaw tree bears pendent white flowers and green fruit directly from its branches. The fruit is ripe when it falls off the tree (usually in early autumn); until then, its taste is mouth-puckering.

Pass under a power line after 500 yards, then another one after 0.2 mile. The extensive woods hosts a great many species of forest-interior birds. A sprinkling of rhododendrons along the way is a foretaste of the splendor to come in the gorge. The trail crosses the red-blazed Loop Trail to the left, turns right, and heads downhill via a steep, slippery rocky trail. After about a mile, you'll reach the bottom and enter the gorge.

Schist is a hard rock that resists erosion but shears off in flat planes. As the stream has cut into the rock over time, carving a 350-foot gash, it has left vertical cliffs standing sentinel over the creek. Wide boulders that have fractured and fallen off the bluffs now line the sides and bottom of the creek bed, their corners rounded by the rushing force of water. Rhododendrons mass on the slopes and along the banks; ferns wave fronds in the breeze from the rushing creek; hemlocks insist on having a presence on precarious landings. Very tall, very old tulip trees and sycamores found a foothold long ago. The deep V-shaped ravine doesn't allow moisture to evaporate easily, so the cliffs and boulders are covered with moss; on certain days mist fogs the valley, rendering the scenery both soft and sublime.

All that moisture makes clambering over the roots and rocks slippery under normal conditions and, in rain or snow, quite treacherous. You'll cross the stream four times on stepping-stones. After the fourth crossing, continue downstream about another quarter-mile, reaching a gravel fire road with a gate to the left. Turn right onto the road and follow it as it narrows to an unblazed path and climbs the hill gradually, first through a dry scrubby area, then through a dry upland woods.

Cross the Conestoga Trail going up steeply to the left (an alternative route, shorter but more strenuous), and follow the less steep red-blazed trail, which turns sharply left after 0.5 mile and again meets the Conestoga Trail. This time, enter the Conestoga Trail and head up the steep dry hill. The orange-blazed Conestoga Trail runs north-south through Lancaster County for 63 miles, from the Horse-Shoe Trail to the Mason-Dixon Trail at Lock 12 (see Trip 23). It winds around to the river side of the ridge, traversing prominent sidehill rock outcrops (requiring careful footwork but no scrambling), which provide excellent river vistas. Along with chestnut oak and pitch pine, blueberries are common on these slopes.

Near the crest you'll come to an old woods road; turn left to continue uphill on the Conestoga Trail (this is also the yellow-blazed Fireline Trail). In summer and fall, hikers nearing the top of the climb will see blackberries and grapes lining the trail.

You'll soon reach a picnic area and parking lot. This is the Pinnacle, the top of an anticline of Wissahickon schist that is folded like a blanket. There are majestic views of the river and Lake Aldred from the official overlook and from a rock outcrop about 300 yards farther along the Conestoga Trail. Invisible to the viewer, too, are 2-mile-long, 125-foot-deep trenches in the river bottom, of unknown origin.

To the right of the picnic area, enter the red-blazed Pine Tree Trail, an old road that winds clockwise around the Pinnacle and through woods that have taken over former farmland, then back uphill to an old road. Make a left downhill, and after about a quarter-mile turn left onto the white-blazed Pinnacle Trail, bearing right and downhill at its intersection with the Pine Tree Trail going uphill; the Pinnacle Trail ends at Kelly's Run Trail.

From here, you can complete the hike by turning left and retracing your steps. Alternatively, you can complete it as a loop with essentially the same distance and effort. The loop is *not* recommended for high-summer hiking, as there is too much exposure to the sun and the river views are obscured. In other seasons, though, the return trail offers a variety of terrain complementary to that of the outbound route.

To complete the loop, turn right onto Kelly's Run Trail, making the fourth stream crossing again. At the old road, turn left past the gate. The road becomes

Rhododendrons grow on the slopes in Kelly's Run and form tunnels along the trail.

macadam and climbs the hill, gaining better and better views of the river as it goes; it ends at a gated (active) road. Take a sharp left turn into the woods; the trail is now blue-blazed. Continue climbing uphill on a wide grassy path through a pleasant deciduous woods. Enter a farm field, follow the blue blazes on poles along the edge and then down the middle of the field, and reenter the woods on the other side. Pass the Loop Trail intersection on the left, go under two power lines, and come out at a gate just below the parking lot.

MORE INFORMATION

A portable toilet is in the lower parking lot; it is open from April through October. The area is open to hunting; wear orange in season except on Sunday. The trails are maintained by the Lancaster Hiking Club (http://community .lancasteronline.com/lancasterhikingclub). Information about the Conestoga Trail is also available from the York Hiking Club (www.yorkhikingclub.com/ conestoga.html). Holtwood Environmental Preserve, 9 New Village Road, Holtwood, PA 17532; 800-354-8383; www.pplweb.com/holtwood/.

TRIP 26
MASON-DIXON TRAIL–HOLTWOOD PRESERVE

Location: Slab, PA (York County)
Rating: Moderate–Difficult
Distance: 7.0 miles
Elevation Gain: 700 feet
Estimated Time: 3.5 hours
Maps: USGS Airville and Holtwood; trail map available at the website
for the Mason-Dixon Trail

**Hike up steep bluffs to take in sweeping views of the Susquehanna
River; trek through gorgeous rugged ravines, and amble through a
bucolic landscape surrounded by farmland vistas. It is almost guar-
anteed you'll see bald eagles and, in breeding season, eagles' nests.**

DIRECTIONS
This is a shuttle hike. Park one car at Lock 12 of the Susquehanna Canal. Take
Route 372 north; just before the bridge over the Susquehanna, turn left onto
McCall's Ferry Road. Park at the lower parking lot (except in winter, when lot
is closed; park in upper lot). *GPS coordinates*: 39° 38.794′ N, 76° 19.691′ W.

For the endpoint, park in the public York Furnace boat launch parking area
(the hike ends a short distance away). Take Route 425 north and turn right
onto Indian Steps Road. Go 0.5 mile to the parking area, where you will find
ample space. *GPS coordinates:* 39° 51.680′ N, 76° 22.450′ W.

TRAIL DESCRIPTION
The rugged cliffs and gorges that line the lower Susquehanna River contain
some of the most beautiful scenery and challenging hiking in Pennsylvania.
These rocky sites are hidden in plain sight; the rural countryside is comprised
of rolling hills farmed for generations. The river itself sweeps in a majestic
slow curve toward its mouth at the Chesapeake Bay. It's only where land meets
water that one can fully experience the drama of plunging ravines and soaring
promontories as well as the gentle beauty of rhododendron-covered hillsides
and mist-haloed streams.

This hike traverses the west side of the Susquehanna River along the Mason-
Dixon Trail (MDT). The 193-mile-long MDT connects the Brandywine Trail

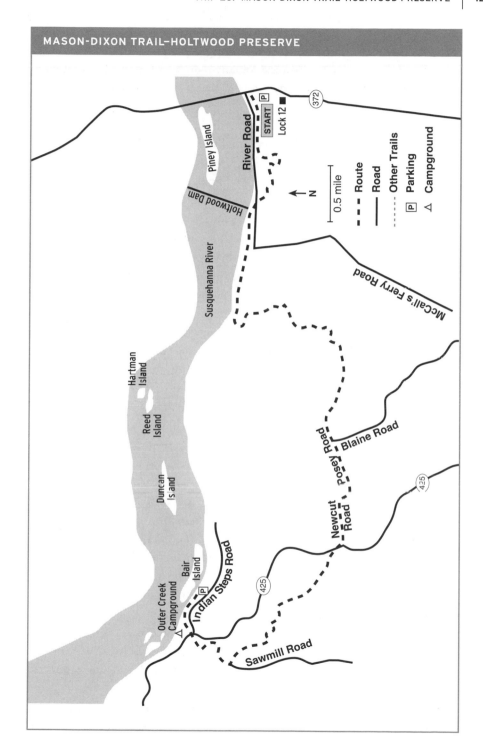

MASON-DIXON TRAIL–HOLTWOOD PRESERVE

Piney Island

River Road

START

Lock 12

372

P

Holtwood Dam

Susquehanna River

Hartman Island

Reed Island

Duncan Island

Bair Island

Outer Creek Campground

Indian Steps Road

McCall's Ferry Road

Blaine Road

Posey Road

Newcut Road

425

425

Sawmill Road

N

0.5 mile

— — — Route
——— Road
········· Other Trails
P Parking
△ Campground

in Delaware to the Appalachian Trail in Pennsylvania. Much of the hike is in the Holtwood Preserve, 5,000 acres straddling the river around the Holtwood Dam. PPL Corporation, the power company that owns the site, has preserved the land for "public use and enjoyment." (The east side of the river is equally terrific for hiking; see Trip 25.)

Begin the hike at the north (river) side of the parking lot, noting the signpost for the MDT. The MDT is exceptionally well-marked; you'll get to know its blue blazes. The trail goes downhill, crossing the remains of Lock 12 of the defunct Susquehanna and Tidewater Canal, a 43-mile waterway between Wrightsville and Havre de Grace built in the 1830s (and closed in the 1890s). The trail follows the old canal's flat, wide towpath for a mile and turns uphill toward River Road, passing foundations of a sawmill, millrace, and cannery. Cross the road, turn right to go over the bridge, and immediately turn left to climb the steep ravine via a narrow footpath. Follow the right bank of Mill Run as it bounds over boulders and slips into mossy pools. Rhododendrons cover the hills, making for a spectacular display in late spring.

Turning sharply right, the trail climbs very steeply up the rocky hillside. It is tempting to hold on to trees as you climb, but take care that they're well anchored in the thin soil. Follow the crest of the ridge to the edge of the sheer bluffs, where several outcrops offer panoramic views of the river, Lake Aldred, and the Holtwood Dam. Looking south below the dam, you can see some of the Conowingo Islands, which are an unusual landform consisting of vertical chunks of very hard Wissahickon schist bedrock, eroded into knobs by the Susquehanna River over eons.

Descend the ridge, going under power lines, to River Road, passing by some old foundations for a hotel. Just above the road, you will pass by a "whispering rock" outcrop that amplifies sounds from below.

At River Road, turn left. Cross the road to the dam overlook. While enjoying the spray and thunder of the waterfall, imagine what it's like to be a fish trying to swim upriver to spawn. Nearest to the overlook is a fish ladder, installed in 1910 to assist migrating shad, herring, and other fish. Prior to the damming of the Susquehanna, hundreds of thousands of shad journeyed annually from the ocean to the upper watershed. The fishway is ineffective; a modern fish elevator (only marginally more effective) is across the river, but PPL plans to install a new fish elevator (similar to that at Conowingo) that collects fish and deposits them on the upriver side.

Follow the road for 1,500 feet, then bear right into the woods; the trail passes through residential yards, joins a dirt road, and bears left up a bank at a cable crossing sign before bearing right into the woods. Descend along the river, which laps at the low shore. Just downriver is where McCall's Ferry once crossed.

Notwithstanding the Susquehanna's hazards for migrating fish, the river's fish population is robust enough to support a burgeoning population of bald eagles. Holtwood Preserve is a prime spot to observe eagles year-round. Eagle nests can often be spotted from this section of the trail. From March to May, look for large nests made of stout sticks high in trees or even on power-line towers. Do *not* disturb!

Turn left to climb up a beautiful ravine along Oakland Run as it plunges down to the river. Rhododendrons crowd the gorge, creating challenging passageways as the trail threads through them, up and along the side of the ridge. Cross the stream, enter a rich woods (now in Pennsylvania State Game Lands—reserves for hunting, fishing, and trapping managed by the Pennsylvania Game Commission), and walk along a woods road tending uphill. After a long, straight climb you will pass a gate. The next section (almost 2.5 miles) of the hike is on picturesque roads, with great views of the surrounding countryside. Turn left on Posey Road and right onto Newcut Road. Cross Route 425 and head straight across a farm field, then right onto Bare Road for about 100 feet before turning left to follow a power line maintenance road for 0.5 mile. Watch the blazes carefully to make a sharp right turn and then a left into the woods, returning to gamelands. You'll cross several streams, including Furnace Run, which seems to change direction while you're not looking. Follow Furnace Run to Sawmill Run. Turn right onto the dirt Sawmill Run Road for 1.0 mile. Turn right off Sawmill Run Road to Route 425, go 0.25 mile to Indian Steps Road, bear left, and follow the road another mile to the parking lot.

MORE INFORMATION

Restrooms are located below the Lock 12 parking lot. The trails are maintained by the Mason-Dixon Trail System (www.masondixontrail.org) and the York Hiking Club (www.yorkhikingclub.com). Holtwood Preserve, 9 New Village Road, Holtwood, PA 17532; 800-354-8383; www.pplweb.com/holtwood.

2

CENTRAL AND SOUTHERN NEW JERSEY

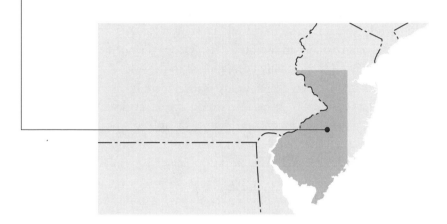

NEW JERSEY CAN BE DIVIDED INTO THREE PARTS: high ground (the mountains of the northwest), middle (the Piedmont of the center), and low (the coastal plain of South Jersey, which roughly follows a northeast-southwest line along Route 1).

South Jersey is all coastal plain. The dominant characteristic of the coastal plain is its soil: flat, sandy, fast-draining, low in nutrients and organic matter, high in iron. While the soil is dry, South Jersey does have access to productive groundwater aquifers, which are fed by rainfall farther north. Surface water is one of the unique attributes as well. Many rivers—including the Mullica, Maurice, Batsto, and Wading—are aquifer-fed rather than depending on runoff, as most Piedmont streams do. As a result, these rivers are cool year-round. And they're brown, from the iron and the cedars. Depending on the availability of water close to the surface, the dominant type of habitat may be a pine forest, a mixed pine-hardwood forest, or a cedar swamp.

The Pinelands National Reserve is a 1.1-million-acre designated federal and state reserve and a unique cultural, historic, and natural area. As the Pinelands Preservation Alliance notes, "It is the largest surviving open space on the eastern seaboard between the northern forests of Maine and the Everglades of Florida." Almost half of the Pinelands National Reserve, which is part of the larger area commonly known as the Pine Barrens, is publicly owned, including the Wharton and Lebanon State Forests. Pinelands hikes include Wharton State Forest/Mullica River Trail (Trip 29) and Wharton State Forest/Batona Trail (Trip 30).

On the coastal plain but not in the Pine Barrens are Cape May (Trip 27) and Parvin State Park (Trip 28), which is on the edge. Rancocas State Park (Trip 31) is on the geographic edge of the Pine Barrens but not in the designated Pinelands Reserve.

The coastal plain extends into central New Jersey. The northern edge of the coastal plain, or Fall Line, roughly corresponds to the line of Route 1. However, none of the hikes in central Jersey are coastal plain hikes.

Hiking in the coastal plain is, as one would expect, typically a trek across flat, sandy soils, whether through pine forests or upland woods or along an ocean beach. Although the routes are flat, they are never monotonous. Hikers can observe little changes and details, from the varying sounds of the wind in the trees to the texture of lichens on tree trunks. Coastal plain hikes are often best in fall, winter, or early spring, before the bug population becomes intolerable and the sunscreen ineffective.

Central Jersey north of Route 1 is part of the Piedmont, or foothills, of the mountains to the north. Piedmont terrain is much more varied than that of the coastal plain, ranging from rolling hills to flat valleys and also including diabase mountains and ridges. (See "Black Rock, Green Forests" on page 159.) Much of it is formed of sedimentary rock created from deposits laid down by inland seas long ago. These sedimentary rocks, having weathered over time, vary considerably in their shape, so the landforms vary as well. The hike at Bull's Island and D&R Canal (Trip 34) traverses the flat floodplain valley along the river, while the hike in the Thomas Breden Preserve at Milford Bluffs (Trip 35) climbs the heights of red shale cliffs. The hike in the Musconetcong Gorge Preserve (Trip 36) follows a ravine.

The diabase ridges are part of a visually, if not geologically, continuous band of forested ridges that extend from Pennsylvania into New Jersey. Because they are rocky, have thin soil, and don't have access to great quantities of groundwater, they were not developed as quickly as the surrounding area. And as a result, they are richer in habitat, with diverse woods and wildlife. Diabase ridge hikes in central New Jersey include Ted Stiles Preserve at Baldpate Mountain (Trip 32) and Sourland Mountain Preserve (Trip 33).

TRIP 27
CAPE MAY

Location: Lower Township, Borough of West Cape May, NJ (Cape May County)
Rating: Easy–Moderate
Distance: 8.0 miles
Elevation Gain: Minimal
Estimated Time: 3.25 hours
Maps: USGS Cape May; a small map showing trails and streets (below the canal) is available at the Cape May Observatory Nature Center, 701 East Lake Drive, Cape May; trail maps available at the Cape May Migratory Refuge.

This route goes along the Jersey Shore, traversing ocean and bay beaches. Cape May is an internationally renowned birding site with a popular, long-established hawk watch. The hike passes through varied habitats: dunes, meadows, ponds, and freshwater and salt-water marshes.

DIRECTIONS

To reach The Nature Conservancy's Cape May Migratory Bird Refuge, take I-76 east to Route 42 south to Exit 13. Take Route 55 south to Route 47 south to Route 9 south to Route 109 south. Merge with the Garden State Parkway as it ends (Exit 0); merge onto Lafayette Street, then right on West Perry Street, which becomes Sunset Boulevard. The refuge is 1.0 mile ahead on the left; you will find ample parking. *GPS coordinates*: 38° 56.277′ N, 74° 56.686′ W.

TRAIL DESCRIPTION

Cape May, a Victorian-era Jersey Shore community two hours from Philadelphia, has long attracted vacationers. Its recognition as a natural area is more recent. Refuges, sanctuaries, and nature centers have proliferated, preserving much of the peninsula's irreplaceable habitat for wildlife as diverse as birds, butterflies, and horseshoe crabs. Cape May's hawk watch sets the standard for migration research.

Given Cape May's unique location, this is the only hike in this book for which the recommended footwear is (in season) either sandals, flip-flops or no footwear at all. Bring binoculars and a beachcombing bucket.

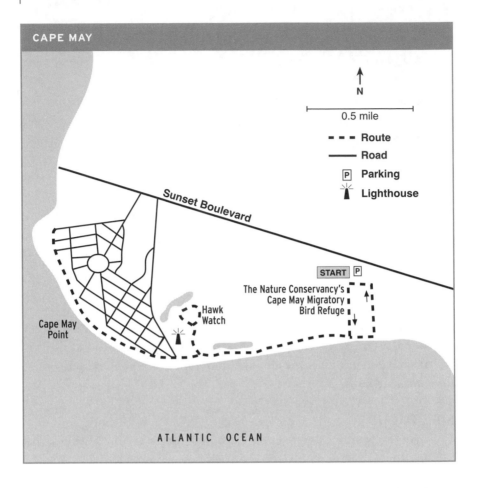

Begin at The Nature Conservancy's 229-acre Migratory Bird Refuge (commonly known as The Meadows) on Sunset Boulevard. In the fall, southbound songbirds rest and feed at Cape May's woods and meadows—full of berries, nuts, and seeds—before the long Delaware Bay crossing. In spring, they stop on their way back. Raptors are attracted to the abundance of prey. Spring through fall, shorebirds and waterfowl congregate in and around meadows, marshes, ponds, and beaches. The Cape May refuge protects coastal habitat, a haven for migrants and nesting birds.

From the entrance, follow the wide, flat, pebbly Main Trail as it passes through extensive wetland meadows. Trails in the refuge go along the tops of levees that enable refuge managers to control water levels in the freshwater wetlands. Their elevation provides excellent angles for viewing ducks, egrets, herons, and other birds in the ponds and marshes. The trail rises to go over a recently restored mile-long sand dune that protects the inland marshes from

The sea, the lighthouse, and the beach: essential components of a walk on the extensive, undeveloped beach around Cape May.

wind and is a unique habitat in itself. Look for the burrows of sand fiddler crabs, inch-wide holes excavated in the sand; you may even spot the white crabs. Follow the trail over the dune to the beach. During part of the year, large portions of the beach are fenced off to protect endangered piping plovers, whose nests on the ground are vulnerable to disturbance.

Turn right, take off your shoes if you feel like it, and head down the beach toward the Cape May Point lighthouse, walking as close to the ocean as you want. The view south is unobstructed, as the shore here is undeveloped. Sanderlings run back and forth with the surf, feeding on small invertebrates; gulls and terns wheel overhead. Depending on the season, you'll see all kinds of birds flying, resting, and feeding along the shore.

Not quite a mile down the beach, is the Bunker, a World War II-era concrete structure, part of a coastal defense system. Turn right at the Bunker, head up the beach (putting your shoes back on), and enter Cape May Point State Park with the parking lot to the left. The large wooden platform to the right is a hawk watch; in prime raptor migration season, it is packed with birders and spectators scanning the sky for hawks, eagles, and vultures.

Continue along the sidewalk and enter the state park trails to your right. The trails, many of them boardwalks, wind through wetlands, around ponds, and among dune forests. Follow the blazes for the Blue Trail, passing through cool, low woods of black gum, bayberry, holly, cedar, pine, and oak trees. The Blue Trail ends at an unmarked trail; turn left on the unmarked trail to go back down to the beach, turning to pass the Bunker. Continue the beach walk, now entering the Borough of Cape May Point; stay between the high-tide line and the water.

As you round the peninsula, you're passing from the ocean side to the bay side. Typically, the waves are smaller here and the sand begins to change from fine to rough, with interspersed pebbles. As the pebbles become more and more dominant in the sand, bare feet don't do well. You'll pass eight stone jetties; the ninth jetty, about 1.5 miles from the Bunker, stretches inland, marking Sunset Beach. This beach faces west and is therefore one of the few on the Jersey Shore from which you can watch a sunset over the water.

Turn around here and head back along the beach. As you near The Nature Conservancy refuge, look for the large interpretive sign next to the dune; otherwise, it may be difficult to pick out the trailhead from the continuous dune line. (Or watch for the end of the plover fencing, in nest season.) Go over the dune, but turn right at the top and follow the trail along the dune; then go left to cross the wetlands via the East Trail, which features a viewing platform. Go left again on a trail paralleling Sunset Boulevard, completing the circuit.

MORE INFORMATION

Many beaches in New Jersey are privately or municipally owned, and those who wish to use the beaches must purchase tags. However, according to state law and Department of Environmental Protection regulation, the public has a right of access to the area between the mean high-tide line and the water, and a beach owner must provide free public access to it. If a hiker desires to use another part of the beach, the owner may legitimately charge a fee.

Restrooms are located at the visitor center for Cape May Point State Park. There is a fee to visit The Nature Conservancy refuge: $3 for members and $5 for non-members. The lighthouse is worth a visit; pay the fee and climb the stairs to the open-air observation deck for a 360-degree view of the point. Cape May Point State Park, P.O. Box 107, Cape May Point, NJ 08212; 609-884-2159; www.state.nj.us/dep/parksandforests/parks/capemay.html.

OUT OF THE BLUE, INTO THE WHITE

Down from the Arctic Circle, along Greenland's coast, and across the Labrador Sea to eastern North America come millions of birds every fall during the migration from northern to southern latitudes. Some winter over in the southern United States; others continue on to Central and South America. Birds reverse direction from south to north in springtime to breed. Along the way, the migrants need to stop, rest, and eat. Some land on the forested ridges of the Delaware and Lehigh valleys and in the tidal wetlands of Delaware and South Jersey during these stopovers.

Because most songbirds migrate at night, even those who know that birds appear and disappear seasonally may not notice this great movement. Scientists use radar to track the movement, though, so we are aware of what the birds are doing under the cover of night. For example, researchers have learned that weather influences flight. The northwest winds of an autumn cold front push birds forward. But when weather conditions are adverse, as when a tropical storm blows in, birds literally drop from the sky, exhausted, particularly if a long water crossing lies ahead or behind.

Unlike the smaller songbirds, raptors (hawks, vultures, eagles) migrate during the daytime, riding the thermals (columns of warming air) and updrafts that form along a ridge. They can be observed "kettling" in groups, spiraling up and up and up the wind elevator. Birds ride the airstream up and then glide along wind pathways that follow ridgelines. Atop ridges throughout the Appalachian and Highlands regions, hawk-watchers gather to count raptors in the fall. The cry of the hawk-watcher, binoculars focused on an infinitesimal spot high in the sky moving through the scattered clouds, arrests the attention of a hiker, who must strain to see a hint of a dot overhead: "There! In the blue, heading to the white!"

Hawk Mountain on Kittatinny Ridge is the most popular hawk watch in Pennsylvania. Perhaps more famous among Delaware Valley hawk-watchers, though, is Cape May, New Jersey. Not a ridge but a peninsula between the Atlantic Ocean and the Delaware Bay, Cape May is a natural funnel for migrants heading south along both shorelines to cross the bay. Tired songbirds collect in the scrubby forests, preparing for the long overwater bay trip. Raptors too are tired and hungry, and those songbirds make a nice lunch; Cape May is a birder's heaven and a raptor's cafeteria.

TRIP 28
PARVIN STATE PARK

Location: Pittsgrove, NJ (Salem County)
Rating: Easy
Distance: 5.0 miles
Elevation Gain: Minimal
Estimated Time: 2.5 hours
Maps: USGS Elmer; trail maps available at park office, with a more accurate map displayed on a signboard outside

This easy, level hike winds through a diverse variety of pine and hardwood forests at the southwestern fringes of the New Jersey Pine Barrens.

DIRECTIONS

From Route 55, take Exit 35 and follow signs to the park. Parvin State Park is located between Centerton and Vineland on Route 540 (Almond Road). The parking lot contains an ample number of spots. *GPS coordinates*: 39° 30.679′ N, 75° 07.935′ W.

TRAIL DESCRIPTION

The word "ecotones" sounds like it means nature's music, and in a way it does. Ecotones are transition zones created by the meeting of different ecosystems, such as pine forests and hardwood swamps. Just as different notes combine to create diverse harmonies and melodies, ecosystems converge to create diverse, distinct plant and animal communities.

Parvin State Park in southwestern New Jersey lies on the margin of the Pine Barrens, where the dry, sandy soil that underlies pinelands meets slow-draining, claylike, peaty uplands. Within this 1,137-acre park are upland pine/oak forests, hardwood swamps, pitch-pine lowlands, and Atlantic white cedar swamps, as well as ecotones in between. Enjoy Parvin's continually shifting "music" as you hike from one kind of habitat to another.

The hike begins at the main office. This white-painted brick building, along with other structures in the park, was constructed by the Civilian Conservation Corps (CCC) in the 1930s. The complex sits by the Parvin Lake Beach, where swimming is popular. Parvin was a private recreational facility long

PARVIN STATE PARK

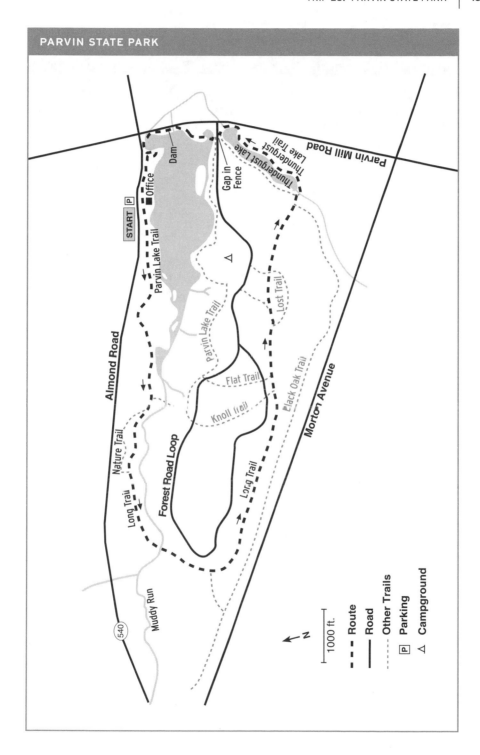

START

Office

Dam

Gap in Fence

Parvin Lake Trail

Thundergust Lake Trail

Parvin Mill Road

Almond Road

Parvin Lake Trail

Lost Trail

Flat Trail

Black Oak Trail

Knoll Trail

Morton Avenue

Forest Road Loop

Nature Trail

Long Trail

Long Trail

Muddy Run

540

N

1000 ft.

- - - Route
—— Road
.... Other Trails
P Parking
△ Campground

Trails in Parvin State Park wind through mixed pine and hardwood forests.

before the state purchased it in 1929. Only a small portion of the lakefront is cleared; otherwise, the shoreline seems carved out of deep forest.

Turn left from the office, heading northeast, to pick up the packed gravel Parvin Lake Trail (green-blazed). Immediately the trail enters a sandy floodplain forest, under a canopy of swamp white oaks, red maples, and sweet-gum trees. The understory consists of dogwood, holly, mountain laurel, blueberry, arrowwood shrubs, and a forest floor of ferns. This changes gradually into a dry, sandy pitch-pine forest, with ground cover that includes Canada mayflower, teaberry, and bracken, and a dense understory that includes the sweet pepperbush. In spring and summer the woods are alive with singing birds. The trail passes to the left of the site of a CCC camp, where the workers stayed while constructing the buildings.

The trails are blazed with colors at intersections, although not all intersections are on the map. Follow the Parvin Lake Trail, with its occasional green blazes, until it intersects the red-blazed Long Trail, at about four-fifths of a mile. This is the dividing line for the official 400-acre "natural area" of the park; bikes are not permitted on trails here, and the trails seem slightly quieter and more remote than those on the eastern side.

The narrow Long Trail parallels the course of Muddy Run, the creek that was dammed to create Parvin Lake. The name seems to refer to the creek's dark brown color, caused by the tannins in the Atlantic white cedars that thrive in pineland bogs. Where the trail crosses these bogs, look for bright green sphagnum carpeting the peaty forest floor. The trail crosses Muddy Run after 0.5 mile; bear right at the fork shortly after (not on map) to continue on the Long Trail, which soon meets a clear-running stream, notable for its contrast with the brown cedar streams. The trail passes through a low, moist area thick with hollies and enters a pine forest, which becomes a pine woods. It then continues into a very open pine/oak forest with tall trees, sparse understory, and a floor of lowbush blueberry and becomes sandy.

As you continue, note the almost ongoing changes in the height of trees, the thickness (or openness) of the understory, the terrain underlying the footpath, and the dryness or swampiness of the surrounding soil. This is the "music" of the ecotones.

After about a mile from the start, the Long Trail reaches a T; continue straight (south) and follow the trail as it bends eastward. About half a mile later, the trail reaches an intersection with the orange-blazed Knoll Trail on the left and shortly thereafter an unblazed trail to the right. You'll soon come to an intersection with the orange-blazed Flat Trail; an unmarked trail leads to the right about 800 feet later, and an intersection with the yellow-blazed Lost Trail follows about 50 feet after that. This area can be confusing; when in doubt, keep heading straight (east) and follow red blazes if you see them.

The Long Trail intersects with the Black Oak Trail, going off to the right at 2.75 miles from its start, then almost immediately ends. Go straight onto the yellow-blazed Thundergust Lake Trail, cross Thundergust Break (a small, quiet, clear-running stream), and continue straight. Thundergust Lake appears on the left. This is a small fishing lake with a bare shoreline. Go halfway around the lake. When the trail comes close to the road, it passes over the outlet; take the next right, cross the paved drive, go about 50 feet to a gap in the fence, and head straight, taking the bridge over Parvin Lake. You are now back on the green-blazed Parvin Lake Trail.

The trail goes around the edge of Parvin Lake, traversing a concave dam from which you can watch the aerobatics of barn swallows as they rocket out from their roosts under the footbridge to twist and turn over the lake, catching insects on the fly. Cross the lovely CCC footbridge; the trail ends at the park office, where it began.

MORE INFORMATION

Hiking is free, although a seasonal fee ($2) is required to use beach facilities. Restrooms are located at the park's main office. The trails are maintained by the Parvin State Park Appreciation Committee (www.friendsofparvin.org/Welcome.html). Parvin State Park, 701 Almond Road, Pittsgrove, NJ 08318; 856-358-8616; www.state.nj.us/dep/parksandforests/parks/parvin.html.

EIGHT LEGS, ONE ORB

If you're the first one down the trail in the morning, a hike through the woods can be downright ticklish—you may find your face, arms, and hands covered in sticky spiderwebs. But neither you nor the spiders whose webs you're displacing are likely to find the situation laughable.

Spiders are consummate environmental opportunists, and a standard footpath 4 feet wide is the ideal infrastructure for an orb web. An orb-weaver spider starts at the end of a branch and plays out a line of silk, letting a breeze carry the line to a branch across the trail. After strengthening this bridge, the spider makes another line and drops down from its center, making a Y shape. It then secures this line below and makes radial lines from the center. The spider spirals around from the center outward, connecting the radials with a silken line; it then spiral backs to the center, replacing the silken line with a stickier one. Then it sits and waits. The long, linear space that is a trail is also a highway for zooming insects. When the web vibrates, the spider rushes out to wrap the prey in silk; if the prey is a tiny, tasty fly, the spider kills it and eats it. If instead the prey turns out to be a human hiker swatting at the sticky threads, the spider spins out a quick dragline and gets out of the way, fast.

If you walk carefully, you may be able to avoid destroying webs and even to spot the weavers. The most commonly seen Philadelphia-area woodland orb weaver is the spined micrathena. Only 0.5 inch long, the dark brown to black spider is nonetheless easily spotted in the center of her web (males of this species don't weave webs). What appears to be a hard, glossy backpack is actually her abdomen. Sharp black spines run along the outside, presumably protecting the spider from predators.

Spiders have been around for 400 million years, but it wasn't until flowering plants arose that spiders' webs evolved from simple ground-hugging catchments to sticky orbs that fill the space between stems—space that happened to be newly populated with all kinds of pollinating insects flying from flower to flower. And then along came people, and their trails—all that space, all those zooming insects. Next time you take an early-morning hike, you'll understand better why orb-weaver spiders choose to share the trails with you.

TRIP 29
MULLICA RIVER TRAIL

Location: Atsion and Batsto, NJ (Burlington County)
Rating: Moderate
Distance: 9.5 miles
Elevation Gain: 25 feet
Estimated Time: 4.0 hours
Maps: USGS Atsion

Walk on soft needle-covered sand trails through shady pine forests, along cedar bogs, and by the beautiful red-brown Mullica River.

DIRECTIONS

To Atsion: From Route 676 east, take Route 30 east over the Ben Franklin Bridge; turn right onto North Elmwood Road, go 0.7 mile, and then turn left onto East Main Street, which becomes Tuckerton Road. Go 6.6 miles to County Road 541; go 5.0 miles and turn right onto U.S. 206. The Wharton State Forest office is on the right side of Route 206 northbound, at Atsion Road, where there is ample parking. *GPS coordinates*: 39° 44.534′ N, 74° 43.553′ W.

To Batsto: Take I-76 east to Route 42 south; go 7.6 miles to Atlantic City Expressway. Take the expressway 15.9 miles to Exit 28, and take Route 54 toward Hammonton/Vineland. Take the ramp to Hammonton, turn left onto 12th Street/Route 54 north and go 2.2 miles. Turn right onto Central Avenue/County Road 542, go 1.7 miles, and turn right onto South White Horse Pike/Route 30/County Road 542. Immediately turn left onto Pleasant Mills Road/County Road 542. Continue to follow County Road 542 about 7 miles. *GPS coordinates*: 39° 38.551′ N, 74° 39.295′ W.

The trailhead is off Route 542, about a quarter-mile west of the office; it is marked "Canoe Launch." A small parking area with room for six cars is located here. If parking is full, or you prefer to park in a monitored location, use the main office lot, where parking is ample.

To drive from Atsion to Batsto, go south on Route 206 and turn left onto Route 613; then turn left onto Route 693, and turn left again onto Route 542, to Batsto on your left.

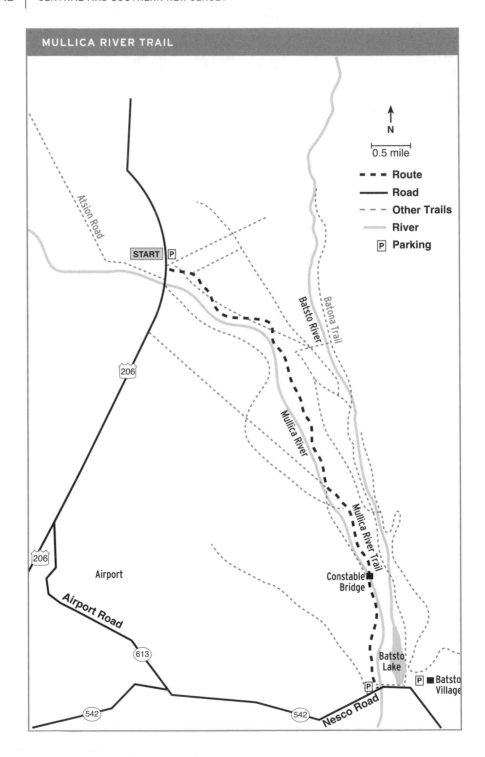

MULLICA RIVER TRAIL

N

0.5 mile

- - - Route
—— Road
- - - Other Trails
—— River
P Parking

Alsion Road

START P

206

206

Airport

Airport Road

613

542

542

Nesco Road

Batsto River

Batona Trail

Mullica River

Mullica River Trail

Constable Bridge

Batsto Lake

P

P Batsto Village

TRAIL DESCRIPTION

The Mullica River is one of the great "little rivers" of the Pine Barrens. Along with the Batsto, Oswego, and Wading rivers, it flows southeast into the Great Bay of the Atlantic Ocean above Atlantic City. This watershed is the largest in the Pine Barrens, and the only one wholly within it.

The Mullica's swift current, broad curves, swimming holes, consistently cool temperatures, shaded banks, and sand beach landings make it a paddling paradise. A hike along its banks lets you experience its beauty, a combination of serenity and dynamism, without having to get wet.

This trail can be hiked between Atsion and Batsto, putting a car at each end or arranging a pickup from a local outfitter, or it may be hiked to the Mullica Wilderness Camp and back. The very ambitious can hike the whole trail out and back for an all-day excursion. There are connector trails to the Batona Trail as well, enabling a 12-mile loop from Batsto via the Wilderness Camps Connector, or a 14-mile loop via the Beaver Pond/Quaker Bridge Trail.

As described here, the hike goes between Atsion and Batsto, allowing the hiker to experience a continuous section of the Mullica as it widens and narrows, rushes and rests. The beginning and end points are reminders of the historical human presence along the river. Both towns were vibrant ironworks settlements in the nineteenth century. Batsto has been restored to demonstrate what it was like when it was a living community, while Atsion exists only in the form of scattered structures.

The Mullica River Trail begins behind the Atsion State Forest Office, across from Atsion Lake, which dams the Mullica on the other side of Route 206. It is blazed with yellow markers on trees. Trailheads, intersections, and road crossings are marked by posts, which may be obscured by vegetation. There are also mileage markers about every half-mile.

Turn left onto Quaker Bridge Road, a sand road, passing by the Atsion church and cemetery, remnants of Atsion Village. The road went over the Batsto River to a long-vanished Quaker settlement.

About 150 yards on, across from an old red wooden building, the trail turns left into the woods along a narrow sand-based footpath pillowed with pine needles. The canopy is provided by the ubiquitous pitch pine and various oaks, the understory by blackjack oak and mountain laurel, bracken fern, greenbrier, sheep laurel, huckleberry, and blueberry. Teaberry (wintergreen) and bearberry form ground covers, along with false reindeer lichen. All of these plants, and the others typical of the upland Pine Barrens, thrive in dry, sandy soil, for that is what you are walking on: sand. There is little else, such as

Mature cedar stands on the Mullica River die off while young ones flourish.

clay or organic matter, mixed in with the finely ground quartzite particles, so the soil doesn't hold rainwater. For the plants here, life is a perpetual drought. Without clay or organic matter, the soil is also nearly devoid of nutrients but very high in iron; it is highly acidic as well. The plants that do grow here are tough—tough but beautiful.

The trail winds through this upland woods with occasional glimpses of the river or small streams. Lowland swampy areas are where you'll find cedars, with their reddish, shreddy bark and flat, lattice-like evergreen leaves. Atlantic white cedar has long been a commercially valuable tree for its resistance to decay—a useful characteristic in a tree that makes its home in swamps. Cedars are to the Pine Barrens what sycamores are to the Piedmont woods: they indicate the presence of water. If you see a stand of cedars, you'll be almost certain to find water or a high water table. Cedars, along with bog iron in the soil, are the source of the tea color of Pine Barrens waterways. In cedar swamps and along the river, look for red maple and black gum trees, sphagnum moss mats, sweet pepperbush, sweetbay, inkberry, and golden spike. The endangered swamp pink is found in cedar swamps.

At about the half-mile mark, you'll cross a railroad track; a quarter mile later, you'll cross an old road and veer around a small, pretty pond. Because the Pine Barrens is so uniformly level, almost all ponds and lakes are the products of human engineering, many dating from the days of mills and forges. Beavers were common in the Pine Barrens until 1850, when they were virtually extirpated; as a result of reintroduction and protection programs, they're making a comeback. Indeed, at about the 3.0-mile mark, you'll come upon the aptly named Beaver Pond Trail (connecting to the Batona Trail), which intersects the Mullica River Trail at a large cedar swamp with active beaver colonies.

The shoreline offers several fine viewing spots. Return to the Beaver Pond Trail intersection to follow the yellow-blazed trail as it goes along a sand road, then veers left after about 20 feet, becoming a narrow footpath that follows the river closely for the rest of its distance. The Wilderness Camps Connector Trail (to the Batona Trail) intersects at about the 4.0-mile mark.

The trail turns onto a sand road and continues in this manner for about 2.5 miles. You quickly realize the benefits of walking on soft, needle-covered sand trails under a pine canopy. On sugar-sand roads, your feet sink with each step. The sunny, open road is harsher on the eyes and ears, too, as even the wind seems to whine instead of whisper.

At around the 4.5-mile mark, you'll pass the Mullica Wilderness campsite along the river. About a mile and a half from the end, you'll reach the Constable Bridge, which spans the Mullica River. This is a popular canoe and kayak put-in/take-out spot and impromptu swimming pool. Cross the bridge. The rest of the way, you'll have the river on your left, with many opportunities for scenic views.

The rest of the trail is through a low, swampy area, apt to be quite muddy; it also serves as a nature walk with interpretive signs. The 9.5-mile trail ends at the edge of Batsto Village. If you parked here, you're done. If you parked at the main office, simply continue on through the gate and go another half-mile, through the restored village and past Batsto Lake, to the parking area.

MORE INFORMATION

There are restrooms at Batsto, none at Atsion (though there are restrooms at Atsion Lake, across Route 206). For information on local transportation, contact Wharton State Forest, 31 Batsto Road, Hammonton, NJ 08037; Batsto Office: 609-561-0024; Atsion Office: 609-268-0444; www.state.nj.us/dep/parksandforests/parks/wharton.html.

BROWN IS NOT DIRTY

Close your eyes for a moment and picture a clean river. What do you see in your mind's eye? Is the water in the river crystal clear? Or is it perhaps a glacial blue?

Your imaginary clean river surely wasn't the rusty brown of a sewer pipe. Not unless you've been to the New Jersey Pine Barrens, an hour's drive from Philadelphia, where brown is clean and the purest water runs russet out of the swamps. Two of the unique features of the Pine Barrens—swamp cedars and bog iron—are responsible for tinting the waters piney brown.

Waterways in the Pine Barrens—including the Batsto, Wading, Mullica, and Maurice rivers and the Rancocas Creek—are primarily fed by the Kirkwood-Cohansey Aquifer, a natural underground storage area that holds 17 trillion gallons of water, replenished as rain filters through the fast-draining sandy soils. Because the Pine Barrens is largely uninhabited, its rivers are cleaner than those fed by surface runoff from developed areas, which carries pollutants with it. Supplied by underground sources, Pine Barrens rivers are also refreshingly cool—a year-round 55 degrees Fahrenheit.

When water from an aquifer reaches the surface, it feeds into swamps, where the water table is high. Dominating the Pine Barrens swamps is the Atlantic white cedar, commonly known as the swamp cedar or bog cedar. Reaching 50 to 80 feet in height, this tall, straight tree with flat, dark green leaves grows in dense stands in seeps, springs, ponds, and riverbanks.

Despite is name, the white cedar has reddish bark. The red color is indicative of the tree's high tannin content, and tannin is one of the two main constituents of the color of Pine Barrens river water. Cedar bogs are also high in iron. Water percolating down through peaty soil composed of decayed cedar is highly acidic. The acidic water reacts with minerals in the sand below the organic layer, precipitating iron out of the water. The iron rises to the surface, where it reacts with air and turns red, then sinks to the bottom of slowly moving waters that have been fed with the bog water. Mining these deposits of bog iron from the rivers, then forging and casting them into ironware, was a major Pine Barrens industry in the eighteenth and nineteenth centuries. No longer a commercially viable product, bog iron today is just the other source of the distinctive brown color of the clean Pine Barrens rivers.

TRIP 30
BATONA TRAIL:
CARRANZA MEMORIAL TO APPLE PIE HILL

Location: Tabernacle, NJ (Burlington County)
Rating: Moderate
Distance: 9.0 miles
Elevation Gain: 110 feet
Estimated Time: 4.0 hours
Maps: USGS Indian Mills; trail map available online

This is a level walk past cedar swamps through pine woods to a spectacular view of South Jersey from the highest point in the Pine Barrens.

DIRECTIONS
Take Route 206 south just past Route 70, turn left onto Carranza Road, and follow for 9.0 miles through Tabernacle and into Wharton State Forest until you reach the parking area for Carranza Memorial on your right, hidden slightly behind the pine trees. Parking is ample. *GPS coordinates*: 39° 46.641′ N, 74° 37.942′ W.

TRAIL DESCRIPTION
Emilio Carranza was a celebrated Mexican aviator, a contemporary of Charles Lindbergh. In June 1928, when he was just 23 years old, he flew from Mexico City to New York, a flight that mirrored Lindbergh's New-York-to-Mexico run. On the return trip, encountering a thunderstorm over the Pine Barrens on July 13, Carranza's plane crashed; he did not survive. The Carranza Memorial, located at the start of this hike, is a stone marker carved in Mexico, commemorating his flight and tragic death. From the memorial, turn right onto the sand road. After about 100 yards you will see the pink blazes of the Batona Trail as it crosses the road.

The Batona Trail is a 50-mile linear trail through the Pine Barrens. Created in 1961, it was designed—and is still maintained—by the decades-old Batona Hiking Club of Philadelphia, whose name is a portmanteau formed from the saying "Back to nature," reflecting the club's original objective of encouraging city dwellers to get outside.

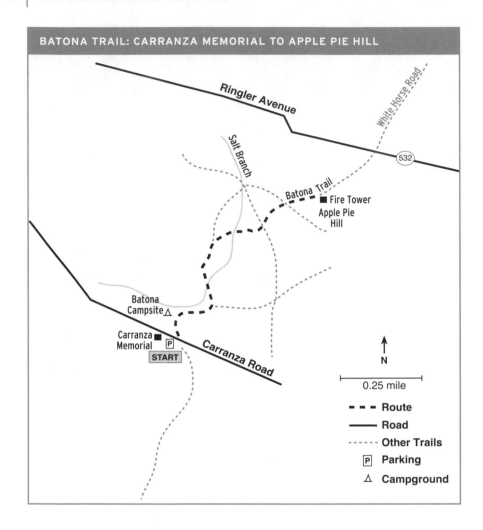

Turn left to follow the trail into the Batona Campground, one of several primitive campsites along the trail. This section of the Batona Trail is representative of its best characteristics: a quiet, easy trek through one of the great overlooked wilderness areas of the Delaware Valley. Like all other Pine Barrens trails, it is best hiked in late fall, winter, or early spring, before the mosquitoes, ticks, and chiggers become unbearable.

The trail winds hither and thither through the campground; the pink blazes are very visible when you catch sight of them but occasionally hide in shadows. Just past a pit toilet, the trail ducks into the woods. Follow the trail, which parallels (and at several points joins) a sand road as it weaves in and out of shrubby highbush blueberry and mountain laurel under pitch pine and blackjack oak. The trail skirts a wide cedar swamp, the Salt Branch of the

A stone obelisk com-
memorates Mexican
aviator Emilio Carranza's
1928 solo flight and
tragic crash in the Pine
Barrens.

Batsto River. After 0.75 mile, it hits the road again and bends left onto a foot-bridge over a bubbling brown creek.

Tea-colored waterways are characteristic of the Pine Barrens. The color results from the Atlantic white cedar, which thrives in the acidic bogs that surround creeks and rivers. The nut-brown tannins of the cedar bark, leaves, and cones seep into the water; these tannins, along with the high iron content of the boggy soil, lend a dark brown color to the area's streams and ponds.

Once over the bridge, the trail turns right into the woods. The soft sand covered with long pine needles makes for easy footing as the narrow, level trail undulates gently over occasional tree roots. All is quiet, except for the wind in the pines, and in spring and fall, the trill of the pine warbler, a cheery yellow bird that, true to its name, favors pine forests.

The trail crosses several small cedar swamps. Sphagnum mosses form dense green mats on the peaty soil. The land is so low and flat and sandy that the swamps and creeks seem to have been carved from the bottom up, and indeed they have: these waters are fed by underground aquifers.

At the 3.0-mile mark, the trail abruptly ascends about 20 feet onto a 10-foot-wide gravel ridge. Named on older maps Tea Time Hill, this ridge has been marked with a sign saying "Mount Korbar," in honor of Walter Korszniak and Morris Bardock, members of the Batona Hiking Club who created the Batona Trail.

Descend the "mountain" and continue on the trail, which crosses several sand roads. After about a half-mile, the trail crosses a long firebreak, a dug ditch that marks the edge of a controlled burn area. The State of New Jersey Forest Fire Service regularly sets controlled fires in the Pine Barrens, limiting the burning by trenching the margins of a targeted burn area so as to prevent the fire from spreading. Controlled burns reduce needles, duff, and other dry tinder, fuel that could ignite from a spark or lightning strike and cause a wildfire. Controlled, or prescribed, burns are intended to contribute positively to the regeneration of the pine-dominated forest, as pitch pine seeds are more likely to take root in fire-burned soil than are the acorns of the blackjack oak.

After another 0.5 mile (about 4.25 miles from the start), the trail crosses a road and suddenly, rising before you, is Apple Pie Hill. This mound of sand atop gravel climbs 100 feet to the highest point in the Pine Barrens, 208 feet above sea level. Even better, there is a 60-foot fire tower at the top. From the tower's highest landings, you have a clear view of the sweep of South Jersey from the Delaware River to the Atlantic Ocean; the Pine Barrens seem a sea of green. On clear days, you can easily see the skyscrapers of Philadelphia and Wilmington and the casinos of Atlantic City. This is one of the most marvelous views on the eastern seaboard.

Both Apple Pie Hill and Mount Korbar are composed of Beacon Hill gravel, an ancient marine deposit of the Pliocene era, some 2 million to 6 million years ago. These deposits are the remnants of an ancient waterway that, like the creeks and streams of our era, left gravel and sediment as it changed course.

To reach to your car, return the way you came.

MORE INFORMATION

The Batona Hiking Club (www.batonahikingclub.org) maintains the trails. There are primitive restrooms at Batona Campground. Camping at Batona Campground requires an advance reservation; the fee is $2/night. Wharton State Forest, 31 Batsto Road, Hammonton, NJ 08037; Batsto Office: 609-561-0024; Atsion Office: 609-268-0444; www.state.nj.us/dep/parksandforests/parks/wharton.html.

TRIP 31
RANCOCAS STATE PARK

Location: Mount Holly, NJ (Burlington County)
Rating: Easy
Distance: 5.0 miles
Elevation Gain: Minimal
Estimated Time: 2.0 hours
Maps: USGS Bristol and Mount Holly

In the westernmost Pinelands state park, you'll walk along the placid Rancocas Creek, traverse a freshwater tidal marsh, and explore varied pine and hardwood forests. The Rancocas Indian reservation museum provides an unusual historical-cultural dimension to the hike.

DIRECTIONS
Take I-295 to Exit 45A (Mount Holly/Willingboro). Head east on Rancocas Road (Route 626); the New Jersey Audubon Society's Rancocas Nature Center is about 1.8 miles ahead on the right, with an ample amount of parking. *GPS coordinates:* 40° 00.190′ N, 74° 49.276′ W.

TRAIL DESCRIPTION
The Rancocas Creek is not your typical pinelands creek, and Rancocas State Park is not your typical pinelands state park. Unlike the creeks and rivers of the eastern pinelands—cedar-lined streams that flow eastward into the Atlantic—the Rancocas, unique among major pinelands waterways, flows westward into the Delaware River. Because it meets the river below head of tide, the Rancocas is tidal. Its freshwater marshes harbor stands of wild rice, more commonly encountered in the slow, wide reaches of the southern and eastern pinelands creeks.

The 1,100-acre state park provides access to the creek as well as its surrounding tidal marshes and woods, the last being a mixture of pitch-pine forest and uplands forests. A unique aspect of this park is that a 350-acre area is leased to the Powhatan Renape Nation, whose Rankokus Indian Reservation occupies a small portion of the land that was occupied by tribes of the Powhatan nation when the area was settled by Europeans. There is a museum on

RANCOCAS STATE PARK

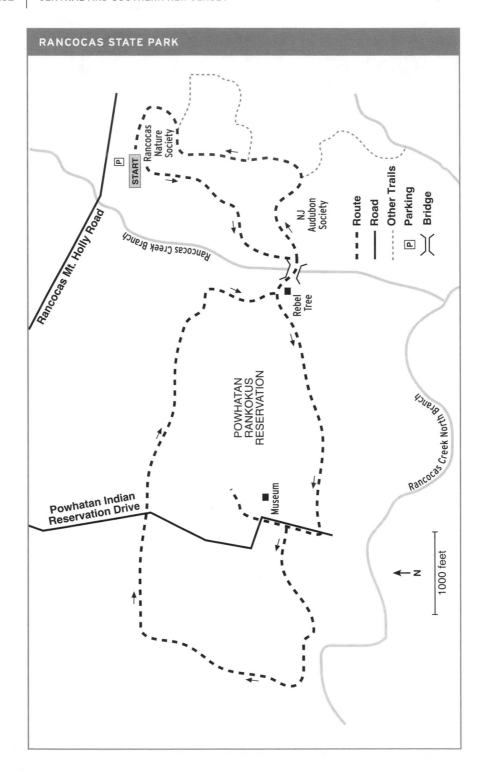

START

Rancocas Nature Society

Rancocas Mt. Holly Road

Rancocas Creek Branch

NJ Audubon Society

Rebel Tree

POWHATAN RANKOKUS RESERVATION

Rancocas Creek North Branch

Powhatan Indian Reservation Drive

Museum

Route
Road
Other Trails
Parking
Bridge

1000 feet

N

the grounds, along with a replica village, and the nation hosts cultural events open to the public.

The hike starts at the Rancocas Nature Center, a 125-acre sanctuary within the park, leased to the New Jersey Audubon Society (NJAS). The NJAS section, though small, is well mapped and prominently blazed. The visitor center houses some modest exhibits about the natural and cultural history of the area (including live snakes and turtles). The state park section, much larger, is not mapped, and is poorly blazed and signed.

Enter the NJAS trail system at the south end of the parking lot, starting at the Yellow Trail. Take the right-hand fork of the Blue Trail loop along a sandy surface trail. You'll enter a flat floodplain forest with many sweet-gum trees and hollies. Bear right at the next fork to cross a bridge over a small, very pretty, sand-bottom stream. The sand is brownish because of the iron content of the soil, characteristic of pinelands waterways. Immediately turn right to follow the stream as the trail leaves the NJAS site and is now in the state park. The woods are quiet, the trail flat, and the footing soft; among sheltering oak trees, this is a comfort-giving spot. It may come as a shock, then, to pass by a beech tree with the word "Rebel" carved in it, but be on the watch for it, as it marks the turn off the trail. At the tree, go left along a narrow, moss-lined footpath.

After 1.5 miles, you'll pass a group of Rankokus Indian Reservation outbuildings. On the reservation, respect the posted boundary lines. At the paved road, turn right. The road crosses an unusual buttonbush wetlands; look for the buttonbush's spherical fruit and seedheads. Pass the museum on the right. In the field beyond the museum, you can detour to view the replica village in the woods, the peafowl and dove cage, and the bison pen.

Opposite the museum is the entrance to a nature trail. Enter this trail, cross a stream, bear left, and then go straight at the next intersection; this trail heads down to the creek toward the left (west). The creek is wide, flat, and slow-moving. Pickerelweed lines the opposite shore. The trail bends away from the creek briefly; turn left at the intersection to return to the creek and walk along its banks. There are plenty of places to pause, look out at the scenery, and observe wildlife.

The trail ends at a woods road; turn right, noting the very twisted trees in the small woods. The trail empties into a large field; continue to the north end and turn right onto the paved path that starts here. Follow the path as it crosses a paved road, turns into a trail, and goes into a woods. (Take the trail that goes slightly left; don't continue straight ahead.) Go straight for 100 yards, then continue straight (not left) when the trail turns right. Where it ends, go straight into the woods and continue heading east on this trail; just when the

The Rancocas Creek is the only major Pinelands waterway to flow west to the Delaware River. Tidal marshes surround it at Rancocas State Park.

stream makes a turn and comes close to the trail, look for the "Rebel" tree on the left. Retrace your steps back to the little footbridge and over the stream. However, after crossing the bridge, bear right at the T. Follow this trail; turn left at the next intersection to follow the Blue Trail through a conifer plantation full of very tall, straight pines.

Keep left at the next intersection, go onto a boardwalk through a wetlands, and turn right at the sign for the nature center. Go along the meadow. The trail is a wide mowed path through tall grasses. It ends at the nature center.

MORE INFORMATION

On Mondays, the Rancocas Nature Center is closed and hiking is not permitted. Restrooms are located at the nature center, which is open Tuesday through Saturday from 9 A.M. to 5 P.M. and Sunday from noon to 5 P.M. Dogs are not allowed on New Jersey Audubon Society properties. Rancocas Nature Center, 794 Rancocas Road, Mount Holly, NJ 08060; 609-261-2495; www.njaudubon.org/Centers/Rancocas/.

TRIP 32
TED STILES PRESERVE AT
BALDPATE MOUNTAIN

Location: Titusville, NJ (Mercer County)
Rating: Moderate
Distance: 6.5 miles (shuttle hike) or 8.0 miles (loop)
Elevation Gain: 350 feet
Estimated Time: 3.25 hours (shuttle hike) or 3.75 hours (loop)
Maps: USGS Lambertville; official map available online at Mercer
County Parks website

**A mere hill compared to the peaks in the Appalachian range farther
north, Baldpate Mountain has features that belie its size. The highest point in Mercer County, it is a mountain-in-miniature whose
deep forests, rushing streams, and ridge-top meadow views make
for a surprisingly wild and remote-feeling hike.**

DIRECTIONS

Take I 95 north into New Jersey to Exit 1, take Route 29 north 4.7 miles and
turn right onto Fiddlers Creek Road. To reach the main parking area, which
has 35 parking spaces, turn in the drive on the left after 0.3 mile. *GPS coordinates:* 40° 19.102' N, 74° 53.429' W.

To reach the Church Road parking area and the Honey Hollow trailhead,
continue on Fiddlers Creek Road 1.4 miles to Church Road; cross the road to a
gravel drive on Brick Road, which is the entrance to Washington Crossing State
Park, where you will find room for six cars. *GPS coordinates:* 40° 19.111' N,
74° 51.966' W.

TRAIL DESCRIPTION

Admit it: you're skeptical. A mountain? In central New Jersey? Ten miles from
Trenton?

Yes, there is a mountain. And this mountain along the Delaware River—at
479 feet the highest peak in Mercer County—boasts not only a view of Philadelphia's skyline from its crest but also rocky forested slopes, rushing streams,
historic ruins, old logging roads, rugged trails, and wildflower meadows.
Within its deep woods breed diverse species of forest-dwelling birds such as
scarlet tanagers and veeries. Such features are the norm for the "real" New

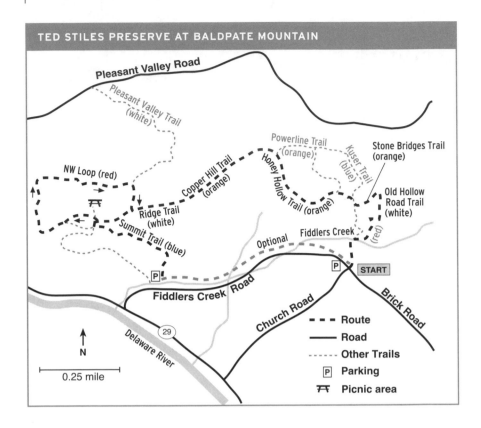

TED STILES PRESERVE AT BALDPATE MOUNTAIN

Pleasant Valley Road

Pleasant Valley Trail (white)

Powerline Trail (orange)

Stone Bridges Trail (orange)

NW Loop (red)

Copper Hill Trail (orange)

Honey Hollow Trail (orange)

Kuser Trail (blue)

Old Hollow Road Trail (white)

Ridge Trail (white)

Summit Trail (blue)

Optional

Fiddlers Creek

(red)

P

P

START

Fiddlers Creek Road

Church Road

Brick Road

29

Delaware River

N

0.25 mile

- - - Route
—— Road
.... Other Trails
P Parking
⚏ Picnic area

Jersey mountains in Warren County up north, where another peak called Baldpate Mountain reaches 1,165 feet. However, the Mercer County Baldpate Mountain has an outsize hiking value compared with its modest reputation.

The late Edmund "Ted" Stiles, for whom the 1,800-acre preserve was named in 2007, had a similarly outsize role in the region. A Rutgers biology professor, avid birder, and tireless conservationist, Stiles was a powerful force in central New Jersey land preservation.

The Sourlands region of diabase ridges, of which Baldpate is a part, extends from Mercer to Hunterdon and Somerset counties. Like its geologic Pennsylvania kin, the region's hard volcanic bedrock discouraged dense settlement, resulting in extensive areas of continuous, relatively undisturbed forest.

This hike explores the forest as well as the ridgeline crest, which was the site of a farmstead, hunting lodge, and estate; many buildings are still extant. Trail designers have not connected the eastern and western sections, so the first alternative uses two parking areas with a short shuttle, beginning at the Honey Hollow Trail and ending at the Summit Trail. The second alternative is to make a loop by walking the 1.4 miles along Fiddlers Creek Road (a wooded but not untraveled road) or by eliminating the Summit Trail (with its stone staircase) or the Honey Hollow Trail (with its wooded stream valley). The color-blazed trails are generally (though not without exception) well marked.

If you and your party have two cars, park one at the Fiddlers Creek Road lot and the other at the Church Road parking area. If you have only one car, put it at the Fiddlers Creek lot and walk to Church Road. Begin at the red-blazed Honey Hollow trailhead by crossing Church Road from the parking area. The narrow trail enters a red-shale hillside woods, where it turns muddy (typical of poorly drained red rock sites); the trail then joins an old wood-chip logging road, descending steeply to cross Fiddlers Creek via a charming wooden bridge. It ascends equally steeply on the other side and bears right at a Y, where it merges with the orange-blazed Cedar Grove Trail. From here on up to the ridge, the trails cross numerous small streams—some via rocks, some via bank-to-bank hops.

The predominant red rock disappears, replaced by light-colored sandstone. As the trail gets deeper into moist beech-maple-ash woods, the vegetation thickens; note that a large patch of skunk cabbage along the stream indicates a wetlands. Turn right where the Cedar Grove Trail diverges, then left onto the white-blazed Old Hollow Road Trail. At its end, go left onto the orange-blazed Stone Bridges Trail, an old stone-laid road. This flat section meets the Honey Hollow Trail; turn right and briefly merge with the blue-blazed Kuser Trail. Go uphill and then turn left at the orange-blazed Copper Hill Trail. Descend, passing by a ruin with a chimney; the trail bends right to climb a long, steep slope. This is one of the best parts of the mountain for seeing birds.

At the top of the hill, turn left (west) onto the white-blazed Ridge Trail, which follows the crest of the mountain along a gentle, flat, but rocky-surface trail. After about 1.25 miles, you'll enter a clearing with several old farmstead structures. Note the blue-blazed Summit Trail intersection. Turn right to follow the Summit Trail, which enters an old orchard, wending around small groves to a meadow. Here, picnic tables with a view provide a perfect rest stop.

From the summit, continue west back on the white-blazed Ridge Trail. After about 200 yards, note the marker suggesting that you look southwest, taking in the expansive long-range view over the Delaware Valley. On clear days, Philadelphia skyscrapers can be seen just above the horizon (binoculars help). Continue west through the meadow, entering the woods, and you'll meet the red-blazed Northwest Loop Trail almost immediately. Turn right, following the trail downhill. On this side of the ridge, sounds of the quarry below frequently echo through the woods and ominous signs indicating blasting in progress are posted on trees.

Turkey-tail mushrooms colonize on dead wood.

The trail descends steeply, then becomes an old road with a flat grade, occasionally muddy, for about half a mile; it then turns right and climbs back up the ridge very steeply, joining the white-blazed Ridge Trail after less than a quarter of a mile. Turn right (to make a loop back to Church Road, turn left and return by backtracking); retrace the Ridge Trail route for about a quarter of a mile (again passing old farm structures), until the blue-blazed Summit Trail intersection. Turn left; the trail descends through rich woods. The descent traverses a remarkable stone staircase built by volunteers from sandstone boulders onsite. After another 0.5 mile, the trail ends at the Fiddlers Creek parking area.

MORE INFORMATION

There are no reliably open restrooms. Horses are permitted on trails. Dogs must be leashed. Trails are open from sunrise to sunset, 7 days a week; hunting is permitted by arrangement in season (except Sundays mid-November to mid-February), and trails may be closed; contact Mercer County Parks for exact dates of closure; www.state.nj.us/counties/mercer/commissions/park/. Trails are maintained by Mercer County Parks, with some assistance provided through New Jersey Trails (www.njtrails.org).

BLACK ROCK, GREEN FORESTS

A ring of cold fire stretches from Adams County to Bucks County, Pennsylvania, and on into Mercer and Hunterdon counties in central New Jersey. About 200 million years ago, magma (molten volcanic rock) spewed from volcanoes deep under the area's sedimentary shale and sandstone bedrock into cracks and crevices in the layers above. Where it found horizontal space between layers, it spread out like melted chocolate in a s'more; where it found vertical space, it oozed up like caulk from a tube. Heat from the intrusive magma baked the surrounding rock and recrystallized it. Then the magma cooled and hardened to become an igneous rock called diabase.

Because diabase is dense and hard, it resists erosion. Over time, as the softer rock around them weathered away, sheets and spikes of dark, fine-grained diabase were left standing alone, forming long ridges and rounded hills. Diabase crops out in the forested ridges of French Creek State Park (Trip 16), Green Lane Park (Trip 17), Nockamixon State Park (Trip 20), Nolde Forest (Trip 22), Clarence Schock Park (Trip 23), and Baldpate Mountain (Trip 32).

It's no coincidence that diabase is found in some of the Philadelphia region's largest and richest natural areas. Because the rock is dense and hard, the soil above it drains slowly, creating swampy areas unsuitable for development. Also, the rocky soil is not conducive to farming. Consequently, many of the places where diabase is prevalent have been sparsely settled. With fewer people around, plants and wildlife have room to thrive. Furthermore, the diversity of wildflowers and other plants tends to be greater in areas with diabase soil than in the surrounding areas of acidic sedimentary rock.

Ridges of diabase typically have talus slopes, mountainsides covered with rock debris that are formed when water gets into cracks at the top of ridge, freezes, and breaks the rocks apart, sending blocks and boulders tumbling down. Large, blocky boulders look like staircases for giants, which is why a local name for diabase in Pennsylvania is traprock, from the German *Treppe*, meaning "stairs."

Rocks were fundamental in the development of human civilization. They underlie the soil from which everything grows, and they form the physical and chemical basis for the community of living things that inhabits a place. Quartzite, also common on Kittatinny Ridge, gets most of the attention, but diabase deserves a hall-of-fame plaque for its role in underlying some of the most treasured natural areas in the United States.

TRIP 33
SOURLAND MOUNTAIN PRESERVE

Location: Hillsborough Township, NJ (Somerset County)
Rating: Moderate
Distance: 5.0 miles
Elevation Gain: 400 feet
Estimated Time: 2.25 hours
Maps: USGS Rocky Hill; trail maps available at the trailhead and on the website for the Sourland Mountain Preserve

Hike up and down a rugged ridge through a rich, rocky woods, highlighted by a ridge-top boulder "amusement park" with rock outcrops, crevices, overpasses, and underpasses.

DIRECTIONS
Take I-95 north to Route 206 north (Lawrenceville). In Princeton, turn left onto Elm Road, which becomes Great Road. Cross Route 518. About 3.0 miles past Skillman Post Office, turn left at East Mountain Road; go approximately 1.0 mile to the entrance of Sourland Mountain Preserve on your left, where you will find ample parking. *GPS coordinates*: 40° 28.431′ N, 74° 41.655′ W.

TRAIL DESCRIPTION
The Sourlands is a discontinuous 20-mile-long region in central New Jersey defined by a unifying geology. Looming over flat valleys of sedimentary rock are vertical ridges of volcanic diabase, including Baldpate Mountain (see Trip 32) at the southwest corner of the region and Sourland Mountain at the northeast corner. Diabase splits into blocks and boulders that tumble off the ridges down the sheer slopes. The name "Sourlands" may derive from the nature of the soil; the stone slopes yielded thin soil and held little water, making "sour" farmland. It may also derive from the word "sorrel," for the reddish color of the surrounding soil. Difficult to farm, the ridges were largely undeveloped (though extensively quarried) and thus remained a rich wildlife habitat and an important resource for protecting water quality.

On the south- and east-facing slopes of Sourland Mountain lies Somerset County's 3,197-acre Sourland Mountain Preserve. Trails access the rocky slopes and provide glimpses of the valley. This hike focuses on the Ridge Trail,

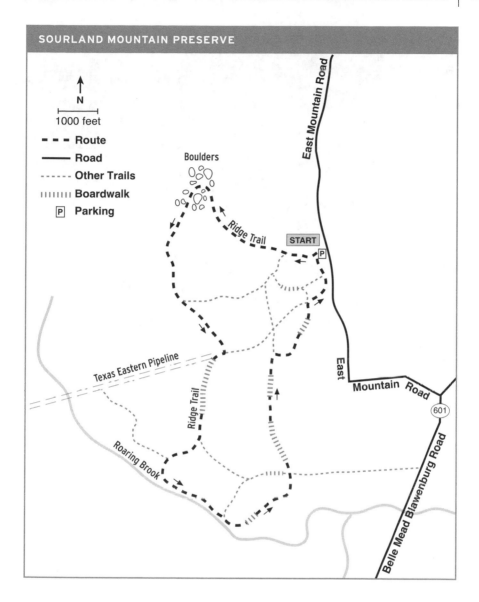

SOURLAND MOUNTAIN PRESERVE

a 5-mile circuit that makes its way up to a boulder field near the crest and me-anders through streams and quiet woods on its way there and back.

The hike starts behind the information kiosk at the main trailhead at the edge of the woods. It begins as a wide gravel path with a few rocks in and around it. Trailside posts with numbers correspond to numbers on the preserve's map so that you can easily discern intertrail connections, assess elapsed distance, and—important in an essentially homogenous landscape—be reassured that

Boardwalks carry the Ridge Trail through wet areas in the diabase woods of Sourland Mountain.

you're not going astray. Trails are marked with distinct shapes. The Ridge Trail is marked with squares.

At marker 1, continue straight (do not cross the bridge). The trail, now a narrow rocky footpath, climbs steeply up and across the ridge. Maple, tulip tree, oak, and beech predominate; as the trail ascends, hickory, birch (gray and black), and basswood trees begin to appear. (Basswood indicates where the woods are wet; it is typically a bottomland tree.) The whistle of the eastern pewee, a forest-dwelling bird resident in spring and summer, indicates that the woods are deep and healthy.

The trail passes by large boulders, first a few, then more and more, until finally near the top of the ridge it begins reeling crazily around an extensive collection of innumerable boulders as if the trail designer became giddy with delight. You'll have to squeeze through, climb over, or brush by boulder after boulder. Just when you think the boulders are done, there is another grouping that the trail enjoys a close encounter with. The tumbled, jumbled, thrown quality of these huge rocks shows the immense power of water to break off pieces from the parent mountain and toss them around and down the slope.

The trail eventually settles into a southwesterly direction downhill. At marker 4 it meets a connector trail that leads to the trailhead. Continue straight, still heading downhill through woods. At marker 5, after a small stream, there is a wide, cleared gas pipeline crossing. This is the best view on the trail. Turn slightly to the right (uphill and away from the view), then quickly turn left to reenter the woods. Boardwalks carry the trail over a particularly muddy section, of which there are many in this woods; the rocks don't percolate, so water sits on the surface. At marker 6, the trail passes through a chain link fence marking a former 3M mining site. Turn left at the next intersection with a red-blazed trail and follow square blazes downhill. (At publication, these trails were being re-blazed.) At a cairn marking the red trail, bear left and pass back through the fence.

There are fewer rocks and more trees and fungi in this section. Musclewood (hornbeam), another stream-loving tree, appears in patches—and, sure enough, a brook appears out of the muddy ground. At marker 8, the Roaring Brook is very close to the trail. Named for the roaring noise it makes as it runs over the boulders, Roaring Brook may have an odd milky color after rain, due to the presence of silt in the sediment, residue from the former mining operations higher on the ridge.

The trail turns back on itself at marker 8, heading down and north, crossing a connector trail at marker 9. More boardwalks take the trail over swampy areas.

Turn right at marker 10 and descend toward marker 11. Cross the lower end of the pipeline clearing, reenter the woods, turn right at 12 and left at 13, and emerge from the woods at the trailhead.

MORE INFORMATION

A portable toilet is located at the parking lot. The park is open dawn to dusk. Bikes are permitted on the trails. The Sourland Planning Council (www .sourland.org) has extensive information on the history and natural resources of the region as well as on conservation initiatives. Sourland Mountain Preserve, East Mountain Road, Hillsborough, NJ 08844; 908-782-1158; www .co.hunterdon.nj.us/depts/parks/guides/Sourland.htm.

TRIP 34
BULL'S ISLAND–DELAWARE CANAL
AND DELAWARE & RARITAN CANAL

Location: Lumberville, PA, and Bull's Island/Raven Rock, NJ
Rating: Moderate
Distance: 9.0 miles
Elevation Gain: Minimal
Estimated Time: 4.0 hours
Maps: USGS Lumberville and Stockton

Walk through an old-growth floodplain forest at Bull's Island, then continue along the canals and along both sides of the Delaware, where mules once towed barges and locomotives pulled trains.

DIRECTIONS
Take I-95 north into New Jersey to Exit 1; take Route 29 north (toward Lambertville). Continue north on Route 29 for about 5.5 miles to Bull's Island State Park. The entrance is on the left; you will find ample parking. *GPS coordinates:* 40° 24.596′ N, 75° 02.140′ W.

TRAIL DESCRIPTION
This portion of the Delaware River, 12 miles upstream from its industrialized tidal segment, is a miracle. In a region that has been growing and developing for centuries, here is a wild, undeveloped riverscape that hasn't changed appreciably since William Penn sailed upstream to his country estate in present-day Philadelphia. The river here runs swiftly, just as it has for centuries, beneath ragged red cliffs, past tree-clad hills dotted with picturesque villages, and around islands populated only by turtles.

Ironically, the best way to experience the untamed river (other than by paddling or tubing with its current) is to walk the vestiges of riverside industry that line its banks. Because the Delaware wasn't navigable above Trenton and Morrisville, canals were built early in the nineteenth century. In Pennsylvania, the Delaware Canal ran between Easton and Bristol, and in New Jersey, the Delaware & Raritan (D&R) Canal stretched from Trenton to New Brunswick, fed in part by a smaller canal from Bull's Island to Trenton. Although water continues to run through them, the canals today are used only for recreation. The towpath (from which mules once pulled boats) and a railroad track along the feeder canal have been converted into trails.

BULL'S ISLAND–DELAWARE CANAL AND DELAWARE & RARITAN CANAL

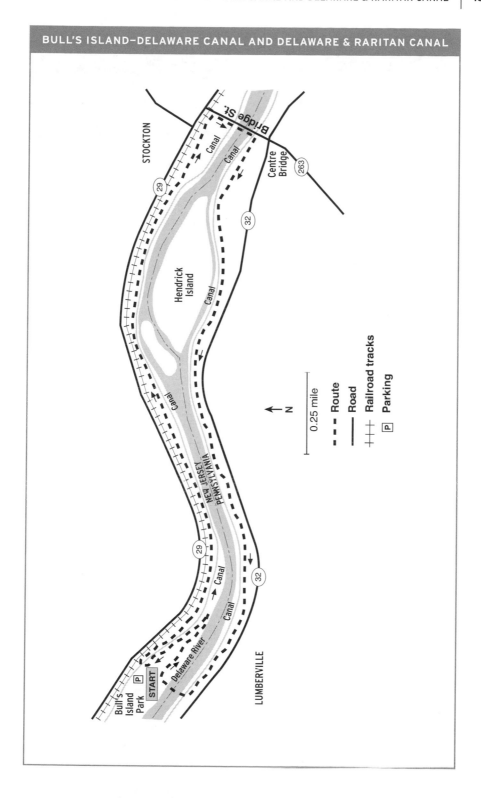

The Delaware & Raritan Canal parallels the Delaware River in New Jersey, as does its Pennsylvania counterpart the Delaware Canal.

The hike begins at Bull's Island, with a 1.0-mile loop to the tip of the island and back. The feeder canal, dug in the early 1830s, enlarged a creek between the river island and the mainland. The downstream portion of the island contains a large and unusual old-growth floodplain forest. The trailhead for the Nature Trail is located opposite the park office mailboxes. Enormous trees—such as sycamore, silver maple, tulip tree, and river birch—wrapped with giant vines soar over a lush, green, primitive bottomland choked with 5-foot-tall ferns. The trees predate the construction of the canal.

Follow the narrow dirt footpath along the canal to the left, with the forest on the right. Be careful of the stems of stinging nettles crowding the trail; although it is harmless and lasts only minutes, their sting is painful. The trail runs right to the endpoint of the island; it stops abruptly at the top of the low dam, with the canal on one side and the river on the other. Don't fall! Turn around here, and after 0.1 mile bear left into the woods. Now the exceptionally large old-growth trees envelop the trail in green and brown.

The trail parallels the river for a mile and emerges onto a paved path just after passing the canoe landing. Follow this to the parking area, turn right, and head over the canal bridge to the D&R Canal Trail, and turn right again. This wide, flat gravel path extends for 3.0 miles, paralleling Route 29 on the left and the canal and floodplain forest on the right; the river plays peek-a-boo through the thick trees. The last 0.5 mile threads past the historic Prallsville mill, passes over the mill dam bridge, and travels through the backyards of Stockton.

Cross Bridge Street, turn right, and go over the river via the bridge to the town of Centre Bridge, Pennsylvania. This bridge, with its open-grate steel truss, replaced the wooden covered bridge whose dramatic demise in a 1923 fire was depicted in a celebrated painting called *The Burning of Center Bridge*, by Pennsylvania impressionist Edward Redfield.

To get to the Delaware Canal towpath, descend the stairs just below the bridge and turn right. To the left is the canal, which is narrower and shallower than the one on the New Jersey side. To the right is the river, which is much closer to the path than it is on the New Jersey side; sometimes it will be just a few feet away, and rarely more than 10 feet.

The towpath is a flat, stabilized turf surface. This section, along with most of the rest of the path, has been reconstructed several times in the last few years, because it has been decimated by flooding on more than one occasion. Unlike the canal on the New Jersey side of the river, the canal in Pennsylvania runs for much of its length along steep rocky slopes. The natural floodplain for the Delaware includes the towpath and the canal. When the river floods, the water washes away the towpath. Some say that it is not worth reconstructing, because the river will take back what belongs to it, but the community has continued to support this beloved amenity.

The towpath continues for 3.5 miles, providing an intimate experience of the river and its islands, as well as the canal and the red rock cliffs above, themselves covered with unusual ferns and wildflowers. The last mile passes below Lumberville on the banks above. Go under the bridge and climb up the stairs to cross over the river to Bull's Island. This historic, pedestrian-only footbridge (one of two on the river) was built in 1947 on an 1856 masonry substructure by John A. Roebling's Sons (of Brooklyn Bridge fame). Follow the paved path to the parking lot.

Note: According to the Pennsylvania Department of Conservation and Natural Resources, the towpath reconstruction on this section was to be completed by end of 2009.

MORE INFORMATION

Restrooms are located at Bull's Island Recreation Area and at Virginia Forrest Recreation Area on the Pennsylvania side of the Delaware River. Bikes are permitted on the canal paths. The Bull's Island Recreation Area and the Virginia Forrest Recreation Area are open from sunrise to sunset. Bull's Island Recreation Area, 2185 Daniel Bray Highway, Stockton, NJ 08559; 609-397-2949; www.state.nj.us/dep/parksandforests/parks/bull.html. Delaware Canal State Park, 11 Lodi Hill Road, Upper Black Eddy, PA 18972; 610-982-5560; www.dcnr.state.pa.us/stateparks/parks/delawarecanal.aspx.

Location: Holland Township, NJ (Hunterdon County)
Rating: Difficult
Distance: 3.0 miles
Elevation Gain: 175 feet
Estimated Time: 2.0 hours
Maps: USGS Frenchtown; location map (not trail map) available at www.nj.gov/dep/njnlt/maps/tfbreden.jpg

Although this rugged, unmaintained site is not for novices, the rewards of exploration include wild and scenic views of the Delaware River and displays of locally unusual plants, particularly the masses of prickly pear along the cliffs.

DIRECTIONS

From the traffic light at the intersection of Bridge Street, Water Street, and Frenchtown Road in Milford, New Jersey, go north on Water Street (Route 519) for 1.25 miles and turn left onto the unnamed dirt road entrance to the preserve, where you will find parking for three cars. *GPS coordinates*: 40° 34.759′ N, 75° 06.617′ W.

TRIP DESCRIPTION

From the top of the 450-foot-high red shale Milford Bluffs, the Delaware River seems to unspool as an endless olive ribbon, from horizon to horizon, swathed in green. The bird's-eye vantage point you will have on this hike gives ample evidence of the river's power and beauty. The 250-acre Thomas F. Breden Preserve is owned and managed by the New Jersey Natural Lands Trust (NJNLT), a unit of the state's Department of Environmental Protection. The NJNLT focuses on protecting the natural diversity of the site, but it also provides limited public access; there are trails, though they are not marked or regularly maintained. Nonetheless, the preserve is a hidden jewel that offers hikers the opportunity to see prickly pear cactus and other locally unusual wildflowers. (The Mariton Sanctuary, Trip 37, also provides dramatic, albeit narrower, views of the river, from the Pennsylvania side, with maintained trails.)

Note that the bluffs are steep and there are no guardrails, and that unmaintained trails have high grasses and thorny shrubs: this is *not* a hike for

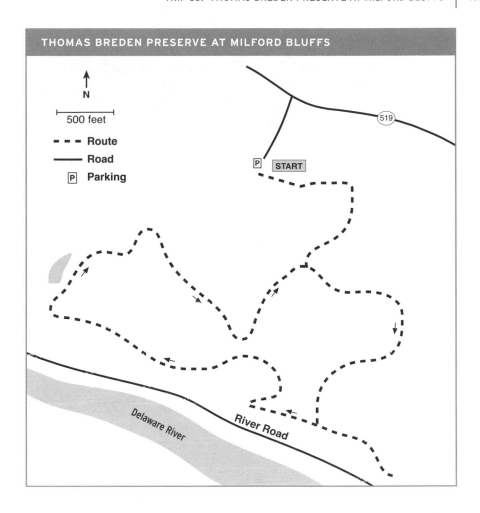

THOMAS BREDEN PRESERVE AT MILFORD BLUFFS

N

500 feet

- - - Route
——— Road
P Parking

519

P START

Delaware River

River Road

unsupervised children. A compass or handheld GPS device is highly advisable. Technically, hikers are not required to stay on trails here at the preserve, but to limit disturbance to the diverse natural area, you should confine your wanderings to defined spaces such as the perimeters of fields.

The hike takes you up wooded hills, across old fields, and along the top of a deep ravine. Start at the parking lot, where an information kiosk displays a hand-drawn map of the preserve and a representation of some trails. (However, as of the time of this writing, the map does not reflect the current ownership or extent of the preserve.) Head east, up the hill by a narrow, natural-surface path along a dry streambed. The hill is composed of red sandstone and shale that fractures horizontally; look closely at any flat red rock and you'll see cross sections that look like pages in a book. These rocks were formed 180 million to 250 million years ago from sediments laid down when the area was a

The Delaware River winds past Milford, New Jersey, across from Upper Black Eddy, Pennsylvania.

shallow sea and the Delaware River flowed north to what is now Newark Bay. Red rocks, as these sedimentary formations are called, are common throughout central New Jersey and in Bucks and Northampton counties in Pennsylvania, across the river. The fragmented rocks turn into clay, so that the typical soil in red rock regions is slow-draining and slightly acidic. In moist woods such as the one that surrounds this gorge, you'll see ash, red and white oak, red maple, sugar maple, beech, hop hornbeam, and hickory trees as well as possumhaw and spicebush in the understory, along with multiflora rose.

The trail climbs steeply for about 500 feet, then turns right (south) and levels off, becoming an old road. It enters a shrubby area and then an old field. This sunny site was once a farm, and this area a pasture, so what you see is early successional shrub-scrub habitat (much of which is invasive non-native autumn olive). This kind of habitat is fast disappearing in the region, as old fields turn into housing developments or timber stands. Follow the perimeter of the field. In any season but winter, if the trail is not mowed, you will be tromping through high grass, pushing aside common meadow vegetation such as dogbane, asters, goldenrod, milkweed, and yarrow; you may be lucky enough to spot wild strawberries at ground level.

Cross a line of trees—an old fencerow separating two farm fields—and continue toward the woods at the far side of the field. At the woods edge, turn left into the woods. A spur trail descends along the edge of a ravine. The road is below and to your left. Go slow. This trail emerges onto an overlook atop the sheer bluffs, with spectacular river views. Be *very* careful; the rocks here are steep, crumbly, and dangerous. *Do not* climb on the rocks. When leaves are not in bloom, you can also see red rock cliffs across the river on the Pennsylvania side. The vertical areas of the bluffs are dry and sun-baked, yet because of the horizontal fracture patterns, there are numerous crevices that collect moisture and create cool, moist microclimates where wildflowers such as red columbine thrive. The cliff sides are also home to native prickly pear cactus plants, which bear bright yellow flowers in the early summer.

From this overlook return to the field. Follow the perimeter of the field (there are side trails going into the woods), reenter the woods, and descend following a trail that parallels the river on your left. It intersects an old road; turn right (northeast), away from the bluffs, and ascend along a rocky old road that crosses an old (now dry) streambed. Just before the trail reaches the top, it passes a small, quiet pond to the left. This is a good place to sit and listen for frogs in spring. The trail emerges from the woods into another field. Follow the perimeter of this field by heading to the right and turning gradually counterclockwise as you go around. You will pass a maintenance building on your right, then just beyond the building, the field ends at an old road. Turn right and follow the road until it ends at the old field. Turn left and follow the field around to the left; watch for the opening in the shrubbery to backtrack down the trail you came in on, bearing right at the Y, returning through the woods to the parking area.

MORE INFORMATION

The preserve is open during daylight hours for passive recreational activities that do not disturb the natural diversity of the site. Rock climbing and scrambling are prohibited, not only because of the danger but to protect the communities of rare plants. There are no restrooms. Hunting is permitted in season (for designated hunters). Thomas Breden Preserve at Milford Bluffs, County Road 627, Holland Township, NJ 08848; 610-746-2801; www.njwildlifetrails .org/SkylandsTrails/Sites/tabid/445/Scope/site/Guide/SKYLANDS/Site/209/ Default.aspx.

HOW GREEN IS MY VALLEY?

Residents of the region surrounding Philadelphia—including the suburbs and exurbs of southeastern Pennsylvania, central and southern New Jersey, and northern Delaware—refer to the area as the Delaware Valley. This may surprise those residents of upstate New York who use the same name to refer to their region. But the river is wide enough, and long enough, to accommodate any number of people who claim it as a geographical frame of reference.

The Delaware basin extends north to the Catskill Mountains of New York, where its west and east branches arise; after passing through reservoirs that supply water for New York City, the branches meet at Hancock, New York, where the main stem of the Delaware River begins its journey south. For the next 331 miles, it flows free to the sea, emptying into the Delaware Bay; it is the longest undammed river east of the Mississippi. Two major rivers empty into the Delaware—the Lehigh, at Easton, Pennsylvania, and the Schuylkill, at Philadelphia—and 214 other creeks and rivers feed into it. All told, the Delaware drains a four-state watershed of 13,539 square miles.

The Delaware is tidal up to the fall line between Morrisville, Pennsylvania, and Trenton, New Jersey, where the sandy Atlantic coastal plain meets the rocky Piedmont province. The line is marked by a mass of large boulders in the river; these inhibited the movement of big ships upriver, so major industry is concentrated below the line. Because it is free-flowing and largely undeveloped, the river has been designated a federal Wild and Scenic River for most of its length.

In the mental geography of the region's residents, the Delaware Valley extends to the confluence of the Lehigh at Easton, where the Lehigh Valley is centered. The Delaware divides Pennsylvania from New Jersey, but it also unites the two states, for it is two sides that make a whole valley.

Much of the lower nontidal Delaware retains the feel of a natural shore. The river flows swiftly between tree-lined hills and alongside red cliffs, small towns hug the banks, herons fish in the shallows, and ospreys soar overhead. A paddlers' delight, this section of the river is also enjoyed by pedestrians because, ironically enough, of the remnants of alternative transportation systems. Canals and rail lines built in the 19th century have been repurposed to serve as walking paths on both sides. Today's hikers have a 21st-century relationship with the river: appreciative of its gifts, accepting of its pace.

TRIP 36
MUSCONETCONG GORGE PRESERVE

Location: Holland Township, NJ (Hunterdon County)
Rating: Moderate
Distance: 4.0 miles
Elevation Gain: 250 feet
Estimated Time: 3.0 hours
Maps: USGS Bloomsbury and Easton; trail map available online

This hike is short in length but rich in challenges and interest. Its rugged terrain includes paths along rocky ravines and waterfalls. It provides views of the Kittatinny Ridge and glimpses of the Musconetcong River. The historical industrial context evident along the route adds an extra dimension.

DIRECTIONS

Take Route 519 north from Milford, New Jersey; at 5.8 miles, turn right onto Dennis Road; continue 0.6 mile to the parking area on the right, where you will find parking for seven to eight cars. *GPS coordinates*: 40° 37.627′ N, 75° 08.151′ W.

TRAIL DESCRIPTION

An irony of hiking in the Philadelphia area is that many of the wooded streams and rivers we enjoy for their scenic beauty and recreation value are reclaimed industrial sites. Early settlers discovered a rich resource in the region's forested valleys. Dammed and channeled, swift-running waterways would power mills and forges; cleared and burned, forests would yield charcoal. The stripped, smoke-filled hillsides resounded with gears turning and millstones grinding. Even after water-powered industries disappeared, rivers continued to be a cheap source of water and a place to dispose of waste.

The Musconetcong Gorge Preserve is a prime example. Mills and forges have been operating along the Musconetcong River for centuries. Hunterdon County obtained the 425-acre preserve, near the river's confluence with the Delaware, in 1974 from a paper company, which had used the river for power and the woods for raw materials; no longer functioning, the mill and dam are still extant, as is a rail bed. Today, the preserve is a cool, quiet forested ravine sloping toward the river. The fresh air is filled with the sounds of birdsong

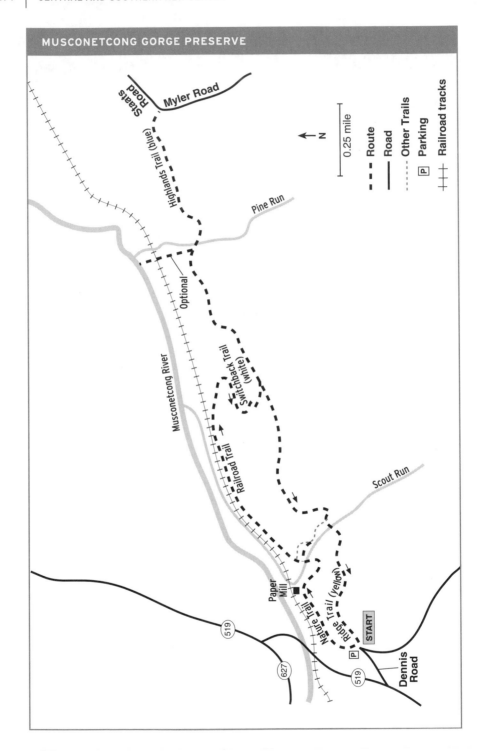

MUSCONETCONG GORGE PRESERVE

Myler Road

Staats Road

Highlands Trail (blue)

Pine Run

N

0.25 mile

Route
Road
Other Trails
P Parking
Railroad tracks

Optional

Musconetcong River

Switchback Trail (white)

Railroad Trail

Scout Run

Paper Mill

Nature Trail

Ridge Trail (yellow)

START

P

519

627

519

Dennis Road

and rushing water, hills so thick with trees that the river is barely visible. Yet reminders of the site's industrial past form as much a part of its fabric as do natural features.

The hike starts at the blue-blazed Nature Trail on the north side of the parking lot, marked by a large wooden sign about 20 feet down the hill—not the yellow-blazed Ridge Trail starting at the eastern end. (This loop hike can be done in the other direction, taking the more difficult option of descending rather than ascending the long, steep Switchback Trail in the middle.) Descend the hill along a narrow rocky footpath (note occasional numbered posts). The trail levels off, then descends steeply into the Scout Run Valley, crossing the stream twice, once on rocks and then on a bridge via a midstream island. Continue about 100 feet to a gravel road (the blue-blazed Gas Line Trail).

Turn right onto the road; after 20 feet bear right into the woods to go up the steep and rocky red-blazed Waterfall Trail; it returns to the Scout Run and follows it uphill to a multilevel waterfall. Return downhill via the same trail; at the three-way intersection, turn right to follow the orange-blazed Railroad Trail into the woods.

Enter a moist, rich hardwood forest of birch, ash, oak, maple, tulip tree, and dogwood, with abundant shrubs and ferns, and wildflowers in spring. This forest is a haven for songbirds, including the deep-woods residents veery and scarlet tanager. The trail continues along the slope of the hill, paralleling the rail bed near the base of the ridge below. In winter there are decent views of the river and the paper-mill dam. The trail is wet and swampy in some places.

After 0.5 mile, just before the trail reaches the rail bed, it intersects the white-blazed Switchback Trail. Turn right and climb the hill. The half mile trail is steep and rocky; note the changes in size and type of rock as you ascend. Near the top, stone steps aid in the climb.

The Ridge Trail is marked with yellow diamonds. The trail is also marked with blue diamond badges indicating that it is part of the Highlands Trail, a long-distance trail under development that traverses the Highlands region of New Jersey and goes into New York. The Highlands Trail will eventually continue through Pennsylvania.

Turn left and follow the Ridge/Highlands Trail blazes. Descend the ridge after 0.75 mile, down the ravine to the Pine Run. Cross the stream on rocks and continue up the other side, up the slope. The trail climbs steeply up the rocky hill, then levels out, winding past sunny fields and wildflower meadows. The preserve, though not the Highlands Trail, ends at Myler Road. (To continue on the Highlands Trail, turn right and follow the blue diamonds.) Turn around, and return down the Highlands Trail until you meet the Pine Run again. Cross the stream.

For an optional, *strenuous* half-mile detour to gain the only access to the river in the preserve, turn right to head downhill along the creek. The descent along the stream is over rocks, along an old trail (not maintained) that is rocky, steep, and slippery, especially close to the stream, as it descends to the bottom of the ravine. It crosses an abandoned gravel rail bed, which had been a spur line for the paper mill. The preserve includes a very small portion of the rail bed several hundred feet on either side of the stream, and the rest is off-limits to the public. Continue along the stream until it joins the river. Return to the Ridge/Highlands Trail the way you came down.

As it winds downhill, the trail passes several charcoal landings. Look for flattened, cleared circular areas with black soil. The landings are remnants of a long-ago industry. Trees were cut down and burned to make charcoal, which was used as fuel in nearby forges or shipped downriver. Because charcoal is lighter than raw wood, it was economically more efficient to burn it onsite than to ship logs. Charcoal-making devastated huge swaths of forest in Pennsylvania and New Jersey, until anthracite coal replaced charcoal as an economical fuel.

Go by several enormous boulder outcrops, excellent vantage points from which to view Kittatinny Ridge to the northwest or just to contemplate the passage of time. Immediately upon passing these rocks, you will hear the sound of a waterfall.

Descend into a rocky ravine via steep wooden steps to cross the Scout Run, passing an artificial waterfall (note the hardened bags of concrete). Bear right to continue uphill and along the ridge via the Ridge/Highlands Trail for another 0.5 mile to the parking area.

MORE INFORMATION

There are no restrooms. Musconetcong Gorge Preserve is open sunrise to sunset. Dogs must be leashed. Hunting is permitted throughout the preserve; during hunting season, wear orange or confine visits to Sundays, when hunting is prohibited.

The Hunterdon Hiking Club maintains the trails. Musconetcong Gorge Preserve, 1020 State Route 31, Lebanon, NJ 08833; 908-782-1158; www.co.hunterdon.nj.us/depts/parks/guides/MusconetcongGorge.htm.

3

LEHIGH VALLEY

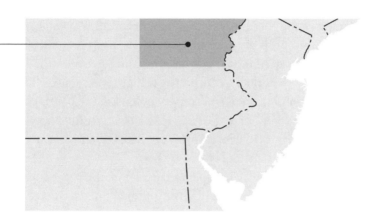

THE LEHIGH VALLEY IS A LABEL FOR A CULTURAL AREA rather than a geographic one, for what is called the Lehigh Valley is a subset of the actual valley of the Lehigh River. The river flows 103 miles south-southeast from the Lehigh Marshes in the Poconos, into the Delaware River at Easton. The Lehigh Valley in Pennsylvania, though, is just the greater Allentown-Bethlehem-Easton metropolitan area, or Lehigh, Northampton, and Carbon counties—three of the seven counties in the river's watershed.

The most prominent geographic feature in the Lehigh Valley is the Kittatinny Ridge, also called Blue Mountain. The 1,500–1,700-foot-high Kittatinny, which is the easternmost ridge of the Appalachian range, marks the southern boundary between the ridge-and-valley province and the Piedmont.

The ridge-and-valley province is a series of parallel ridges, composed of hard metamorphic rock, primarily quartzite, and valleys of softer sedimentary rock like shale, sandstone, and limestone. All the ridges, including the Kittatinny, tend in a southwest-northeast direction. Finding Blue Mountain in its way as it sought to head south, the Lehigh River decided to make its own path. It excised a gap in the ridge (the Lehigh Gap) and then proceeded south before turning to go east toward the Delaware.

Driving north toward the Kittatinny Ridge from Philadelphia never fails to elicit in me chills of delight. As my car approaches from the south and the long ridge comes into view, stretching across the horizon, I usually exclaim, "There it is! The Appalachian Trail!" That the Appalachian Trail (AT) could actually go more than 2,000 miles, from Maine to Georgia, is such a tremendous feat of the imagination of the planners, the determination of the builders, and the devotion of its contemporary maintainers that it deserves commemoration every time we see it. Hikes on the AT go along the top of the ridge. These include Appalachian Trail/Route 309 to Bake Oven Knob (Trip 44) and Lehigh Gap West and East (Trips 45 and 46).

To the south of the Kittatinny is the Piedmont section of the Lehigh Valley (described more fully in the Southeastern Pennsylvania and Delaware section), a region of varied topography and terrain. The southern boundary of the Lehigh Valley is marked by South (or Lehigh) Mountain. Hikes in the Lehigh Valley Piedmont include Louise W. Moore Park (Trip 38), Jacobsburg Environmental Education Center (Trip 39), Monocacy Trail (Trip 40), Walking Purchase Park (Trip 41), Lehigh Parkway (Trip 42), and South Mountain Preserve (Trip 43).

North of the ridge, in the ridge-and-valley section, the rugged terrain and dramatic topography make for a qualitatively different hike. The hikes in this area include Hickory Run State Park (Trip 47) and Glen Onoko Falls/Lehigh Gorge State Park (Trip 48).

Many hikes in the Lehigh Valley are located in the Highlands region. If you are looking for more places to hike in the Pennsylvania Highlands, you can also consult the AMC's *Pennsylvania Highlands Regional Map and Guide* and AMC's *Hike the Highlands* hiking cards. Both are available at www.outdoors. org/hikethehighlands.

TRIP 37
MARITON WILDLIFE SANCTUARY

Location: Williams Township, PA (Northampton County)
Rating: Easy–Moderate
Distance: 3.5 miles
Elevation Gain: 500 feet
Estimated Time: 2.0 hours
Maps: USGS Riegelsville and Easton; trail map available at nature center

Trails in the Mariton Sanctuary wind up and down steep, rocky forested hills in a dramatic cliffside location above the Delaware River.

DIRECTIONS
From the Pennsylvania Turnpike's Willow Grove exit (Exit 343), take Route 611 north to Riegelsville. Turn left onto Spring Hill Road (at the north border of the town), go about 0.5 mile, then turn right onto Sunnyside Drive and go another 0.5 mile (crossing over County Line Road). The sanctuary is on the left, where you will find parking for nineteen cars. *GPS coordinates*: 40° 36.450′ N, 75° 12.283′ W.

TRAIL DESCRIPTION
The Mariton Wildlife Sanctuary packs more diversity, history, and scenic beauty into its 200 acres than many larger natural areas have in theirs. In part this is because of the sanctuary's heritage—forest, then farmland, then country residence, now forest again. In part it is because of Mariton's location—on the slopes of Bougher Hill along the Delaware, on the border between two geologic provinces. And in part it is because the sanctuary is so well laid out and well maintained, balanced between the interests of wildlife and humans.

Begin the hike at the nature center, which has exhibits relating to the site's natural history. Take the lower of the two trailheads that begin at the woods' edge behind the building—not the Woods Trail (your return route) but the Main Trail, which is slightly downhill past the residence. Note the wooden post, painted yellow at the top. Each trail is blazed with a different color, and the colors are noted on the trail map. The posts are well spaced—not obtrusive, but frequent enough to reassure you that you're on the trail you want.

The wide natural-surface trail heads downhill and into a middle-aged woods (50–75 years old) with many tall tulip trees. Mariton is an excellent

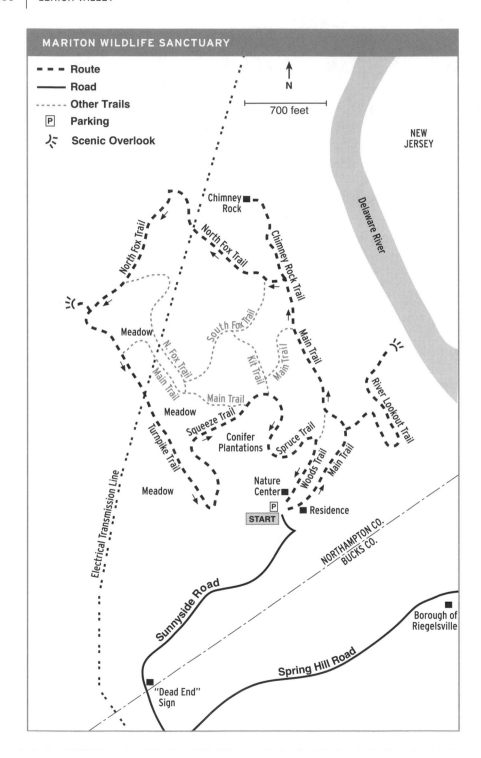

MARITON WILDLIFE SANCTUARY

- - - Route
—— Road
····· Other Trails
P Parking
ᒉ Scenic Overlook

N

700 feet

NEW JERSEY

Delaware River

Chimney Rock

North Fox Trail

North Fox Trail

Chimney Rock Trail

Meadow

South Fox Trail

N Fox Trail

Kit Trail

Main Trail

Main Trail

Main Trail

Main Trail

Meadow

Squeeze Trail

River Lookout Trail

Conifer Plantations

Spruce Trail

Turnpike Trail

Woods Trail

Main Trail

Meadow

Nature Center

Electrical Transmission Line

P
START

Residence

NORTHAMPTON CO.
BUCKS CO.

Sunnyside Road

Borough of Riegelsville

Spring Hill Road

"Dead End" Sign

place to observe the stages of forest succession. Until the mid-1900s, the formerly wooded slopes were mostly cleared for farming, but by the time Mary and Tony Guerrero (the "Mar" and "Ton" of Mariton) acquired the property in 1949, cultivation had ceased. Forests regrew in abandoned fields. The first trees to colonize fields in this area have long been (and still are) sassafras and eastern red cedar; eventually tulip trees, oak, birch, hickory, maple, and others shade them out. Under the tall trees you can spot sassafras and red-cedar skeletons. In younger woods, the sassafras and red cedar are still vigorous; in very old woods they have disappeared.

The trail passes a bird blind after about 250 yards, then goes through a gap in an old wall of local fieldstone. Such walls in the woods are remnants of boundaries between former farm fields, which offered up the stones when they were plowed.

About 350 feet later, turn right onto the narrower River Lookout spur trail (blazed dark blue). The trail heads downhill, levels, and turns sharply left to traverse the east-facing slope. You can see the Delaware River through the trees, which are older and larger here than on the slope above. After about a quarter-mile, a rustic sign warns of sheer cliffs; the trail turns right and steeply downhill, becoming increasingly rocky; it passes through a profusion of rhododendrons and, after another 350 feet, abruptly ends at a bluff overlooking the river to the northeast. Edge out onto the outcrop and, in winter, take in excellent views.

The knobby light-pink, black-speckled rocks are granitic gneiss, a rock characteristic of the Reading Prong, which underlies the Highlands region that stretches from southeastern Pennsylvania into Connecticut. Many exposed gneisses in this area are Precambrian, 1 billion years old—some of the oldest rocks in North America. These stand in contrast to the red Triassic-era shales and sandstones, much younger (200 million to 250 million years old), which can be seen just south along the Delaware below the Monroe border fault at Riegelsville—spectacularly exposed at the Nockamixon Cliffs in Pennsylvania and the Milford Bluffs in New Jersey (see Trip 35).

Backtrack to the Main Trail; turn right and continue through woods, paralleling the River Trail below. The deer "exclosure" to the right, a fenced area, is a long-term experiment to assess whether excluding deer affects the diversity of vegetation. You shouldn't see much difference, though, between the exclosure and the rest of the woods. Many properties surrounding the sanctuary are hunted; deer density has not yet adversely affected the quality of Mariton's woods.

Old roads following stone walls indicate these woods were former farm fields.

Continue slightly uphill on the Main Trail, bearing right at the next intersection. At the next junction, bear right onto the black-blazed Chimney Rock Trail, which begins as a continuation of the old road, going downhill gradually, then more steeply, becoming narrow and rocky. About a third of a mile from the start, it turns sharply left to Chimney Rock, an eroded remnant of a scarp of Precambrian gneiss. The rock formation is easy to climb, affording a 360-degree view of the woods and (in winter) a 90-degree bend in the Delaware.

Backtrack, but before reaching the Main Trail, turn right at the red-blazed Fox Trail, then right again after 0.1 mile onto the North Fox Trail, a narrow footpath that parallels the Chimney Rock Trail below. Head downhill, passing under a power line after 0.25 mile, then continue very steeply down for another 0.15 mile (rocks may be slippery) to a hairpin turn back uphill. At the hilltop, bear right onto the gray-blazed Pine Circle. After 0.1 mile, take the very short spur trail (right) to the Stouts Valley overlook. In winter, the northwest-facing cliff affords a view of the valley of the Frya Run, toward Elephant Rock (right) and Hexenkopf (Witch's Head) Rock (far left), outstanding formations of extremely old Precambrian gneiss. (Stouts Valley, like Bougher Hill, is a Highlands Critical Treasure.)

Return to Pine Circle (note the private drive to the right), then bear right as the trail makes a Y. Stay straight at the intersection with Main Trail, continuing uphill. Exit the woods and wander the unmarked mowed paths that crisscross the meadows. The meadows, primarily sassafras saplings and wildflowers, are in the first stages of forest succession—and they'll never get to the next stage. Preserve managers mow these 15 acres annually to prevent them from becoming forest, adding diversity to the sanctuary's habitat to support such wildlife as ground-nesting birds and butterflies.

Return to the trail. At the Y, bear slightly right onto the Turnpike Trail (blazed light blue); follow the power line for about 100 feet, then veer left downhill through a grassy area to woods. The trail, an old straight road, follows a stone wall downhill. Contrast the size and density of tree species to the right and left of the trail; the woods to the right is at least 25 years younger.

At the Y after about 0.2 mile, bear left onto the sand-blazed Squeeze Trail. (To shorten the hike by 0.5 mile, bear right instead and return via Turnpike Trail to the nature center.) The Squeeze Trail begins steeply uphill, then, following an old road, levels off. To the right are conifer plantations (Norway spruce planted in the 1950s and 1960s as erosion control). Bear right at the Main Trail intersection, then take a sharp right at the Spruce Trail (blazed green). The dense, dark-green conifers on the right contrast dramatically with the light, open canopy of oak, gray birch, hickory, and other hardwoods to the left. Owls nest in the conifer woods.

The trail winds downhill, ending at the Woods Trail (blazed brown); turn right and continue another 0.2 mile to the nature center, where you began.

MORE INFORMATION

Restrooms are located at the nature center and are accessible 24 hours a day, 7 days a week. Trails are open sunrise to sunset 7 days a week. Dogs must be leashed. Mariton Wildlife Sanctuary, 240 Sunnyside Rd., Easton, PA 18042; 610-258-6574; www.natlands.org/preserves/preserve.asp?fldPreserveId=48.

At Riegelsville, in Bucks County just to the south, there is a gem of a suspension bridge over the Delaware, built in 1904 by the John A. Roebling firm of Brooklyn Bridge fame. In Ringing Rocks County Park, nearby, enjoy a fun short hike to see a field of diabase boulders.

SHINING GEMS IN A GREEN RIBBON:
PENNSYLVANIA HIGHLANDS CRITICAL TREASURES

The Pennsylvania Highlands, part of the four-state Highlands conservation region, span 1.9 million acres and 13 counties arching from the Lehigh Valley along the Delaware River to South Mountain on the Mason-Dixon Line. The Highlands are an irreplaceable resource, providing clean air and water, wildlife habitat, farmland, and recreational lands for millions of people who live in southeastern and south-central Pennsylvania, as well as New Jersey, Delaware, and Maryland.

Within the Pennsylvania Highlands are numerous diverse natural areas, cultural resources, and historic places. Forming a greenway—a corridor of undeveloped land—is the objective of the Pennsylvania Highlands Trail Network. Led by the Appalachian Mountain Club, the trail network is a partnership among nonprofit and governmental organizations; its activities complement similar ones in the New York and New Jersey Highlands and will eventually create a multistate regional recreational system.

The 130-mile Highlands Trail traverses the New York Highlands and almost all of the New Jersey Highlands. The Pennsylvania Highlands Trail Network will extend the Highlands Trail into the Pennsylvania Highlands. Within and adjacent to the Pennsylvania Highlands are many existing trails, including both long-distance trails and short trails contained within individual parks and natural areas. The Pennsylvania Highlands Trail Network will create connections between existing trails and will add new trail segments, connecting the spine of the trail to nearby communities and local trails.

To increase awareness of the Highlands' ecological and recreational value, the Pennsylvania Committee of the Highlands Coalition has identified 47 Critical Treasures, top-priority areas for conservation within the region (see Appendix A for a list). These natural areas offer opportunities for public recreational access and in many cases need protection from development. In Pennsylvania, the Critical Treasures include public parks and wildlife management areas as well as entire watersheds and bioregions.

To find out more about the Pennsylvania Highlands Trail Network, the Critical Treasures, and other conservation/recreation opportunities, visit www.outdoors.org/hikethehighlands. For more information about the Highlands, see "The Highlands Conservation Act and AMC" on page 104.

TRIP 38
LOUISE W. MOORE PARK

Location: Lower Nazareth, PA (Northampton County)
Rating: Easy
Distance: 2.5 miles
Elevation Gain: Minimal
Estimated Time: 1.25 hours
Maps: USGS Nazareth; sign with a map located at the park; trail map available online

Louise W. Moore Park provides a novice- and family-friendly experience on a 5-mile multiuse trail system just outside Bethlehem. This open, grassy setting includes a windmill and small wetlands; the surrounding farmlands provide picturesque landscape views.

DIRECTIONS
Take the Pennsylvania Turnpike Northeast Extension (Route 476 North) exit to Exit 56, U.S. 22 east toward Allentown. From Route 22, take the exit onto PA 33 north toward Stroudsburg. Exit at Hecktown Road, turn right, and go 0.3 mile. Turn left onto Country Club Road. After 0.1 mile, you'll see the park entrance on the right; turn here to reach the park's trail system. The remainder of the park is located on the left side of the road and includes playgrounds and tennis courts. The parking lot has space for approximately 30 cars. *GPS coordinates*: 40° 41.519′ N, 75° 17.675′ W

TRAIL DESCRIPTION
Despite its proximity to the city of Bethlehem, the 100-acre Louise W. Moore Park seems to belong to a more remote area, with its woods and rural vistas. A portion of the park has been designed as an arboretum. Trees from North America, Europe, and Asia have been planted and are identified with markers. There is also a small mature woodland with a self-guided nature trail. This park is a nice place for a walk and a picnic with children or with anyone who doesn't have much experience in the outdoors. The route includes various loop trails with options for increasing the mileage of the walk.

From the parking lot, face the restroom and head toward the perimeter of the park at the upper right-hand corner of the parking lot. You will find the beginning of the 2-mile Perimeter Trail, a flat, worn path through the

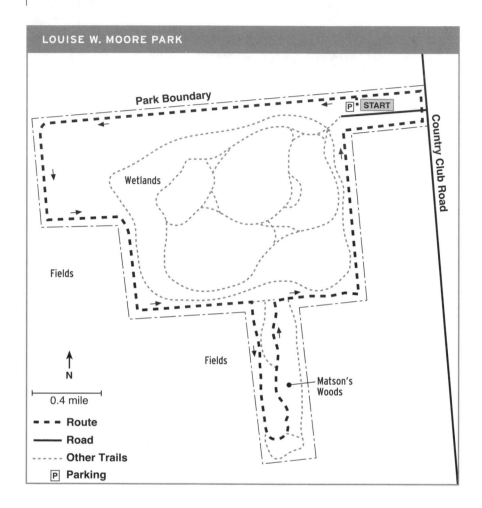

LOUISE W. MOORE PARK

Park Boundary

P START

Country Club Road

Wetlands

Fields

N

0.4 mile

- - - Route
—— Road
----- Other Trails
P Parking

Fields

Matson's
Woods

grass that follows the park's boundary along a fencerow of native black walnut, hackberry, and Osage orange trees to your right. These trees were planted long ago to create living boundaries between farm fields or along property lines. (Honeysuckle, privet, and other non-native invasive shrubs have grown up here too.) The arboretum trees to your left were planted more recently, as decorative elements in the park's landscape. Feel free to stray off the trail and examine the many trees on either side. The route is easily followed by keeping the boundary on your right.

Continue along the perimeter until you reach a wooded area to the right; follow the Self-Guided Nature Trail loop through the woods and back to the Perimeter Trail. This area, known as Matson's Woods, contains 6.6 acres of mature oak woodland. A nice place to explore in spring, it features an abundant amount of blooming wildflowers in April and May.

Once you leave Matson's Woods, turn right to continue on the Perimeter Trail, heading toward the parking lot. At this point you have hiked approximately 2.0 miles.

To continue, walk toward the kiosk at the park entrance and take the paved path that loops around the cattail wetlands and the windmill. The windmill, which was installed in the park as a decorative feature near the pond, seems reminiscent of the farm that existed here before Louise W. Moore purchased the property and donated it for use as a park and an arboretum. (Moore, a philanthropist in the Lehigh Valley, was married to industrialist Hugh Moore, who founded the Dixie Cup Company.) The wetlands are remnants of former ponds. Rainwater soaks into the limestone bedrock under the park, resulting in wet areas that don't hold water for long. The windmill pumps water into the wetlands for demonstration purposes.

MORE INFORMATION

Restrooms, picnic tables, and rentable pavilions are available at the park. The trails are mostly used by walkers and joggers; bicycles and horses are also allowed. Louise W. Moore Park is managed by Northampton County's Parks and Recreation Division; 610-746-1975; www.recreationparks.net/PA/northampton/louise-w-moore-park-nazareth.

TRIP 39
JACOBSBURG ENVIRONMENTAL
EDUCATION CENTER

Location: Wind Gap, PA (Northampton County)
Rating: Easy–Moderate
Distance: 2.5 miles
Elevation Gain: 200 feet
Estimated Time: 1.75 hours
Maps: USGS Wind Gap; trail maps available at trailhead and at the website for the Jacobsburg Environmental Education Center

This is a short, easy hike with great variety. It winds through ridge-top meadows to an old-growth forest along a dramatic ravine, in an area resonant with history.

DIRECTIONS
From the south: Take Route 33 north to the Belfast exit; turn right onto Henry Road and then take the immediate left onto Belfast Road. Cross Bushkill Creek and look for the parking lot on the left. You will find ample parking.

From the north: Take Route 33 south to the Belfast exit, turn left onto Henry Road, and follow the directions above. *GPS coordinates:* 40° 46.966′ N, 75° 17.599′ W.

TRAIL DESCRIPTION
The peace and beauty of the Jacobsburg district belie its history. The deep, hemlock-studded ravine through which the Bushkill Creek flows seems as if it has been wild forever; the ridge-top fields seem to have been placed exactly where the mountain views are best. Yet it was here that the William Henry family manufactured guns used in the American Revolution and the Civil War, as well as by the settlers who explored the western frontier. A century ago, Jacobsburg was an industrial community; nature was not celebrated but ravaged—the Bushkill Creek was dammed for water power, the hills were cleared of trees to fire the furnace, and the ravine echoed with the sounds of small-arms manufacturing.

You can hike through Jacobsburg's 1,168 acres of woods, meadows, and streams without contemplating its historical significance. But knowing the historical context adds another dimension to the hike. The essential characteristic

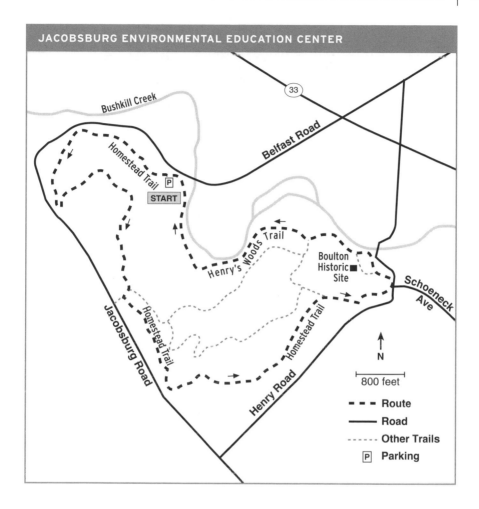

of this place is not the despoliation of nature, but rather its redemption through preservation and conservation; indeed, it was James Henry, a gunsmith and forester and descendant of the William Henry family, who in 1883 championed the first Pennsylvania stream protection regime to promote reforestation of cleared stream banks.

The hike begins at the main Belfast Road parking lot. Head south (away from the information kiosk) to the trailhead for the Homestead Trail (blue blaze). Trails in this park are generally well signed at intersections and blazed consistently. The Homestead Trail is a multiuse trail open to bikes and horses as well as hikers.

The trail gradually ascends through a meadow and then enters young woods of oak, ash, hickory, walnut, and cherry trees. In spring and summer, wildflowers abound on the forest floor and warblers sing in the treetops.

Follow the Homestead Trail as it bends away from Belfast Road below, climbing the hill. Bear left when the trail forks just past a power-line crossing. Pass under the power line again, then reach a meadow, where the trail once again forks. Bear right, following the blue blazes, and go through a meadow of summer-blooming wildflowers. Pass through a hedgerow to reach another meadow, a former farm field. After a cluster of park maintenance structures, the trail turns right, continuing through meadows where bluebird boxes have been placed. Tree swallows are just as likely to have taken up residence here; both of these blue species like to dart out from fieldside perches to snag insects.

As the trail passes the Jacobsburg Road entrance (small parking lot), you reach another fork. Both paths here are part of the Homestead Trail; take the right-hand one (not the spur to the parking lot) to go along the edge of the field. The trail then reaches its high point, a ridge-top meadow with expansive views of Kittatinny Ridge (Blue Mountain); Wind Gap is directly to the north.

The trail descends past private residences on the right, then reaches a T; turn right, heading southeast. The way becomes steeper, reaching the bottom of the hill at the intersection of Henry Road and Schoeneck Avenue. Follow the yellow-blazed trail along Henry Road, then bending left to parallel the creek. The trail passes through the Boulton Historic Site, which preserves for public access some of the buildings from the small-arms manufacturing era. Interpretive signs along the trail describe the economically self-sufficient Boulton community.

Follow the All Trail Traffic signs around the site, to the bridge over the Bushkill Creek. At this point the orange-blazed, pedestrian-only Henry's Woods Trail begins. It is a loop that follows the creek from the parking lot, so you can take either side to get to your car. Each has its merits; if you have time, try both. The far, flatter side (0.75 mile) traces the course of the creek in the valley and offers views up the gorge; the near, steeper side (0.5 mile) climbs up the ravine and looks down through the dense forest. The steep side is the one described here.

Henry's Woods is an old-growth forest, one that has not been logged; spared by the Henrys, its stands of hemlock, birch (yellow and black), oak (red, white, and chestnut), sugar maple, basswood, and sycamore contain huge trees up to 350 years old. Like all hemlock ravines, this one is dark, shady, moist, mossy, and often misty; its rocky slopes are covered with ferns, maple-leaf viburnum, and rhododendron. And this ravine, with its giant trees, seems deeper, darker, and mistier than most, a primitive forest that stayed into the modern era.

The narrow, steep trail has slippery roots, but the signs warning of danger seem overly dramatic, perhaps in keeping with the outsize scale of the place itself. The trail ascends steeply to a crest, offering some views to the east, then drops steeply and continues down a set of wooden steps to a path along the creek to the parking lot.

MORE INFORMATION

The center office on the corner of Belfast and Jacobsburg roads is open 8 A.M. to 4 P.M., Monday through Friday. The main parking area on Belfast Road is open from sunrise to sunset, 7 days a week. There are more than 18.5 miles of trails in the park. There are portable toilets at the trailhead for Homestead Trail. Jacobsburg Environmental Education Center, 835 Jacobsburg Road, Wind Gap, PA 18091; 908-879-1339; www.dcnr.state.pa.us/stateParks/parks/jacobsburg.aspx.

SONG OF THE ETERNAL MORNING

This is the only bird whose note affects me like music, affects the flow and tenor of my thought, my fancy and imagination. It lifts and exhilarates me. It is inspiring. It is a medicative draught to my soul. . . . It changes all hours to an eternal morning.
—Henry David Thoreau, on the wood thrush

Its song is arrestingly beautiful: a trill, followed by a flutelike *ee-oh-lay* and a bubbling coda. The song may be distinctive, but the singer is not. The robin-sized wood thrush is not spectacularly colored; it is brown and has a white breast speckled with brown spots. It spends the spring and summer breeding seasons in the deciduous woods of the eastern United States, and during those months the male can be heard singing from treetops in remote forests, parks, and even suburban backyards all over the Delaware Valley.

What it seems to require above all else is woods. That does not mean just trees—trees alone do not make a woods. A woods requires three layers: a high canopy of mature trees; an understory (middle layer) of shrubs and medium-sized trees; and a ground layer of leafy plants (vines, wildflowers, and ferns) and plenty of leaf litter (decaying organic matter). A healthy woods has rich soil to provide nutrients, a balance between old and young growth, and a diversity of scales to accommodate a wide spectrum of wildlife.

One reason wood thrushes need woods is their diet. In spring and summer, they eat spiders, caterpillars, beetles, ants, and flies, which proliferate in areas with diverse shrubs and wildflowers and a rich bottom layer of soil and leaf litter; in fall, they eat fruits and berries, which are produced by small trees, shrubs, and vines. Because they nest close to the ground in shrubs or low tree trunks, a dense layer of vegetation provides cover from predators.

The wood thrush is the "poster bird" for the decline of neotropical migrant songbirds. Its numbers have been decreasing rapidly throughout its range since the 1970s. Loss and fragmentation of habitat—both in Central America, where the wood thrush winters, and North America, where it breeds—are the most probable culprits.

When you hear a wood thrush singing, you are hearing the sound of a healthy, intact woods. That sound may be especially comforting to those who hear it as a sign of the natural world in harmony.

TRIP 40
MONOCACY TRAIL

Location: Bethlehem, PA (Northampton County)
Rating: Moderate
Distance: 6.0 miles
Elevation Gain: Minimal
Estimated Time: 3.0 hours
Maps: USGS Catasauqua; trail map available online at the website for the Monocacy Creek Watershed Association

The Monocacy Trail parallels the scenic Monocacy Creek while unveiling the past and present of the city of Bethlehem. The hike is an out-and-back route with flat terrain traversing wooded areas and the historic downtown.

DIRECTIONS
Take the Pennsylvania Turnpike Northeast Extension (Route 476 North) exit to Exit 56, Route 22 east toward Allentown. Take the Center Street/Route 512 exit. Turn left at Bath Pike/Center Street/Route 512 and go 1.7 miles. Turn right onto Illick's Mill Road. At the bottom off the hill, take the first left after Monocacy Creek Road to enter the parking lot across from Illick's Mill or across the street from it. The parking lot has space for 40 cars. *GPS coordinates*: 40° 38.519′ N, 75° 22.787′ W.

TRAIL DESCRIPTION
The Monocacy Trail parallels the last 3.0 miles of the 20-mile-long Monocacy Creek, a small but very high-quality waterway, as it winds through historic Bethlehem. Naturally cool, the creek harbors a rich aquatic wildlife population, including wild trout, and attracts many species of migratory birds. The hike traverses a history-in-miniature of industry in southeastern Pennsylvania, from grain mills to steel mills. Its turnaround at the Lehigh River connects to the Lehigh Canal Towpath, a trail running along the river between Easton and Allentown. The hike provides opportunities to explore the heart of the city's historic district.

From the parking lot, face away from the road and enter the trail marked "Monocacy Nature Center." It begins on a grassy path that winds through a brushy area next to the creek. The Monocacy Creek is fed in part by springs

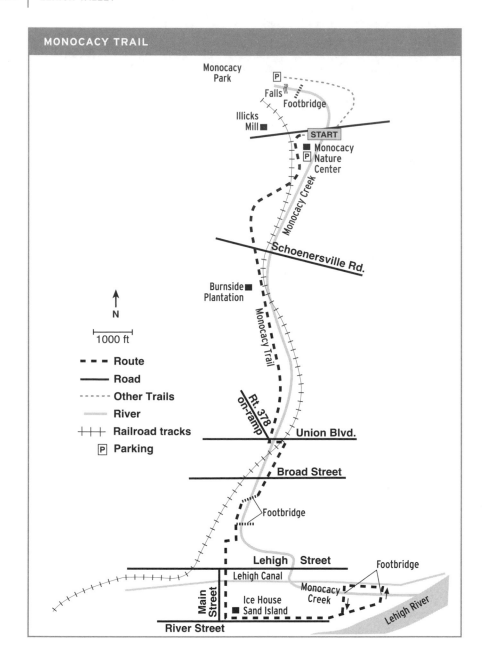

MONOCACY TRAIL

Monocacy Park
Falls
Footbridge
Illicks Mill ■
START
■ Monocacy Nature Center
Monocacy Creek
Schoenersville Rd.
Burnside ■ Plantation
Monocacy Trail

N
1000 ft

- - - Route
—— Road
----- Other Trails
—— River
+++ Railroad tracks
P Parking

Rt. 378 On-ramp
Union Blvd.
Broad Street
Footbridge
Lehigh Street
Footbridge
Lehigh Canal
Main Street
Monocacy Creek
Ice House ■
Sand Island
Lehigh River
River Street

flowing from underground beds of limestone. The rock is naturally alkaline, and the springs remain at a constant temperature of 55 degrees. The combination of cool temperature and low acidity creates conditions that support a complex aquatic food web, including a naturally reproducing brown trout population.

Across from the parking lot is the historic 1856 Illick's Mill, which was an operational water-powered gristmill until 1915, one of seven such mills on the creek. It has been converted to a community environmental center. The center works to restore the creek to its natural state through stream bank plantings, cleanups, channel modification, and other projects. Surrounding the mill is Monocacy Park, built in the 1930s by the Civilian Conservation Corps (CCC).

From the parking lot, enter the trail at the sign for the Monocacy Nature Center, a city-owned sanctuary that extends for a mile along the creek and is a local haven for migratory birds. The trail starts out paved and then becomes grassy. It winds though floodplain woods for about a quarter-mile, then crosses a railroad tracks (Caution: this is an active railway).

After crossing, bear left and follow the trail along a wide-open area for 0.6 mile. Reach an intersection with busy Schoenersville Road, and cross it. The trail merges with the driveway to Burnside Plantation, an eighteenth-century farm that was the homestead of James Burnside, a Moravian missionary. Today it is a living history museum. You can take a self-guided tour of the gardens and buildings, including a 1748 farmhouse. Moravians (a German Protestant sect) founded Bethlehem on the banks of the Monocacy Creek in 1741. The other side of the creek is an industrial area.

The trail is a grassy path as it passes behind Burnside Plantation. It hugs the creek for 0.6 mile on a red-shale gravel surface with some wooden walkways. At Union Boulevard, turn left and walk along the sidewalk. At the first traffic light, turn right and cross Union Boulevard to pick up the trail. Follow the red-shale surface along the creek and walk through Johnston Park. Here, the creek's pools and riffles provide an excellent habitat for trout, evidenced by the ubiquitous anglers. The attractive walls were built by the CCC.

Pass under the Broad Street Bridge. To the left is the Historic Bethlehem Museum's Colonial Industrial Quarter, a group of restored historic buildings. Here, you'll find the Water Works (built in 1762), site of America's first pumped town water system, tannery (built in 1761), and Luckenbach Mill (built in 1869), as well as ruins of other early manufacturing buildings. You can explore this area and return to the trail. This is also an access point to walk around historic downtown Bethlehem, including the Moravian Museum. The Historic Bethlehem Visitor Center is at 505 Main Street, up the hill past the restored area. To continue on the Monocacy Trail, turn right and cross over the stone bridge. Turn left along the railroad line into a parking lot and pass under the Hill-to-Hill Bridge.

The official trail ends as it intersects with Spring Street, but the hike continues, following streets and other trails. Cross the street, turn left, and continue on Spring Street until you reach Main Street. Turn right and go along the creek (on your left). Cross Lehigh Street, and continue on Main Street, passing an old railroad depot that has been converted into the Main Street Depot restaurant. Cross a bridge over the Lehigh Canal and Towpath.

You are now on Sand Island. Turn left onto River Street. Continue to a gravel-surface trail, cross under the New Street Bridge, and pass a footbridge on your left. Continue to the end of the trail. Here is the mouth of the Monocacy Creek at its confluence with the Lehigh River. Across the river is an iconic view of the mighty, now-stilled blast furnaces and rolling mills of Bethlehem Steel Corporation, once the second-largest steel producer in the United States. The mill ceased steelmaking operations in 1995. In 2009, it was converted into a casino. You have now completed your journey through industrial history along the Monocacy Creek.

Turn left to cross the small steel footbridge (made of steel manufactured in Minnesota). Turn left again, and walk along the Lehigh Canal on the gravel towpath, with the creek on your left. The towpath reaches a footbridge at a historic canal lock. Turn left over the bridge, and retrace your steps back through Bethlehem and along the creek to return to Illick's Mill.

MORE INFORMATION

Restrooms are available in Illick's Mill Park and at Sand Island. Illick's Mill Park also includes pavilions and picnic tables. The multiuse Monocacy Trail is managed by Bethlehem Parks and Recreation. Anglers often use the trail to access the Monocacy Creek. Additional information can be found at the websites for Monocacy Watershed Association (www.pipeline.com/~rlfreed/monoc .htm) and Illick's Mill (www.illicksmill.org). Bethlehem Parks and Recreation; 610-841-5831; www.bethlehem-pa.gov/parks/index.htm.

TRIP 41
WALKING PURCHASE PARK

Location: Fountain Hill, PA (Lehigh County)
Rating: Moderate
Distance: 4.0 miles
Elevation Gain: 450 feet
Estimated Time: 2.0 hours
Maps: USGS Allentown East

Offering more than 10 miles of multiuse trails, Walking Purchase Park is a hidden gem in the Lehigh Valley metropolitan area. This multiloop hike traverses the Lehigh Mountain's rocky and diverse deciduous forest.

DIRECTIONS

Take the Northeast Extension of the Pennsylvania Turnpike (I-476 North) to Exit 44 toward Quakertown. Drive on Route 663 for 3.4 miles then turn left onto Route 309; continue for 6.4 miles then take a right onto Route 378 toward Bethlehem and drive for 4.3 miles. Turn left onto Seidersville Road and go 1.4 miles before turning slightly right onto Broadway. Then take a left onto Weil Street and drive 0.5 miles and turn left onto Cardinal Drive. Continue on Cardinal Drive even though there is a sign indicating no outlet. Cardinal Drive will turn into a dirt road known as Constitution Drive. Proceed slowly down to the bottom of the road. A parking lot will be on the left of the road just before the road comes to a T and railroad tracks. The parking lot can accommodate up to ten cars. *GPS coordinates*: 40° 36.346′ N, 75° 25.707′ W.

TRAIL DESCRIPTION

On September 19, 1737, three Pennsylvania colonists and three members of the Lenape nation set off from Wrightstown, Bucks County, on a walk to measure out a land purchase supposedly agreed to in a long-ago treaty. The six men were to walk for a day and a half. The Lenape did not know that the three colonists were accomplished runners who were hired by William Penn's sons to cover as much ground as possible in the allotted time. The runners—Edward Marshall, James Yates, and Solomon Jennings—"walked" 65 miles in 18 hours. As a result, the Penns acquired 750,000 acres of land from the

WALKING PURCHASE PARK

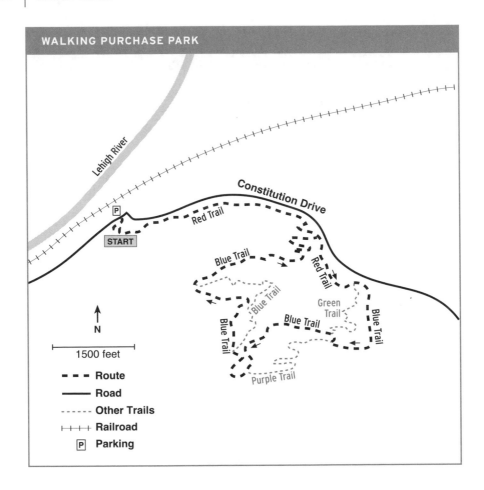

Lenape. Walking Purchase Park, which encompasses what was once Solomon Jennings's farm, is thought to be the location where the runners crossed the Lehigh River between Allentown and Bethlehem. This area is also referred to as South Mountain or Lehigh Mountain.

In the parking lot, face the railroad tracks and turn left to reach the beginning of the Red Trail. There is a red blaze on a tree and a small Walking Purchase Park sign. Although there is a large kiosk with a map in the parking lot, it does not include the portion of the park with the 10-mile trail network described here.

Begin on the Red Trail. The rocky path parallels the road (including three switchbacks) for two-thirds of a mile before intersecting with the Blue Trail. At this intersection, turn right. Follow the blue blazes through a series of five switchbacks with uphill climbs for a third of a mile. The trail levels at the top of the hill then meanders through the woods past a rock outcrop.

Walking Purchase Park features one of the largest relatively undisturbed woodlands along the Lehigh River south of Blue Mountain.

The surrounding forest is a large and relatively contiguous second-growth forest, an area that has experienced regrowth after a major disturbance. In this case the disturbance was timber harvesting. In the nineteenth century, Lehigh Mountain was an ideal place for harvesting trees, with the adjacent river suitable for transporting the logs to the growing cities of Bethlehem and Allentown. The mountain was also a source for iron ore.

The Blue Trail forks just after it begins to curve sharply left, away from the road. Take the right fork. The trail goes uphill and then downhill into a sort of bowl; noise from the nearby freight yard disappears. The dominant tree species in this forest are tulip tree, sassafras, red maple, black birch, and mixed oaks. This large tract of forest, one of the largest relatively undisturbed woodlands left along the Lehigh River south of Blue Mountain, supports habitat for a large number of species, including nesting and migratory birds. This is especially remarkable in light of its proximity to the developed areas surrounding Bethlehem and Allentown.

Remain on the Blue Trail until it forks again. Bear right to continue on the Blue Trail, going uphill on the other side of the bowl. The trail traverses a small series of switchbacks and winds through the woods past a built-up stone wall. At the intersection with the Purple Trail, go left to continue on the Blue Trail.

The trail goes downhill, away from the transmission line, then curves back to pass under the transmission line. The wide opening provides a view of Allentown and the Kittatinny Ridge. Continue on the Blue Trail. Pass the Green Trail (left) and the Purple Trail (right). After 0.25 mile, pass along a stream to the right. Soon the trail crosses it on a tiny wooden bridge. Shortly before the road (visible ahead), the Blue Trail ends at the Red Trail.

Turn left to follow the Red Trail, passing the obscure Green Trail to the left and then the transmission line. After crossing a stream, the Red Trail comes to an old road (a linear depression in the ground). Turn right and follow the red blazes left as the trail leads uphill. The road is visible straight ahead. After about 300 feet, the Red Trail intersects with the Blue Trail. You are now back to the first intersection you encountered. Go right to continue on the Red Trail back to the parking lot.

MORE INFORMATION

The park offers an extensive network of multiuse trails for mountain biking and hiking. Many of the trails have been built and maintained by the Valley Mountain Bikers. Walking Purchase Park is owned and managed by Salisbury Township, the city of Allentown, and Lehigh County. Allentown Department of Parks and Recreation, 3000 Parkway Boulevard, Allentown, PA 18104; 610-437-7750; www.allentownpa.gov/Government/DepartmentsBureaus/ParksandRecreation/tabid/112/Default.aspx.

TRIP 42
LEHIGH PARKWAY

Location: Allentown, PA (Lehigh County)
Rating: Easy–Moderate
Distance: 6.5 miles
Elevation Gain: 125 feet
Estimated Time: 2.75 hours
Maps: USGS Allentown East; trail map available online

Lehigh Parkway's trail runs along scenic, wooded Little Lehigh Creek with a multitude of historic, cultural, and natural sites to visit, including the Museum of Indian Culture and Lil-Le-Hi Trout Nursery. This park is family-friendly with mostly flat gravel-surface trails that have short and long loop options.

DIRECTIONS

Take the Northeast Extension of the Pennsylvania Turnpike (I-476 N) to Exit 44. Go north on Route 663 for 3.4 miles and turn left onto Route 309. After 9.2 miles, take I-78 west for 2.0 miles to Exit 57. Head north on Lehigh Street, bearing left at 15th Street, which becomes Jefferson Street. Take a sharp left turn onto Lehigh Parkway South, and enter the park at the main entrance. Follow the road to its end, next to the Klein Bridge, adjacent to a maintenance shed and a stone barn. There is a parking lot on the right. There is space for twenty or more cars, with additional parking lots nearby. *GPS coordinates*: 40° 34.748′ N, 75° 29.139′ W.

TRAIL DESCRIPTION

Lehigh Parkway is one of Allentown's most prominent and picturesque parks. Wending through woods and open areas along both sides of the lovely Little Lehigh Creek, it provides nature and outdoor enthusiasts with opportunities for scenic, family-friendly hikes. Along the way are delightful creekside historic and cultural sites. Because several bridges cross the creek, hikers can create short or long circuit routes. From the starting point of the hike described here, there are options ranging from 4.0 to 6.5 miles.

From the parking lot, head toward the crushed-stone trail by the creek and turn left, passing under Klein's Bridge. After the bridge, you'll see a series of signs marking the Rev. Dr. Ernest F. Andrews Memorial Planet Walk. This

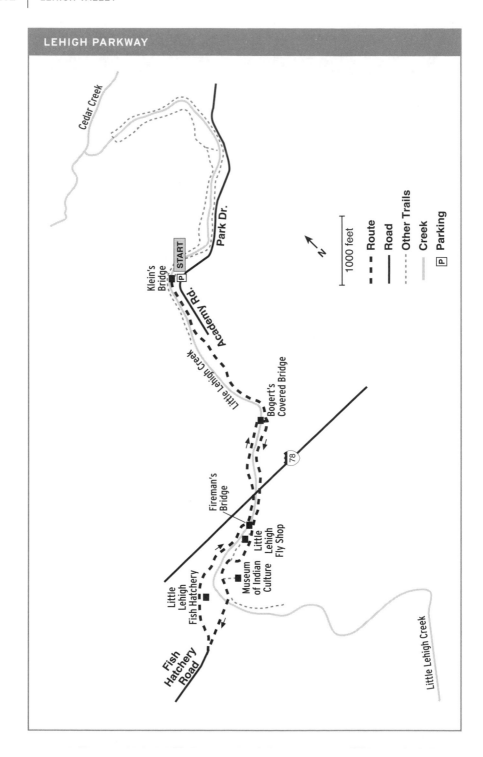

LEHIGH PARKWAY

unique 0.8-mile trail is a scale model of the solar system, designed to give hikers a true appreciation of the vastness of outer space. The trail leads past the police shooting range and into a mature oak-hickory woods. After the final sign (for Pluto), the trail passes Bogert's Bridge, one of seven covered bridges in the Lehigh Valley. Built in 1841, it is listed on the National Register of Historic Places. After following the trail past (not across) the bridge, you walk uphill and steeply downhill before passing under I-78.

Woods and open areas alternate along both banks of the creek. The banks may be flat or steep. The wide, shallow creek runs swiftly over rocks. It is easily accessible for fishing or viewing, yet its banks are well shaded with trees and shrubs. Listen for the rattling call of the belted kingfisher, a white-breasted blue-gray bird whose presence is a sure sign of a healthy fish population in any waterway.

Continue 0.6 mile, passing an old iron furnace stack on the left and Fireman's Bridge on the right. Little Lehigh Fly Shop is by the creek just beyond the bridge in a nineteenth-century spring house, across from a stone barn (with parking area and restrooms). Lessons in fly fishing, fly tying, and rod building are available at the shop. Fed in part by limestone springs, the creek's cool temperatures and its complex riffle-and-pools (shallow, fast-flowing gravel-bottom areas interspersed with deeper, calmer spots) help support a naturally reproducing population of brown trout.

At the shop, take the trail to the left of the Y. This leads to a garden and the Museum of Indian Culture to the left. Exhibits at the museum are designed to educate adults and children about the culture of the Lenape and other woodland Indians of the Northeast. At 0.2 mile past the museum, the trail reaches Fish Hatchery Road. Turn right and walk along the road, crossing the creek and turning immediately right to walk along the grassy path next to the creek toward the Lil-Le-Hi Trout Nursery. The fish hatchery is owned by the city of Allentown and managed by several local sporting clubs. Brook, brown, rainbow, and golden rainbow trout are raised here. More than 25,000 of these fish are annually released to stock the city's waterways, including the Little Lehigh Creek.

At the end of the grassy path is the White-Snyder House, where you can purchase trout food. The paved path to the left of the house leads to a gravel trail heading uphill sharply to the right. Follow this trail 0.4 mile to the Fireman's Bridge, but don't cross the bridge. Continue 0.6 mile to Hunter's Cabin, a restored structure dating from 1739 that is typical of an early German settler's dwelling. Pass under Bogert's Bridge. The trail then bears left past a stone barn.

Walk another 0.7 mile to return to Klein's Bridge. At this point you have hiked about 2.6 miles. If you would like to end the hike here, cross Klein's Bridge to return to the parking lot. Otherwise, continue along the creek.

If you do choose to continue, the trail reaches a parking area at a Y intersection. To end the hike here, go right to follow the trail over the Robin Hood Bridge, turn right and hike the last portion of the trail back to the parking lot by Klein's Bridge. At this point you have hiked 5.0 miles. To extend the hike another 1.5 miles, go to the left at the Y. This paved loop passes old furnace stacks, a series of exercise stations, a disc golf course, and a beautiful stone wall. At the parking lot at the top of the loop, cross the Lehigh Parkway North Bridge over the creek and turn right onto the gravel trail. Follow this trail past Robin Hood Bridge and end at the parking lot at Klein's Bridge.

MORE INFORMATION

Restrooms are located at the fly fishing shop, at the White-Snyder House, and elsewhere along the route; portable toilets are at the trailhead and other parking areas. Dogs are permitted if they are leashed. Fishing is allowed (and encouraged) at the park. Horses are permitted on gravel trails. The Museum of Indian Culture is open Friday through Sunday from noon to 4 P.M.; admission fees are $5 for adults and less for children (www.lenape.org). Lehigh Parkway is managed by Allentown Parks and Recreation, 3000 Parkway Boulevard, Allentown PA, 18104; 610-437-7757; www.allentownpa.gov/Government/DepartmentsBureaus/ParksandRecreation/tabid/112/Default.aspx.

TRIP 43
SOUTH MOUNTAIN PRESERVE

Location: Emmaus, PA (Lehigh County)
Rating: Easy–Moderate
Distance: 3.3 miles
Elevation Gain: 500 feet
Estimated Time: 1.5 hours
Maps: USGS Allentown East; trail map available online

Explore looping hillside trails that wind around boulders, surrounded by nineteenth-century quarries and a mature forest of hardwood trees.

DIRECTIONS

Take the Northeast Extension of the Pennsylvania Turnpike (I-476) to Exit 44. Take Route 663 north for 3.4 miles and turn left onto Route 309 north. Drive 9.2 miles and take I-78 west 0.2 miles to Exit 57. Go south on Lehigh Street toward Emmaus for 0.3 mile. Turn left onto 31st Street and travel for 0.3 mile. Turn right onto Emmaus Avenue and continue for 0.5 mile. (Emmaus Avenue turns into Dalton Avenue.) Stay left where the road forks to remain on Dalton Avenue. Turn left onto Alpine Street and go 0.2 mile, where the street will dead-end. Parking is permitted along the street and in the parking lot to the left, with room for more than ten cars. *GPS coordinates:* 40° 32.894′ N, 75° 28.997′ W.

TRAIL DESCRIPTION

South Mountain marks the southern edge of the Lehigh Valley, forming a cultural as well as topographical border. Sometimes called Lehigh Mountain, South Mountain is geologically part of a province of the Appalachian Range called the Reading Prong, a 45-mile long region of low hills and ridges. It is composed of hard, billion-year-old metamorphic rocks, such as granite, gneiss, and quartzite, which have been pushed up by forces from the southeast, where they now sit on 450 million-year-old sedimentary rocks (limestone and shale). The hard rocks are very resistant to erosion, so the hills and ridges stand markedly higher than the softer sedimentary rocks that surround them. About 150,000 years ago, glaciers covered the northwestern slope of the mountain. Melting and refreezing water broke up the hard rock; as the glaciers

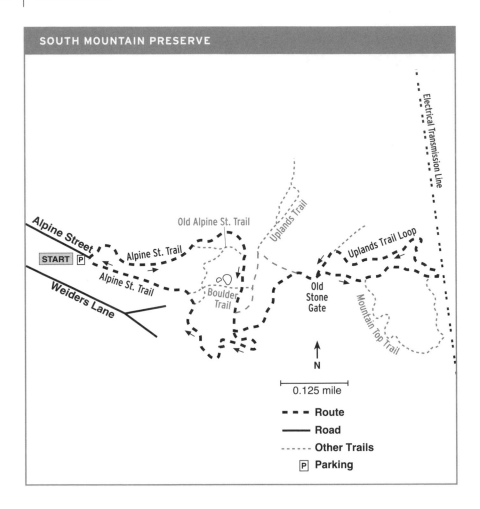

receded they left huge boulders littering the slopes. The mountain's rocky soils were not conducive to farming, but its forests were cleared for timber and charcoal in the eighteenth and nineteenth centuries; the mountain also was a resource for iron ore, magnetite, and sandstone (the stones for many buildings of Lehigh and Moravian universities were quarried here.)

From the parking lot at the end of Alpine Street, walk to the trailhead and turn left to proceed along the Alpine Street Trail. (As you hike the preserve, follow the map above closely because trails may not be blazed or marked by signs, but note that trails are often rerouted. You may encounter mountain bikers, as the trail system is multiuse, and bikers maintain the trails.)

Enter a maturing, second-growth forest consisting mostly of tulip tree and oak, as well as black birch, shagbark hickory, red ash, and beech. (A second-growth forest is a forest that has regrown after a major disturbance, in this case the century-old charcoal timbering.) Because of the forest's fertile, moist soils, wildflowers such as black cohosh, Indian cucumber-root, liverleaf, rue anemone, wild ginger, and wood geranium abound. The preserve also provides a prime breeding habitat for amphibians and nesting habitat for more than 59 species of birds.

At 0.3 mile, the rerouted Alpine Street Trail intersects with the old Alpine Street Trail section. The reroute goes to the left and may be hard to see. The closed section may still be evident. Do not use the trail that goes straight ahead; that section of the trail was closed to protect sensitive wetland areas. The area that you hike through includes vernal pools, seasonal wetlands that fill with fall and spring rain and snowmelt, and dry out in the hot summer months. (See "Jump in the Pool" on page 80.) The vernal pools on South Mountain provide critical habitats for many types of amphibians. Species such as the wood frog, spotted salamander, Jefferson salamander, and marbled salamander breed in these temporary pools. Some of the pools are artificial; they are remnants of mines for jasper (by American Indians) or iron ore (by European settlers). It is important to avoid these areas so that you do not disturb the amphibians, especially during the breeding season in the spring.

The Alpine Street Trail curves to the right and continues another 0.1 mile to the massive boulders of the preserve. These are a popular spot for bouldering or for taking a break to enjoy views of the South Mountain Preserve or glimpses of the Lehigh Valley.

After the boulders, the Alpine Street Trail and red-blazed Uplands Trail overlap briefly. Pass the first intersection, where the Uplands Trail forks sharply to the left (it may be obscure). Where the Uplands Trail forks, going left uphill and right downhill (coinciding with the yellow-blazed Alpine Street Trail), take the left fork. (If you miss the obscure first intersection, this one should be obvious.) After 0.3 miles, the Uplands Trail passes an old stone gatepost to the right. It is evidence of a road that ran perpendicular to the trail. The roadway was once used by horse-drawn carriages that hauled iron ore.

Just past the old stone gate, the Uplands Trail splits. Bear right at the Y and go uphill 0.5 mile, to the point where the trail bears left and comes close to a power line. Go downhill for about 0.5 mile, away from the power line, and meander to a T. Turn left and go 0.1 mile, to the point where the Uplands Trail coincides with the old road, going left to an old stone gate. After passing the old stone gate, bear left through the stone wall at the Y and hike downslope for 0.2 mile on the Uplands Trail. Be careful, as the trail is uneven in this section.

At the bottom of the downslope, the trail forms a T. Go to the left and continue on the Uplands Trail to where it overlaps with the Alpine Street

Trail. Turn left, continuing downhill on switchbacks, following the red/yellow blazes as the Uplands and Alpine Street trails overlap. Gradually descend the mountains on switchbacks, following the yellow-blazed Alpine Street Trail for 0.3 mile. After completing the switchback, continue another 0.2 mile on the trail, crossing over intermittent streams. Pass Boulder Trail twice on the right (it may be closed) and continue for 0.3 mile, crossing over an elevated walkway leading to the trailhead and parking lot.

MORE INFORMATION

South Mountain Preserve is managed by Wildlands Conservancy, a nonprofit organization dedicated to land preservation, river restoration, trail development, and environmental stewardship through education in the Lehigh Valley. The 300-acre South Mountain Preserve, along with adjacent Allentown parkland, comprise the 650-acre Robert Rodale Preserve. Many of the trails at the preserve have been built and rerouted by the Valley Mountain Bikers, a regional club. Mountain biking and bouldering are allowed on the preserve. A restroom is located near the parking lot at the Alpine Street trailhead. In the spring and fall, some trails are closed due to sensitive areas such as vernal pools. Because the preserve is surrounded by private property, be sure to stay on the trails and respect boundary markers. Wildlands Conservancy, 3701 Orchid Place, Emmaus, PA 18049; 610-965-4397; www.wildlandspa.org.

Location: New Tripoli, PA (Lehigh County)
Rating: Moderate–Difficult
Distance: 11.0 miles
Elevation Gain: 200 feet
Estimated Time: 5.5 hours
Maps: USGS New Tripoli and Slatedale; Pennsylvania Appalachian Trail map Section 3

On this scenic, rugged stretch of the Appalachian Trail along the crest of Kittatinny Mountain, challenge yourself to a ridge-top scramble over the Cliffs (the Knife Edge) and up Bear Rocks. Enjoy marvelous vistas along the way and at the rock outcrops at Bake Oven Knob, a celebrated hawk watch site.

DIRECTIONS

Take I-78 or Northeast Extension to Route 309 north; after approximately 23 miles Route 309 crests Blue Mountain. The State Game Lands 217 parking lot is on the right, where you will find space for twenty cars. If you miss it, turn around at the Blue Mountain Summit restaurant parking lot (AT crossing here). *GPS coordinates*: 40° 42.474′ N, 75° 48.478′ W.

The hike can be done as a two-car shuttle by parking at the Bake Oven Knob Road State Game Lands 217 lot. To reach Bake Oven Road, go south on Route 309 about 2.75 miles from the Blue Mountain Summit restaurant, and turn left onto Mountain Road. Go 2.0 miles and turn onto Bake Oven Knob Road (a gravel road); go 2.0 miles to the lot, where there is ample space for parking.

TRAIL DESCRIPTION

The Appalachian Trail (AT) in Pennsylvania has the reputation (exaggerated but not altogether unjustified) of being a long, green tunnel with a carpet of pointy rocks. The section of the AT from Route 309 to Bake Oven Knob is a glorious exception, with splendid views and challenging rock scrambling, which more than make up for the bits in between that consist of a long, green tunnel with a carpet of pointy rocks.

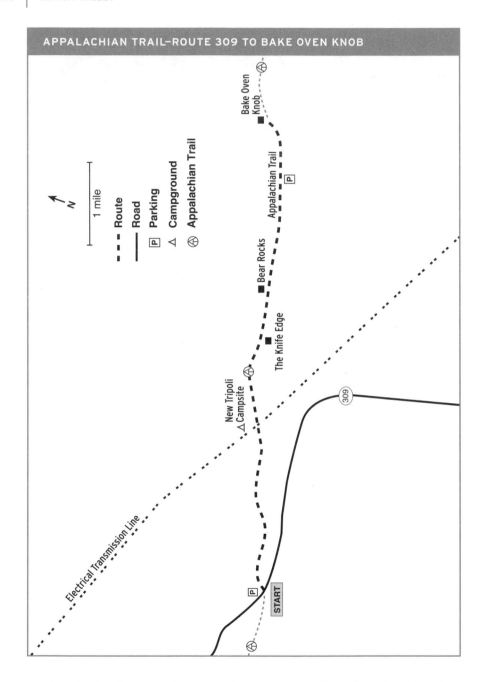

APPALACHIAN TRAIL–ROUTE 309 TO BAKE OVEN KNOB

Start by heading east from the State Game Lands parking lot (downhill toward Route 309), where a blue-blazed trail enters the woods. After just 20 yards it meets the Appalachian Trail, with its distinctive rectangular white blazes. Turn left on the AT—and follow those blazes!

Scrambling over the cliffs along the Appalachian Trail tests agility and strength and rewards the hiker with fine views.

This is a typical dry Appalachian ridge-top woods, featuring chestnut oak, red oak, pitch pine, black gum, and hickory. Witch hazel, mountain laurel, maple leaf viburnum, and blueberry and huckleberry shrubs also grow here, with teaberry covering the ground. The forest is thick and healthy, a haven for birds and other wildlife.

The trail begins as a natural footpath, then after 0.25 mile joins an old woods road, which is wide and rocky, with views of the rural landscape to the right (south). At 1.8 miles, go by the power line, with views to the north. The trail to the New Tripoli campsite goes off to the left just beyond. The trail narrows, becomes very bouldery (predominantly conglomerate) for 0.6 mile, then narrows to a rocky footpath.

At 2.6 miles, the trail crosses a 200-yard exposed section of rock atop the ridge, known as the Cliffs or the Knife Edge. The slabs of quartzite rock slope diagonally, like one side of a pitched roof, and the ridge drops off steeply to either side. This traverse requires agility; you have to hold on to the rocks while stepping across them. But there are plenty of footholds and handholds in the rocks to steady the course. If the rocks are wet or there is a wind, it is more challenging. But even a scrambling-averse hiker should be able to easily cross the Cliffs—and enjoy the exhilarating views to both sides—by being attentive. As with other exposed rocks on the ridge, watch for snakes.

After the Cliffs the rocky trail continues through the woods, passing the blue-blazed trail to the Bear Rocks outcrop, immediately to the left at 3.6

miles. (You can take this detour now or wait until the return trip.) At 4.5 miles turn right at the fork, onto a grassy woods road. At 4.9 miles, you'll pass a metal gate and cross a gravel road (Bake Oven Knob Road); go through the State Game Lands parking lot and reenter the woods, going uphill on a wide rocky trail.

At 5.3 miles you'll reach Bake Oven Knob, a flattish, open area with exposed conglomerate and quartzite rock outcrops on both sides of the ridge. There are beautiful vistas on both sides of the valley and along the spine of the Kittatinny Ridge. According to lore, the name "Bake Oven" refers not to the outcrops (though on sunny summer days they are indeed very hot) but to a depression in the rockface below the crest that resembles an oven.

Bake Oven is a popular hawk watch site where birders congregate in fall to observe and count migrating raptors as they surf on thermal updrafts rising along the ridge.

Return the way you came, detouring to climb up Bear Rocks. This quartzite outcrop was formed by a series of weathering processes over millions of years that left the ridge in a serrated form with upturned edges. The edges fractured vertically; as water froze in the fractures and expanded, blocks broke off and slid down the mountain, leaving standing towers lining the ridge crest like the crenellations of a craggy ruined castle.

The Bear Rock scramble is strenuous, but the route across the rocks is well marked with blue blazes. If you can make it across the cliffs, you can make it up Bear Rocks. At the top, enjoy a marvelous 360-degree view of the valley. Also note the fine exposures of weathered quartzite, displaying both horizontal bedding and vertical fracturing. Return via the same route, holding carefully to the rocks—don't be embarrassed to slide on the seat of your pants.

Now that you have done the Cliffs and Bear Rocks, the second Cliffs crossing may tempt you to become overconfident; be sure to exercise the same care as you did on the outward-bound leg. Follow the trail back to the blue-blazed access trail and to the parking area.

MORE INFORMATION

There are no restrooms. The AT is open 24 hours a day, 7 days a week. For overnight stays along the AT, Bake Oven Shelter and Campsite is 0.6 mile beyond Bake Oven Knob. This section of the AT is maintained by the Allentown Hiking Club, www.allentownhikingclub.org.

TRIP 45
APPALACHIAN TRAIL–LEHIGH GAP WEST

Location: Slatington, PA (Lehigh County)
Rating: Moderate
Distance: 6.0 miles
Elevation Gain: 900 feet
Estimated Time: 4.0 hours
Maps: USGS Palmerton and Lehighton; Appalachian Trail
Pennsylvania Section 2; map of Lehigh Gap Wildlife Refuge available
at the Lehigh Gap Nature Center website

**This loop hike features long-range scenic views from the north side
of Blue Mountain into the Lehigh Valley, as well as a climb down
the steep rock-debris slope of Devil's Pulpit with views into and
across the Lehigh Gap.**

DIRECTIONS

Take the Northeast Extension of the Pennsylvania Turnpike (I-476 north) to
Exit 56 and drive on Route 309 north toward Tamaqua. At 7.8 miles, turn right
onto Route 873, continuing through Slatington (approximately 6.0 miles).
Immediately before reaching the Lehigh River bridge, turn left into an unpaved parking lot, where you will find parking for up to ten cars. *GPS coordinates:* 40° 46.873′ N, 75° 36.524′ W.

TRAIL DESCRIPTION

On its southeasterly run to the Delaware at Easton, the Lehigh River passes
through a spectacular gap that it carved into Kittatinny Ridge. The V-shaped
Lehigh Gap dramatically exposes Blue Mountain's rock layers and, with those
layers, 400 million years of geologic history. Many barren acres of rock tell the
story of the most recent, human-made history of the gap.

Because of a century of zinc smelting in nearby Palmerton, 2,000 acres
of Blue Mountain on both sides of the gap were extensively defoliated. In
1980, the Environmental Protection Agency designated an 8-mile stretch of
the ridge (5 miles east of the gap and 3 west) as a Superfund site. The soil-free
slopes of rock debris near the gap have a stark, otherworldly beauty. South of
the gap, though, the north side of the ridge is full of green acres; many have

APPALACHIAN TRAIL–LEHIGH GAP WEST

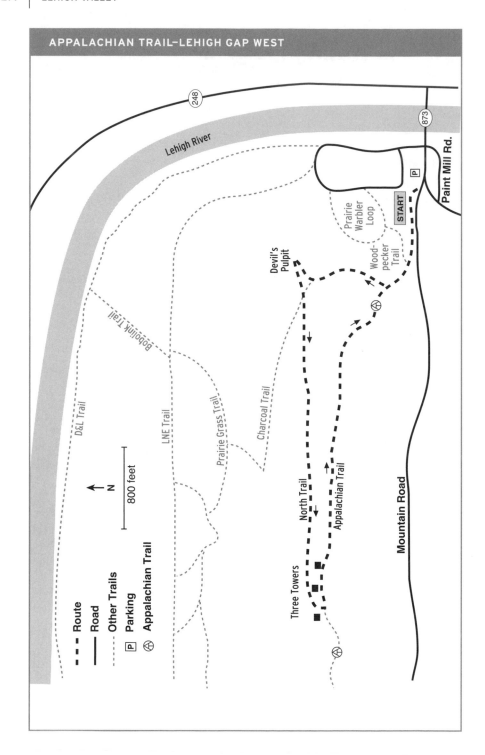

been replanted with grass, shrubs, and trees; some have experienced natural revegetation.

The Appalachian Trail (AT) descends the southeastern face of the ridge and crosses the Lehigh River at the gap, continuing up the east side. This hike uses the North Trail, a scenic route on the northwestern face of the ridge, to create a loop with the AT.

The hike begins at the small parking lot. Note the sign for the AT and proceed south toward the Outerbridge shelter, following the white blazes. The trail begins climbing immediately, at first through a grassy open area and then into the woods, becoming the typical "Rocksylvania" trail that challenges a hiker's agility. Under your feet are the sedimentary rocks conglomerate and sandstone. The typical Kittatinny forest of striped maple, black birch, and chestnut oak is accented occasionally by paper birch (a.k.a. white birch), a species often found in New England, not Pennsylvania. The shade-intolerant paper birch is an early successional tree, which indicates that this is a young forest.

The climb is steep and rocky, and this section seems to have a microclimate of extreme high humidity during summer. At 0.6 mile, the trail passes a spring, immediately followed by the Outerbridge shelter. After about 200 yards, the blue-blazed North Trail goes off to the right while the AT continues straight. To do a counterclockwise loop, follow the North Trail. (You may do the loop in either direction, although to connect with the Lehigh Gap Nature Center trails via the Charcoal Trail, you should go clockwise.)

Continue to ascend the ridge for another 0.3 mile. At the crest, turn right onto the spur (also blue-blazed) for Devil's Pulpit. At a lookout after 0.1 mile, enjoy a superb 180-degree view of the east side of the ridge across the gap. This is the best vantage point from which to observe the dramatic bare rock "nose" of the ridge, over which AT hikers must scramble (see Trip 46), as well as the surrounding valley and the town of Palmerton.

Scramble down 0.2 mile over large quartzite boulders (watch for snakes) to a view of the rocky prominence that has been known as Devil's Pulpit for centuries. Although the surrounding ridge is bare because of the smelter emissions, Devil's Pulpit is an erosional remnant of hard quartzite that was left standing as softer surrounding rock was washed away over eons. From here, take in the splendid view of the bend of the Lehigh River.

Go back uphill the way you came, but not all the way back up to the lookout; turn right on the blue-blazed North Trail to proceed southbound, sideways along a slope of rock boulders. Pass the trailhead for the Charcoal Trail on your right. Follow blazes across the rocks, through scrubby growth (some

The scenic North Side Trail along the Kittatinny Ridge (Blue Mountain) west of the Lehigh Gap offers expansive views of the valley below and a pleasant, relatively rock-free footpath.

of which obscures the blazes), bearing left and uphill. Cairns also mark the trail, which climbs to the ridge crest and turns right at the main North Trail.

For the next 2.0 miles, the trail hugs the north slope of the ridge, passing through patches of scrubby trees. The Lehigh Valley extends before you, with towns, highways, railroads, factories, hills, and of course the river—all spread out below like a miniature train set.

In spring and summer, you'll be tempted to run your hands through the native wavy hairgrass as you pass, as if dangling your fingertips in the water from a canoe. Here too lowbush blueberries cover the slopes. In late June through July, the ripe berries make this a bear's paradise. Watch for snakes and listen for the distinctive calls of the towhee (*drink-your-teeeee!*), the indigo bunting (descending pairs of notes), and the prairie warbler (a rising trill), all of which frequent these slopes.

Note the first of three communications towers on the left. At the third tower (about 0.5 mile from the first), the trail turns left over the ridge, into woods, and rejoins the white-blazed Appalachian Trail (AT). Turn left to follow the AT northbound. The rocky footpath traverses the south slope below the crest, where white pine, oak, hickory, striped maple, and remnant chestnuts abound; fragrant hay-scented ferns grow in the understory. Smelter emissions did not affect this side of the mountain. There are no scenic views from this side, unless you count the continuous view of the beautiful forest.

After 1.5 miles, pass the turnoff of the Blue Trail. Continue on the AT, retracing your path past the shelter and the spring, descending steeply downhill to the parking lot.

MORE INFORMATION

Restrooms are at the Lehigh Gap Nature Center, located on Paint Mill Road 0.5 mile south of the trailhead off Route 873. The center offers much information on the Lehigh Gap and the 750-acre Lehigh Gap Wildlife Refuge, which has a number of trails, including some that connect with the hike described here via the North Trail's Devil's Pulpit spur and the Charcoal Trail. The D&L Trail, a 10-mile rail trail, parallels the river along the ridge, passing through the gap and continuing south. Lehigh Gap Nature Center, 8844 Paint Mill Road, Slatington, PA 18080; 610-760-8889; www.lgnc.org/.

TRIP 46
APPALACHIAN TRAIL–LEHIGH GAP EAST

Location: Slatington, PA (Lehigh County)
Rating: Difficult
Distance: 2.75 miles
Elevation Gain: 900 feet
Estimated Time: 2.0 hours
Maps: USGS Palmerton; Appalachian Trail Pennsylvania Section 2

This short but challenging hike begins with a steep scramble up and over a narrow, barren ridge. The stark landscape has a unique beauty, hosts unusual plants, and provides scenic views of the Lehigh Valley.

DIRECTIONS
Take the Pennsylvania Turnpike Northeast Extension (I-476 north) to Exit 56, and then take Route 309 north toward Tamaqua; at 7.8 miles, turn right onto Route 873, continue on 873 through Slatington (approximately 6.0 miles) and over the Lehigh River bridge. Turn right at the light onto Route 248; bear left to stay on Route 248 where Route 145 bears right. After 100 yards, make a very sharp left onto an unmarked gravel road (note the National Park Service sign) going up the embankment to the parking lot, where you will find parking for 30 cars. *GPS coordinates*: 40° 46.984′ N, 75° 36.244′ W.

TRAIL DESCRIPTION
The east side of Lehigh Gap is a short but intense challenge to the courage, agility, and fortitude of the hiker. It also exemplifies the effect that humans can have on the environment. Pennsylvania mining and manufacturing industries have altered the landscape in many ways: acid mine drainage, slag heaps, slate hills, abandoned quarries, underground coal fires. It's unusual for a hiker to be able to experience firsthand the effects of the still-vital mining sector. The trek up Lehigh Gap East evokes the barren desert beauty of the far West, although the Gap's magnificent desolation is of human origin.

Palmerton, in the Blue Mountain valley northeast of the Lehigh Gap, was home to a zinc smelting operation from 1898 to 1980. Carried on prevailing winds, sulfur defoliated Blue Mountain and heavy metals ended up in the soil, preventing natural revegetation. In 1980, the Environmental Protection

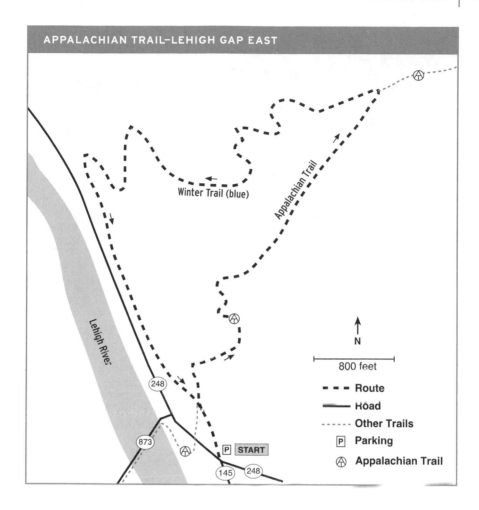

Agency designated Blue Mountain near Palmerton as a Superfund site. Restoration projects have not yet succeeded in reforesting the ridge. Defoliation has left the nose of the Lehigh Gap's east side bare, exposing sandstone, conglomerate, and shale blocks of the Shawangunk Formation. Although Blue Mountain is a Superfund site, the area is perfectly safe for hiking.

The hike begins at the parking lot, part of a former rail bed. The Appalachian Trail (AT) climbs the embankment, entering north of the parking lot. Look for the AT sign; follow the AT's white rectangular blazes. The blue-blazed Winter Trail branches left from the AT; you will take this on the return leg.

The narrow, rocky trail climbs uphill steeply, traversing a scrubby area of hemlock, sassafras, chestnut oak, pitch pine, and the unusual paper (white) birch. The Lehigh River, hidden below the embankment, slowly appears at your left as the trail ascends. At 0.4 mile, the trail begins a traverse of exposed

Lehigh Gap East features a challenging rock scramble.

boulders. Follow the blazes, which mark the best route. Continue up the rock face, using the ledges as handholds and footholds. Look down if you dare; this is not a place for those with a paralyzing fear of heights. Take it one step at a time and know where you are heading before taking each step, but don't be reluctant to stop and enjoy the view.

While not a knife edge, the crest of the ridge is narrow. The weather on the north side can be surprisingly different from that on the south, as it is from here that wind and storms approach and collide with the great mass of the ridge. Clamber down the rock face, then begin a long scramble over boulders (not as steep as the south side). There are long views of the northwest side of the valley. At 0.65 mile, the trail flattens out along the crest and scrubby vegetation reappears.

The north side hosts several plants that seem to thrive on contaminated soils. Sandwort, a low plant with ebullient sprays of tiny white flowers, is found in the state only on Lehigh Gap's east ridge. Chivelike thrift seapink, a garden flower, spreads over the bare rocks in great drifts. Wild bleeding heart, an endangered plant with pink heart-shaped flowers, grows more profusely around both sides of the gap than anywhere else in the state. Blueberries are abundant as well. Lehigh Gap hemlocks are reported to have developed resistance to the hemlock woolly adelgid, an insect that feeds on and kills the trees. Scientists are studying whether the unusual growth patterns are due to the presence of metals, nutrients in amended soil added in restoration projects, or some other factor(s).

The trail proceeds along the crest, a wide boulder field, occasionally marked by cairns rather than blazes. At 1.4 miles the blue-blazed Winter Trail branches off to the left. The AT continues, and the hike can be lengthened as far as you please by continuing north. (The northern endpoint, at Katahdin in Maine, is only 928 miles away.)

Follow the Winter Trail along the crest via a trail with grassy, easy footing; it heads through a grove into a clearing that's a sea of wavy hairgrass, an elegant, ruddy-stemmed native plant that flourishes on dry, rocky sites. The trail descends into shady woods, following a ridge cove around to the north. At several points there are good views of the bare ridge to the south. Emerging from the woods, the trail descends down a wide, exposed rock path. Near the bottom it passes a double-decker spring. A mile down, the trail meets an old rail bed that parallels the road below. Turn left. The trail is occasionally muddy or swampy, as water from the spring above spills down the ridge.

The trail passes through the gorge cut by the river and augmented by rail and highway roadcut construction, giving you a river's-eye view of the spectacular rock layering and the bare nose of the ridge above. After 0.6 mile, the trail ends at the junction with the AT at the parking lot.

MORE INFORMATION

The Winter Trail is aptly named; ice, snow, and wind make the main trail treacherous, so the blue-blazed trail is the only reasonable route. This is not a four-season hike, but it can be an out-and-back over the Winter Trail; however, it is also exposed during storms. The Philadelphia Trail Club maintains the trails. There are no restrooms.

TRIP 47
HICKORY RUN STATE PARK

Location: White Haven, PA (Carbon County)
Rating: Difficult
Distance: 12.0 miles
Elevation Gain: 550 feet
Estimated Time: 5.0 hours
Maps: USGS Hickory Run; trail maps available at park office and at website for Hickory Run State Park

This long but rewarding hike explores numerous rich forests with diverse wildlife, climbs across ridge tops with fine views of the Lehigh Valley, and ends with a creekside trek down a beautiful rhododendron-filled ravine.

DIRECTIONS
Take the Pennsylvania's Turnpike's Northeast Extension to Exit 95, proceed west on Route 940 for 3.0 miles, then east on PA 534 for 6.0 miles. You will find ample parking at the lot. *GPS coordinates*: 41° 01.473′ N, 75° 42.588′ W.

TRAIL DESCRIPTION
This hike is the northernmost—and at 12.0 miles, the longest—in the book. Its rewards, however, make the effort more than worthwhile. This hike concentrates on its western section, but eastern trails (including the celebrated Boulder Field) are just as enjoyable. There are more than 15,500 acres and more than 43 miles of trails in the park; the extensive rich, healthy forests support a great variety of wildlife. Forest-interior-dwelling birds such as veery, scarlet tanager, and Swainson's thrush are resident in spring and summer. Black bears are not uncommon, though you're more likely to encounter a porcupine, a wood frog, or a chipmunk. Hickory Run shows the influence of glaciers on the landscape. The hike primarily traverses a "terminal moraine," a pile of debris left by glaciers that covered portions of the park 20,000 years ago. It is characterized by sand, gravel, and loose rocks (glacial till); conifer forests; boggy, swampy soil; and steep-sided valleys.

Although this lengthy hike follows a series of trails, it's not complicated. The trails are blazed in colors indicating permitted uses (e.g., hiking, skiing), not to distinguish one from another. It's therefore advisable to carry a trail map.

HICKORY RUN STATE PARK

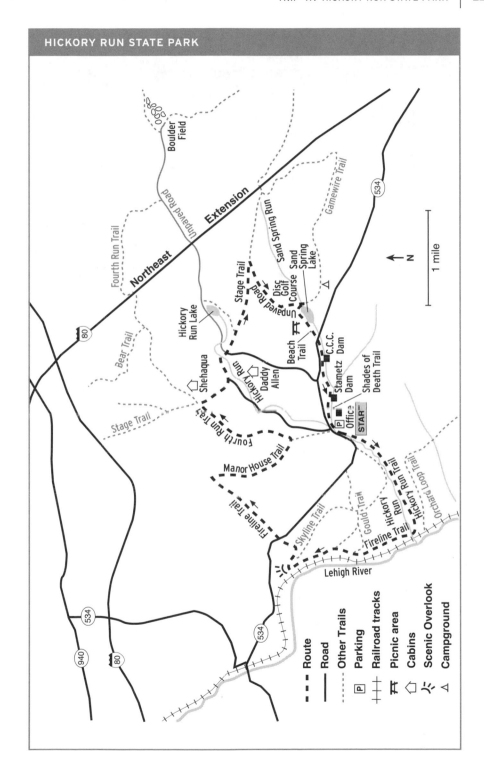

Boulder Field

Fourth Run Trail

Unpaved Road

Northeast Extension

Gamewire Trail

534

Sand Spring Run

Stage Trail

Disc Golf Course

Sand Spring Lake

△

Unpaved Road

N

1 mile

80

Bear Trail

Hickory Run Lake

Hickory Run

Beach Trail

C.C.C.

Stametz Dam

Shades of Death Trail

Shehaqua

Daddy Allen

Stage Trail

Fourth Run Trail

P Office

STAR

Manor House Trail

Hickory Run Trail

Hickory Loop Trail

Fireline Trail

Skyline Trail

Gould Trail

Fireline Trail

Orchard Loop Trail

Lehigh River

534

534

940

80

- - - Route
——— Road
····· Other Trails
P Parking
+++ Railroad tracks
⌂ Picnic area
⌂ Cabins
ᨑ Scenic Overlook
△ Campground

Although the trail following the dramatic, rhododendron-filled ravine surrounding Sand Spring Run is called Shades of Death, it is full of life's wonders.

Start the hike by heading south along Route 534, keeping to the left and staying behind the guardrail. At 0.25 mile bear left, following Hickory Run Trail as it follows the stream down into a boggy meadow with a fine display of summer wildflowers. The trail comes close to the creek, then at 0.75 mile enters the woods along the bottom of a steep ravine. This is a moist woods with big trees—yellow birch, hemlock, red maple—accompanied by an understory of ferns. Rhododendrons are abundant here. Continue to follow the wide, flat trail. (Caution: It has become common for hikers to walk along the railroad tracks ahead; the tracks are private property—and actively used—and it is not permissible to walk on them.)

Turn right onto the Fireline Trail which after about 2.0 miles, goes uphill, overlooking the helicopter pad below. Climb steadily for 0.25 mile past a field with meadowsweet along with white birch and blueberries, leading to a much larger open meadow affording views of the hills surrounding the Lehigh Gorge. The trail continues alternating between open areas and woods. Cross the stream on rocks and pass stone walls and foundations that indicate this was a former settlement. In the open areas, blueberries and blackberries are abundant in season. At a bend in the trail, an old spring flows downhill to a vanished cove. At about 3.0 miles, there are fine north-facing views of Kittatinny Ridge. This is a good area to pay attention to the rocks in and around the footpath, noting the change in type and orientation. About three-quarters of a mile on, you see a view of the Lehigh Gorge.

At 4.2 miles, cross Route 534 to the Manor House Trail, another old road. Here the rocks in the trail are granitic boulders. There are many fungi in this section of the woods. The woods are successional; beech and striped maple dominate. It is a steady uphill climb. Then the trail goes downhill, crossing Irishtown Run several times. At the bottom (6.4 miles) take the Fourth Run Trail to the left. The trail goes along a power line where highbush blueberries and huckleberries ripen in summer. Another plant growing here is sweet fern, which despite the name is not a fern but rather a shrub that grows on dry, sterile soils and produces highly aromatic fernlike leaves. Return to the woods and at 7.75 miles, you'll reach the Stage Trail. Turn right onto this old red-gravel road. The trail is flat, wide, and shady.

At 8.0 miles, pass Camp Shehaqua, then the Saylorsville Dam. Mallows line the small lake. Pass Camp Daddy Allen, then about half a mile later the trail breaks off the road (before the stop sign). Cross the road and stay on the Stage Trail, passing through a pine/hemlock woods with many mountain laurels. At 9.5 miles, you'll reach a gravel road; turn right and pass a well-hidden water tower. At 9.75 miles, the trail enters the Sand Spring Lake day use area, passing by a disc golf course. Keep the disc course on your left and head for either the restrooms across the field (if needed) or the lake bathhouse to the far left. Pass by the lake and go below the dam to the right, then pick up the Beach Trail, a red-gravel road. Continue on this trail, with the stream to your left.

At 10.8 miles, cross the road to enter the Shades of Death Trail, marked with a sign. (Explanations for the name vary, but one account suggests that the swampy area the trail traverses was the site where a large group of settlers fleeing Indians died.) The trail, which is blazed yellow, is the most beautiful and challenging on the hike, though it is not nearly as difficult as the park's literature suggests. The trail goes along the edge of the Sand Spring Run as it tumbles down the gorge. The deep hemlock ravine has many falls and rock pools. Overhanging the trail are masses of rhododendrons. There are many spots where you can stop, sit on the rocks, and take in the drama.

The roaring creek quiets as it nears another dam, installed long ago for a sawmill. This dam has a pretty spillway. At about 12.0 miles, you reach Route 534; follow it to return to the parking lot.

MORE INFORMATION

A portable toilet is located at the parking lot. Full facilities are at Sand Spring Lake. Hickory Run State Park, RR 1, Box 81, White Haven, PA 18661; 570-443-0400; www.dcnr.state.pa.us/stateparks/parks/hickoryrun.aspx.

TRAILSIDE FRUITS AND BERRIES

There is no food more local than the one growing beside the trail. And there is no finer-tasting food than one you've picked yourself. You can find many edible plants in the woods if you take the time to look and know what you're looking for. Picking out what's good to eat changes your relationship with the woods; they become as much a home as a place to visit.

However, it is essential to know what you're gathering. Unlike mushrooms, the edible and tasty fruits and berries you find by the trail are easy to identify and to distinguish from inedible, distasteful, or (very rare) toxic plants. The more you know, the more confident you'll feel. Get a good field guide, attend a presentation, or take a walk with an expert. If you're unsure, go foraging only with someone you trust. Learn to recognize all parts of the edible plants, and learn when the fruits will be in season (elevation makes a difference; at higher elevations fruits appear earlier than in the valleys). If you recognize flowers, you can predict when the fruits will appear.

Tree fruits are a good place to start. There are few wild fruiting trees in the Philadelphia area, so it's hard to confuse them. The following are some of the more easily identified:

- Persimmons have dark, blocky bark. The round fruits ripen from inedible astringent green to tropical-tasting orange-red; they drop when ready, in late summer or early autumn. What fun to gently shake the tree just enough to free a soft red globe, and catch it in midair!
- Pawpaws, shaped like mangoes and tasting like nothing else, ripen in late summer on the small understory tree, under its broad, elliptical leaves. The fruit can be gathered while green, and left to brown and ripen. You'll find pawpaw patches in very rich soil, moist or wet, typically (but not always) south of Philadelphia. However, as noted in the trail description for Trip 10 (Alapocas Run State Park), picking pawpaws is illegal in Delaware state parks.
- Hackberries grow in moist rocky soil. The bark of the tall hackberry trees forms corky furrows. The dark berries, ripe in autumn, taste like very sweet raisins.

Berries on shrubs are so widespread that it is hard not to encounter them on a hike. The following are some of the most common:

- Blueberries—including their less-familiar cousins, huckleberries—can be found in many different habitats: woods, mountains, bogs, sandy soils, rocky soils, wet soils, dry soils. Blueberry shrubs have small, elliptical toothless (or barely toothed) leaves, multiple short twigs, and white urn- or bell-shaped flowers. Shrubs can be knee-high (lowbush) or shoulder height (highbush). The small berries are ripe when they're dark blue (or black, for huckleberries); the stem separates with nary a tug. Depending on the variety, blueberries can be eaten from June to September. All blueberries are edible, though some (the dewberries or deerberries) are not as sweet. And a blueberry patch is a great place to look for bears.
- Blackberries and raspberries—with their many tiny globules of sweet seedy pulp—are so distinctive that even the most skeptical hiker will accept a freshly picked specimen. Look for the thorny canes (stiff curving stems) in sunny openings: fields, meadows, and railroad right-of-ways, often the same places that poison ivy thrives. Black raspberries ripen in early summer, turning black as they sweeten; blackberries and bright red wineberries (an Asian fruit widespread in the Philadelphia area) are best in high summer.
- Serviceberries grow on shrubs or small trees (the difference is height); the serviceberry bush, or smooth shadbush, is common in rocky woods, in thickets, and on roadsides. The long-petaled white flowers appear very early in spring along with serrated leaves (reddish at first). The sweet, juicy dark red or purple berries arrive in June or July.

Don't pick the flowers? That's true. It is, as a general rule, not permitted to pick or collect plants (especially in large quantities) in parks. But most parks and public places do make an exception for fruits and berries. People, after all, have been eating plants and their fruits far longer than there have been rules to tell us not to. Gathering wild edibles is consistent with Leave No Trace ethics as long as you gather sustainably: take no more than you can eat out of hand, don't take rare or (or even locally uncommon) plants, and don't deplete the plant's ability to reproduce or an animal's food source. Provided the edibles are abundant, there's no harm in eating them—and plenty of pleasure. The best rule to follow is "Gather ye blueberries while ye may, for tomorrow the bears may have eaten them all."

TRIP 48
GLEN ONOKO FALLS/
LEHIGH GORGE STATE PARK

Location: Jim Thorpe, PA (Lehigh County)
Rating: Difficult
Distance: 10.0 miles
Elevation Gain: 950 feet
Estimated Time: 4.5 hours
Maps: USGS Weatherly and Christmans

Climb up a rugged steep gorge with numerous waterfalls; enjoy ridge-top bird's-eye views of the Lehigh Gorge; descend along a misty mountain creek.

DIRECTIONS

Take Exit 74 of the Northeast Extension of the Pennsylvania Turnpike. Follow Route 209 south to Jim Thorpe. Then take Route 903 north across the river. At the stop sign, continue straight to Coalport Road. Turn left to Glen Onoko, where you will find ample parking. *GPS coordinates*: 40° 53.017′ N, 75° 45.604′ W.

TRAIL DESCRIPTION

Plunging 860 feet from the top of Broad Mountain to the Lehigh River, generating a series of cascading waterfalls, Glen Onoko is one of the most spectacular yet little-known hiking sites in eastern Pennsylvania. On summer weekends, it attracts a steady stream of local visitors who come to cool off among the splash and spray. Many seem content to go only partway up the gorge, and many others seem frightfully unprepared for the steep and slippery path (especially coming down it). The mile-long trail all the way to the topmost falls is challenging, but even more rewards are in store for the hiker who continues along the crest, down the mountain, and by the river. A long circuit hike, it offers a complete panoply of forested ridge and riverside experiences.

From the state park parking lot, follow signs for Glen Onoko Falls access. The trail goes down to the river, under railroad tracks, and then steeply up a wooded hill. Follow the stone steps, bearing left at all trail forks. (The stone steps are remnants of trails from a nineteenth century resort hotel.) The trail

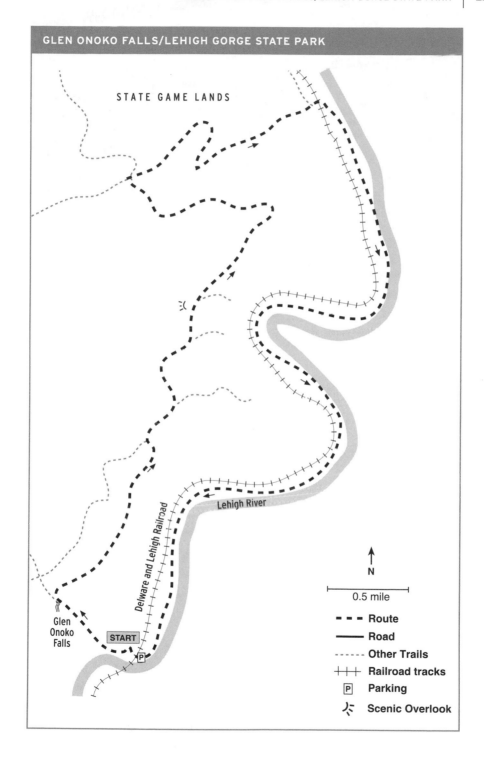

GLEN ONOKO FALLS/LEHIGH GORGE STATE PARK

STATE GAME LANDS

Delware and Lehigh Railroad

Lehigh River

Glen Onoko Falls

START

P

N

0.5 mile

- - - Route
——— Road
------ Other Trails
+++ Railroad tracks
P Parking
ﾊ Scenic Overlook

From the top of Glen Onoko, where the falls begin, the water seems to disappear into the abyss.

enters Pennsylvania State Game Lands; it is blazed red or orange. Follow the trail up the canyon, scrambling over large boulders. On the left, the water falls in sheets, tumbles over boulders, and rests in quiet pools. A cool mist hangs over the glen. Mountain laurel, rhododendron, yellow birch, hemlock, mosses, and ferns cling to the rock ledges. Huge fallen trees tossed here and there like matchsticks among the boulders testify to the power of falling water. A cascade over a wide concave rock face creates a veil of water that you can walk behind. At the top of the canyon, the water lazily spills out over a table ledge and seems to disappear into the sky high over the valley.

The trail turns to the right, entering the woods and ascending to the crest. The dry rocky woodland here is completely different from the moist glen, with completely different types of vegetation: chestnut oak, black birch, pitch pine, blueberry, and sheep laurel. After 0.3 mile from the turn, you'll pass an overlook with stone steps to the right. These steps, more remnants of the hotel, lead down to a trail that descends the mountain, enabling a short return-loop option that is much less treacherous than a descent of the falls would be.

Continue north along the ridge on the rocky, flat trail. To the right (southeast) are excellent winter views of the valley. At about the 4.3-mile mark, there is an overlook right above the Oxbow Bend of the Lehigh River. A perfect place for a rest stop, you will be provided free entertainment: at eye-level or

Glen Onoko features a series of splendid water-falls, each one unique.

below, turkey vultures habitually soar, spiral, and glide along the 1,500-foot-high sheer cliffs of the gorge.

Continue on the crest trail as it bends left; then about 750 feet later, turn right onto a 10-foot-wide unpaved fire road, passing shortly under a power line. The flat, open ridge-top terrain continues. About a mile after the overlook (5.3 miles in), the fire road splits into a Y. Just *before* this intersection, turn right onto a narrow, rocky trail leading into a thick woods. Mountain laurel and blueberry abound.

After proceeding through this dry woods for about half a mile, the trail descends the mountain through a beautiful, intimate ravine. At first you go down gradually, but then the grade gets steeper; your footsteps will accompany the sound of rushing water as the creek and trail descend the mountain in parallel. Eventually the trail meets up with the creek and follows it closely, crossing it once. The trail may be muddy and slippery. Here you find rhododendron, hemlock, yellow birch, and hornbeam. Look for shade-loving native wildflowers such as foamflower and wild ginger.

At the bottom of the ravine, the trail emerges from the woods at railroad tracks. Be aware that these tracks are active. Stop, look, and listen! *Carefully* cross the tracks and descend quickly by going down the embankment. (About 50 feet to the right of the trail, the embankment becomes less steep and more easily passable.) Turn right at the paved trail.

The last 3.5 miles of the hike are along the Delaware & Lehigh (D&L) Trail, part of a 21-mile segment (White Haven to Jim Thorpe) of a planned 165-mile route from Wilkes-Barre to Bristol over which millions of tons of anthracite coal were shipped to port by canal and rail through the 1930s. The D&L Trail includes the Delaware Canal (see Trip 34). This segment follows the bed of a coal railway. The paved multiuse trail runs alongside the Lehigh River. Scenic and flat, quiet (except for the occasional freight or tourist train), this paved section of the hike can nevertheless be fatiguing. It is therefore advisable to take a pair of lightweight shoes to replace heavy hiking boots (especially in hot weather). Follow the trail to the Glen Onoko parking lot.

MORE INFORMATION

Restrooms are located at the parking lot. State park land, including the parking lot, is open from sunrise to sunset. State Game Lands and Delaware & Lehigh Trails are always open. Lehigh Gorge State Park, RR 1, Box 81, White Haven, PA 18661; 570-443-0400; www.dcnr.state.pa.us/stateparks/parks/lehighgorge .aspx. Information about the Delaware & Lehigh Trail can be found at www .delawareandlehigh.org/index.php/trail/.

TRIP 49
APPALACHIAN TRAIL–
THE PINNACLE AND THE PULPIT

Location: Hamburg, PA (Berks County)
Rating: Difficult
Distance: 9.25 miles
Elevation Gain: 825 feet
Estimated Time: 4.5 hours
Map: USGS Hamburg

Climb through rich woods, up and over rugged, steep, rocky mountain trails, to stunning views of the Appalachian Mountains and the bucolic valley below; this is the most well-known vista on the Pennsylvania Appalachian Trail.

DIRECTIONS
Take I-78 west to Exit 35 (Lenhartsville), turn right at bottom of ramp, and turn right onto West Penn Street in Lenhartsville. Drive 2.0 miles to Reservoir Road on the right, and continue 1.0 mile to the parking area, where you will find parking for twenty cars. *GPS coordinates*: 40° 36.803′ N, 75° 54.694′ W.

TRAIL DESCRIPTION
The view from the Pinnacle is the most celebrated of any on the 229-mile Pennsylvania segment of the Appalachian Trail, and one of the most renowned of any trail in the state. The hike to the Pinnacle is a must for any collection of day hikes in southeastern Pennsylvania. Indeed, there are hikers who will tell you they could do this hike every day and not be bored. Some know it and love it so much that they hike it in moonlight. That said, it is a challenging hike, with steep, rocky trails and boulders to climb over. And the trail, always popular, gets so crowded on nice weekends that the view may be obstructed. Nonetheless, this is a hike that makes people fall in love with hiking—and hiking in Pennsylvania.

Head from the parking lot past the yellow gate, and continue uphill along the gravel road (blazed blue) about half a mile until it reaches an unpaved road. Note the wooden Appalachian Trail (AT) sign straight ahead indicating that the AT crosses here, going south to the left and north to the right. (AT convention is that toward Maine is north and toward Georgia is south, although here

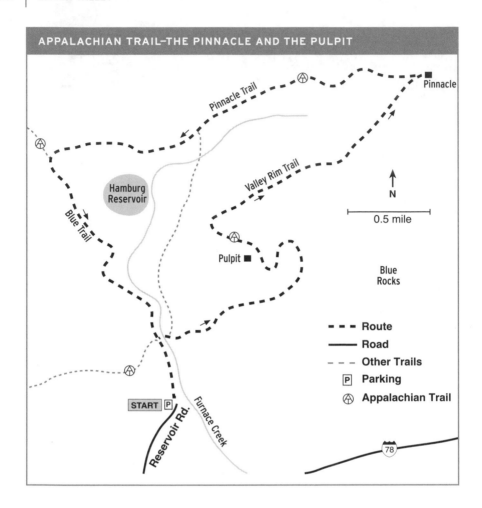

APPALACHIAN TRAIL–THE PINNACLE AND THE PULPIT

Pinnacle Trail

Pinnacle

Valley Rim Trail

Hamburg
Reservoir

Blue Trail

N

0.5 mile

Pulpit ■

Blue
Rocks

- - - Route
——— Road
– – – Other Trails
P Parking
Ⓐ Appalachian Trail

START P

Reservoir Rd.

Furnace Creek

78

"AT north" is heading east according to the compass.) Turn right, onto the road, following the AT heading north. As with all sections of the AT, the trail is marked with white rectangles; two blazes indicate a turn in the direction of the offset upper blaze.

The trail crosses the Furnace Creek via a little footbridge, then bends right and into the woods, where it quickly narrows to a footpath. The trail begins to climb the hill. Pass the spur trail to the Windsor Furnace shelter (blue-blazed), turning right to follow the Valley Rim Trail (still on the AT). The trail is narrow, natural surfaced, and rocky.

This is a rich, high-quality forest; at the height of the growing season, the woods are so thick from canopy to ground that you cannot see through them. Red and white oaks, hickories, tulip trees, ash, and striped maple trees predominate; you'll also see many chestnut saplings. Witch hazel, dogwood, rhododendron, pinxter flower (native azalea), and viburnum shrubs form a middle layer. Cinnamon fern, wood ferns, mayapple, and a variety of wildflowers are common on the ground layer, as are greenbrier and Virginia creeper vines. Mountain laurel, the state flower, is also abundant, blooming on evergreen shrubs from late May to mid-June.

The number of young tree seedlings indicates a healthy woods that can regenerate itself (unlike deer-devastated woods). "Healthy" does not necessarily mean "ancient"; this is not an old-growth forest. As the nearby place name "Furnace" indicates, it was cleared for charcoal production in the nineteenth century. This forest is part of a 13,000-acre protected area along the ridge (including Hawk Mountain Sanctuary, the Appalachian Trail corridor, State Game Lands 106, Hamburg Borough Watershed Lands, and Weiser State Forest) that comprises one of the largest protected tracts of contiguous forest in southeastern Pennsylvania. The quality and extent of the forest attracts diverse wildlife, such as the many songbirds you may hear in spring and summer.

The trail bends left after about a mile from the point where you turned onto the AT, climbs a long hill, then bends sharply left and climbs steeply to the crest of the ridge. Near the crest, the rocks in the trail start getting bigger and bigger until the trail is all rock. Mountain elders greet you to let you know you are in the mountains now.

Climb the rock steps, then make a sharp right to an exposed expanse of rock. As with all exposed rocks on this trail, watch carefully for basking snakes. Pass this outcrop, and cross a grassy expanse to reach the Pulpit Overlook at 1,582 feet. The views here are marvelous. The Pulpit is more than an appendage to the Pinnacle.

Continue on the AT as the trail traverses the dry, rocky ridge. Chestnut oaks are the dominant tree, and hemlocks are scattered throughout the woods; lowbush blueberry is abundant here, as is sarsaparilla, with its distinctive three-part spherical flower heads.

Shortly after leaving the Pulpit, you'll pass a communications tower on the left. The trail continues along the rocky ridge, descending and ascending briefly. You'll pass a yellow-blazed trail on the right heading down to Blue Rocks Family Campground (private).

You'll reach the Pinnacle spur trail 0.4 mile later; head to the right, past a huge (15-foot-high and growing) hiker-made rock cairn. The overlook is about 250 feet from the AT. To the northeast, view the long stretch of Kittatinny Ridge (also called Blue Mountain), the southeastern edge of the Appalachian Mountains; it runs from the Delaware Water Gap to the Maryland border. "Kittatinny" means "endless hills," and from here the ridge does seem to stretch without end to the horizon, broken by water gaps (such as the Lehigh Gap and, much farther in the distance, the Delaware Water Gap) and wind gaps (where water no longer flows). Views to the east and southeast are of the Great Valley. Blue Mountain is composed of quartzite, a hard, blocky sedimentary rock; in the valley below you can see a "river of rocks," or boulders that have tumbled from the ridge top and ended up in a "river" as a result of frost heaves in the soil as the last glaciers (far to the north) retreated. Turkey vultures soar above and below you on the breezes that rise and fall along the cliffs.

After you've given the view its due, head back to the AT and continue past the cairn. You are now bearing west, even though you are traveling north on the AT. After about half a mile, the rocky trail becomes a wide woods road with easy footing and a gentle descent; this is what the trail is like from here to the end of the hike. After another mile, pass a wide, flat, grassy field on the right called the Helipad. On the left is a blue-blazed trail. This trail heads down the east side of the reservoir via Furnace Creek and is an alternative about a mile shorter than the descent followed by the route described here. Continue on the AT and pass (or detour down-and-back) a spur trail to the pretty Gold Spring, 100 feet off the trail.

After another mile, you'll reach a T with another woods road. The AT turns right here, heading to Eckville. Instead, turn left, following the blue blazes. Descend past the Hamburg Reservoir on the left after about 1.25 miles, and after another 0.5 mile you'll reach the road you came in on; head back to the parking lot.

MORE INFORMATION

There are no seasonal or daily time restrictions on the trails. Because hunting is permitted (except Sundays) at Hamburg Reservoir property, wear orange in season. Bikes are not permitted on the AT. Although children may delight in the rock climbing and the views, these are dangerous cliffs and young hikers must be supervised closely; this hike may not be suitable for very young children. There are no restrooms. The Appalachian Trail portion of this hike is maintained by the Blue Mountain Eagle Climbing Club (www.bmecc.org).

Continuing northbound on the AT at 4.0 miles past the Hamburg Reservoir turnoff, toward Eckville, there is a blue-blazed trail to Hawk Mountain Sanctuary (fee charged), a world-renowned center for raptor migration research and conservation.

THE KING IS DEAD; LONG LIVE THE KING

Tall, durable, and long-lived, the oak is a beloved tree, prized for its lumber and for its use in landscaping. Oaks dominate the forests in the Philadelphia area; found in virtually every habitat, they are invaluable in the Delaware Valley, providing food, shelter, and cover for wildlife. It is hard to imagine our woods without oaks, but the story of another tree should caution us that a dominant species can disappear. The American chestnut once held a place in the pantheon of trees that was as great as that of the oak today.

A century ago, there were 4 billion chestnuts on 200 million acres of eastern forests. Tall, straight, and fast growing, chestnuts created a continuous canopy. Wildlife relied on their nuts, which the trees produced annually (in contrast, oaks produce nuts every 2–5 years); the result was an abundance of game. People relished chestnuts too; their sweetness contrasted with bitter acorns, which had to be boiled before eating. Chestnut wood was renowned for its resistance to rot. Nuts, bark (for tanning), and lumber provided cash crops on which many rural Appalachian communities based their economies.

A fungus—chestnut blight—accidentally introduced from Asian chestnut trees attacked American chestnuts in the late nineteenth century. First identified in 1905, the blight effectively wiped out the American chestnut within 50 years, altering the makeup of eastern forests, destroying rural communities, and perhaps (though research is lacking) reducing the abundance of wildlife. Oaks took over the role of dominant tree.

The American chestnut is not entirely extinct. Though most succumb to the blight when they reach maturity (but before they produce flowers and nuts), some trees continue to sprout from stumps or from old seedlings. The sprouts can get to be 8 inches in diameter. The chestnut's elongated, sharp-toothed leaves are common in healthy forests. You can get a sense of how dominant the chestnut was by observing the number of immature sprouts along a trail; a 2008 survey of the Appalachian Trail by volunteer hikers counted thousands within 15 feet of the trail in Pennsylvania.

Today, researchers are using cross-breeding with blight-resistant Asian strains and genetic engineering in an effort to reintroduce the American chestnut. Even if they succeed, however, regenerating a chestnut canopy will take another century or more. Perhaps one day American chestnut trees will see the top of the forest, and future generations will know a different forest than we do.

TRIP 50
SAND SPRING TRAIL AND TOM LOWE TRAIL

Location: Shartlesville, PA (Berks County)
Rating: Moderate
Distance: 5.25 miles
Elevation Gain: 500 feet
Estimated Time: 2.75 hours
Maps: USGS Friedensburg and Auburn; Appalachian Trail
Pennsylvania, section 5

**Hemlock ravines, rocky creeks, and an unusual walled sand-bottom
spring greet hikers on these remote, quiet mountainside trails.**

DIRECTIONS
Take I-78 to Exit 23 (Shartlesville), go north on Mountain Road for 0.3 mile,
bear left onto Forge Dam Road, and continue 1.5 miles to Northkill Road.
End at the State Game Lands 110 parking lot, where you will find parking for
twenty cars. *GPS coordinates*: 40° 32.266′ N, 76° 07.405′ W.

TRAIL DESCRIPTION
The Appalachian Trail (AT) traverses the crest of Kittatinny Ridge (Blue
Mountain) in eastern Pennsylvania, offering valley views, peaceful woods, and
a demanding rocky footpath. Although you will certainly want to hike the AT,
other rewarding hikes in the area beckon.

Below the AT on Blue Mountain's south slope, streams tumble over rocks,
thick forests harbor multitudes of wildlife, and the human-made trail melds
into wilderness. The Sand Spring Trail/Tom Lowe Trail loop skirts the AT,
never meeting it. Those who hike this footpath will feel they've spent time getting to know the mountain, not just getting across it.

Blue Mountain stretches across the landscape like one of summer's ubiquitous (and harmless) black rat snakes. Clad in luscious green, it conceals its
inner structure: layers of rock laid down while ancient continents were drift-
ing and colliding, oceans forming and disappearing, muddy currents swirling.
Here, its top layer is light-colored quartzite, sandstone, and conglomerate; the
band below, dark mudstones.

Water and rock tell the continuing story of the mountain. Sand Spring Trail
follows the course of a stream that is cutting into the rock layers. The hike

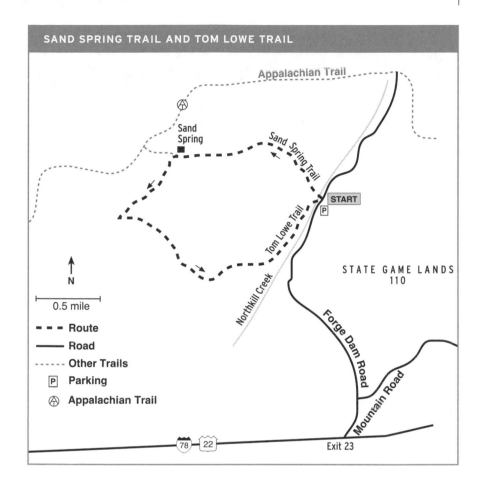

SAND SPRING TRAIL AND TOM LOWE TRAIL

begins in a hemlock ravine, a deeply incised valley formed as the Northkill Creek tumbles down the mountain, breaking it up into pieces and carrying sediment with it. Hemlocks and rhododendrons thrive in the cool, moist, rocky environment of these ravines, as do ferns and fungi.

From the parking lot, head past the gate up the road for 0.1 mile; the blue-blazed Sand Spring Trail begins to the left. The rocky trail follows a tributary of the Northkill, crossing it many times (the rocks may be slippery) and even running up the stream's center. Even over the sound of rushing water, the thick, extensive forest resounds with the calls of birds that thrive in deep woods, such as veery, pewee, and scarlet tanager. Chipmunks are everywhere, chirping and scampering over the mossy rocks. Along the forest floor run partridgeberry, wood strawberries, trailing arbutus, and teaberry. Pink lady's slippers abound in spring, ghostly white Indian pipes in summer. In sunlit openings, butterflies bask and dragonflies hunt.

A simple two-log bridge crosses a stream in a hemlock ravine on the Tom Lowe Trail.

The well-blazed trail climbs the ravine steadily but for the most part gently; there are light- and dark-colored boulders and pebbles in the stream, eroded from one of the two rock layers. At 2.0 miles, the trail reaches Sand Spring. Surrounded on three sides by low walls, the spring percolates silently, bubbling into a clear sand-bottom pool before flowing down the ravine. The fine white sand comes from the underlying quartzite and sandstone that caps the ridge, which is eroded slowly by the water.

Turn off the Sand Spring Trail (which continues 200 yards north to the AT) to take the orange-blazed Tom Lowe Trail, which heads left, to the southwest. The Tom Lowe Trail ascends gradually for 0.2 mile through a dry, deciduous woods, flattens briefly over a hillcrest, then descends 0.2 mile steeply into another quiet, cool, shady hemlock ravine. The trail follows the stream gently downhill for 0.5 mile, then crosses it via a two-log bridge. (Walking upright on this narrow bridge may be disconcerting; either scooch along it or walk on the stones below, using a log as a railing.) More stream crossings follow—some easy step-overs, some more difficult balancing acts. The trail veers away from the creek; at 3.8 miles, it crosses a small open marshy area (a former gravel pit); note the catalpa trees, which indicate former human occupancy. Watch care-

Indian Pipes, common in rocky woods in summer, lack chlorophyll and obtain nutrients by partnering with underground "mycorrhizal" fungi that feed from roots of green plants.

fully for a faded blaze at 3.9 miles, where the trail turns left; head back uphill into the woods.

From here, the trail twists and turns, uphill and downhill, and continues in a counterclockwise direction around the lower slope of a mountainside bulge. At 4.9 miles, Northkill Road comes into sight through the trees; the rushing Northkill Creek is audible. The trail follows the creek, crossing it at 5.1 miles. (Be prepared for wet feet: The creek may overtop the stepping-stones, and an alternative crossing—leaping over the foundation of an old dam—is challenging.) After another 0.2 mile upstream along the creek, the trail exits at the road, just below the parking lot.

MORE INFORMATION

In hunting season (except on Sundays), wear blaze orange. There are no restrooms. Several other trails can be accessed from this location. Continue on the Sand Spring Trail past the Sand Spring to reach the Appalachian Trail; or, follow the Game Lands access road past the Sand Spring trailhead, to the Appalachian Trail, and follow it north to Auburn Lookout. The Blue Mountain Eagle Climbing Club (www.bmecc.org) maintains the trails.

APPENDIX A: CRITICAL TREASURES OF THE HIGHLANDS

Critical Treasures, or areas in the Mid-Atlantic Highlands region threatened by development and sprawl, offer green getaways that are a stone's throw from many metropolises. These areas are also focal points for the Appalachian Mountain Club's conservation work in the Highlands. For more information, visit www.outdoors.org/hikethehighlands and see page 184.

PENNSYLVANIA

Adams County
Buchanan Valley
Narrows
The Fruit Belt

Berks County
Birdsboro Waters
Glen Morgan Lake
Hay Creek Watershed
Mount Penn
Neversink Mountain
North Branch French Creek
    Watershed
Oley Hills
Pine Creek Watershed
Saucony Creek Watershed
Schuylkill River Watershed
Upper Perkiomen Creek
    Watershed

Bucks County
Cooks Creek Watershed
Durham Mine/Mine Hill/Rattlesnake
    Hill
Haycock Mountain
Quakertown Swamp
Rapp Creek Watershed
Ridge Valley Creek
Roaring Rocks Watershed
Rock Hill
Tinicum Creek Watershed
Tohickon Creek Watershed
Unami Hills and Ridge Valley Creek
Upper Perkiomen Creek Watershed

Chester County
Great Marsh
North Branch French Creek
    Watershed

Lancaster County
Furnace Hills
Middle Creek Wildlife Management
    Area
Welsh Mountain

Lebanon County
Middle Creek Wildlife Management
    Area

Lehigh County
Hosensack Swamp
Lehigh Canal & Corridor Greenway
Little Lehigh Creek Watershed
Lower Lehigh Valley Reach of the
    Lehigh River
Upper Perkiomen Creek Watershed

Montgomery County
Schuylkill River Watershed
Spring Mountain
Stone Hill
Unami Hills
Upper Perkiomen Creek Watershed

Northampton County
Bougher Hill
Lehigh Canal & Corridor Greenway
Lower Lehigh Valley Reach of the
    Lehigh River
South Mountain Preserve
Stouts Valley

NEW JERSEY

Hunterdon County
Musconetcong Mountain
Musconetcong River Valley
North Branch Raritan River
    Watershed
Ramapo Mountains and Ramapo
    River Watershed
Upper South Branch Raritan River
    Watershed

Morris County
Farny Highlands
Musconetcong River Valley
North Branch Raritan River
    Watershed
Pequannock Watershed
Rockaway River Watershed
Schooley's Mountain
Sparta Mountain Greenway
Upper Passaic River Headwaters
Upper South Branch Raritan River
    Watershed

Passaic County
Pequannock Watershed
Ramapo Mountains and Ramapo
    River Watershed
Wyanokie Highlands/Wanaque
    Watershed

Somerset County
Upper Passaic River Headwaters

Sussex County
Hamburg Mountain
Rockaway River Watershed
Sparta Mountain Greenway
Wallkill River Valley

Warren County
Musconetcong River Valley
Pequest River Valley
Pohatcong Creek Valley
Pohatcong Grasslands
Pohatcong Mountain
Scotts Mountain

APPENDIX B: RESOURCES

HIKING CLUBS IN THE PHILADELPHIA AREA

Joining a hiking club is a great way to learn about local places to hike and to meet others who share your interest in outdoor recreation. Most area hiking clubs also maintain trails, which can include activities as diverse as brush clearing and building bridges, steps, and shelters. Many clubs welcome volunteers without requiring them to join their organization.

Appalachian Mountain Club
www.outdoors.org
www.amcdv.org

Allentown Hiking Club
www.allentownhikingclub.org

Batona Hiking Club
www.batonahikingclub.org

Chester County Trail Club
www.cctrailclub.org

Lancaster Hiking Club
community.lancasteronline.com/
lancasterhikingclub

Outdoor Club of South Jersey
www.ocsj.org

Wilmington Trail Club
www.wilmingtontrailclub.org

York Hiking Club
www.yorkhikingclub.com

APPENDIX C: FURTHER READING

NATURAL HISTORY OF THE DELAWARE VALLEY

Barnes, John H. and W.D. Sevon. *The Geological Story of Pennsylvania*. Harrisburg, Pa.: Pennsylvania Geological Survey, 2002.

> A good general introduction to the geological processes that shaped the state and the physiographic provinces. Available online at www.dcnr .state.pa.us/topogeo/education/es4.pdf

Boyd, Howard P. *A Field Guide to the Pine Barrens of New Jersey*. Medford, N.J.: Plexus Publishing, Inc., 1991.

> This is a guide to the flora, fauna, ecology, and history of the Pine Barrens.

Collins, Beryl Robichaud and Karl H. Anderson. *Plant Communities of New Jersey*. New Brunswick, N.J.: Rutgers University Press, 1994.

> Applicable throughout the Delaware Valley, this reference describes the plants that are typically found together in specific habitats.

Fergus, Charles. *Wildlife of Pennsylvania and the Northeast*. Mechanicsburg, Pa.: Stackpole Books, 2000.

> Comprehensive nontechnical reference for birds, mammals, amphibians and reptiles.

New Jersey Geological Survey. *Geologic Map and the Geology of New Jersey.* 1999.

>Includes a summary of New Jersey geology and physiographic provinces. (Available online at www.state.nj.us/dep/njgs/enviroed/freedwn/psnjmap.pdf)

Plank, Margaret O. and William S. Schenck. *Delaware Piedmont Geology.* Special Pub. 20. Delaware Geological Survey, 1998.

>Provides an excellent description of the geology of the Piedmont province. Unfortunately, nothing comparable is currently available for the coastal plain. Available online at www.dgs.udel.edu/publications/pubs/SpecialPublications/sp20.pdf

Rhoads, Ann Fowler and Timothy A Block. *Trees of Pennsylvania.* Philadelphia: University of Pennsylvania Press, 2005.

>An illustrated reference to native trees.

Van Diver, Bradford G. *Roadside Geology of Pennsylvania.* Missoula, Mont.: Mountain Press Publishing Company, 1990.

>A bit more technical than *The Geological Story of Pennsylvania*, this book has the benefit of enabling a more specific focus on rocks in southeastern Pennsylvania.

RECREATION GUIDES

Appalachian Mountain Club, *AMC Pennsylvania Highlands Regional Recreation Map and Guide,* 2009. (To get a copy, visit www.outdoors.org/hikethehighlands.)

Appalachian Mountain Club, *Hike the Highlands* cards, 2009. (Download the cards at www.outdoors.org/hikethehighlands.)

Case, Dan. *AMC's Best Day Hikes near New York City.* Boston: Appalachian Mountain Club Books, 2010.

Cramer, Ben, ed. *Pennsylvania Hiking Trails,* 13th ed. Mechanicsburg, Pa.: Stackpole Books, 2008.

Gross, Wayne, ed. *Appalachian Trail Guide to Pennsylvania,* 12th ed. Harper's Ferry, W. Va.: Appalachian Trail Conservancy, 2008.

Kenley, Kathy. *Quiet Water New Jersey and Eastern Pennsylvania.* Boston: Appalachian Mountain Club Books, 2010.

Scherer, Glenn. *Nature Walks in New Jersey.* Boston: Appalachian Mountain Club Books, 2003.

INDEX

ABOUT THE AUTHOR

SUSAN CHARKES writes frequently about the outdoors, nature, and the environment. She has a column, "Nature's Way," and a podcast, "Because Nature Tells Me So." An avid hiker and paddler, she is a hike leader with the Appalachian Mountain Club Delaware Valley Chapter, and a member and Appalachian Trail maintenance leader with Batona Hiking Club. She formerly practiced law, and works in the environmental nonprofit field. Learn more at www.susancharkes.com.

Appalachian Mountain Club

Founded in 1876, the AMC is the nation's oldest outdoor recreation and conservation organization. The AMC promotes the protection, enjoyment, and understanding of the mountains, forests, waters, and trails of the Appalachian region.

People

We are more than 100,000 members, advocates, and supporters; 16,000 volunteers; and more than 450 full-time and seasonal staff. Our 12 chapters reach from Maine to Washington, D.C.

Outdoor Adventure and Fun

We offer more than 8,000 trips each year, from local chapter activities to major excursions worldwide, for every ability level and outdoor interest—from hiking and climbing to paddling, snowshoeing, and skiing.

Great Places to Stay

We host more than 140,000 guests each year at our lodges, huts, camps, shelters, and campgrounds. Each AMC destination is a model for environmental education and stewardship.

Opportunities for Learning

We teach people the skills to be safe outdoors and to care for the natural world around us through programs for children, teens, and adults, as well as outdoor leadership training.

Caring for Trails

We maintain more than 1,500 miles of trails throughout the Northeast, including nearly 350 miles of the Appalachian Trail in five states.

Protecting Wild Places

We advocate for land and riverway conservation, monitor air quality and climate change, and work to protect alpine and forest ecosystems throughout the Northern Forest and Mid-Atlantic Highlands regions.

Engaging the Public

We seek to educate and inform our own members and an additional 2 million people annually through AMC Books, our website, our White Mountain visitor centers, and AMC destinations.

Join Us!

Members support our mission while enjoying great AMC programs, our award-winning *AMC Outdoors* magazine, and special discounts. Visit www.outdoors.org or call 800-372-1758 for more information.

APPALACHIAN MOUNTAIN CLUB
Recreation • Education • Conservation
www.outdoors.org

The AMC Delaware Valley Chapter

THE AMC DELAWARE VALLEY CHAPTER offers a wide variety of hiking, backpacking, climbing, paddling, bicycling, snowshoeing, and skiing trips each year, as well as social, family, and young member programs and instructional workshops. The chapter also maintains a 15-mile section of the Appalachian Trail between Wind Gap and Little Gap, as well as trails at Valley Forge National Historical Park.

To view a list of AMC activities in Pennsylvania, Central and South Jersey, Northern Delaware, and other parts of the Northeast, visit trips.outdoors.org

AMC Book Updates

AMC BOOKS STRIVES TO KEEP OUR GUIDEBOOKS AS UP-TO-DATE as possible to help you plan safe and enjoyable adventures. If after publishing a book we learn that trails are relocated or route or contact information has changed, we will post the updated information online. Before you hit the trail, check for updates at www.outdoors.org/publications/books/updates.

While hiking or paddling, if you notice discrepancies with the trail description or map, or if you find any other errors in the book, please let us know by submitting them to amcbookupdates@outdoors.org or in writing to Books Editor, c/o AMC, 5 Joy Street, Boston, MA 02108. We will verify all submissions and post key updates each month.

AMC Books is dedicated to being a recognized leader in outdoor publishing. Thank you for your participation.

AMC BOOKS & MAPS

EXPLORE THE POSSIBILITIES

More Books from the Outdoor Experts

AMC's Best Day Hikes near New York City

BY DANIEL CASE

You don't have to travel far from New York City to find some of the best day hikes in the Northeast. This guidebook takes you to 50 of the best excursions in New York, Connecticut, and northern New Jersey.

ISBN: 978-1-934028-38-4
$18.95

Nature Walks in New Jersey

BY GLENN SCHERER

Explore 40 of the state's most beautiful natural areas – from the beaches of Cape May to the lush countryside of the Highlands. Includes information on the flora, fauna, and history of the region.

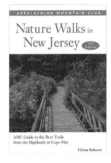

ISBN: 978-192917340-2
$14.95

Quiet Water New York, 2nd edition

BY JOHN HAYES AND ALEX WILSON

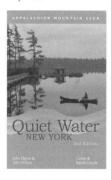

From clear and quick-flowing waterways to picturesque ponds surrounded by mountain peaks, this guide allows paddlers to explore the great variety of water adventures New York has to offer with 90 spectacular quiet-water destinations.

ISBN: 978-1-929173-73-0
$19.95

Quiet Water New Jersey and Eastern Pennsylvania

BY KATHY KENLEY

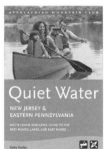

Great for families, anglers, canoeists, and kayakers of all abilities, *Quiet Water New Jersey and Eastern Pennsylvania* features 80 trips, covering the best calm-water paddling in the region.

ISBN: 978-1-934028-34-6
$19.95